Start Your Own

BAND!

A JET LAMBERT GUMPTION GUIDE

**Everything you need
to know to take
your band to the top!**

Start Your
Own
BAND!

A JET LAMBERT GUMPTION GUIDE

by
Marty Jourard

HYPERION

New York

ISBN: 0-7868-8216-6

Library of Congress Cataloging-in-Publication Data

Jourard, Marty
    Start your own band / by Marty Jourard. — 1st ed.
       p.   cm. — (A Jet Lambert gumption guide)
    Includes bibliographical references (p.   ).
    ISBN 0-7868-8216-6
    1. Music—Vocational guidance. 2. Music trade—United States. I. Title. II. Series.
    ML3790.J68   1997
    782.42164'068—dc21   96-53285
                        CIP
                        MN

Designer: Stewart Williams
Art Director: Simon Sung
becker&mayer! Editor: Jennifer Worick
Hyperion Editor: Lisa Jenner Hudson
Hyperion Production Editor: David Lott

Produced by becker&mayer!, Ltd.

FIRST EDITION

10 9 8 7 6 5 4 3 2 1

To Sydney and Jack

CONTENTS

ACKNOWLEDGMENTS

Thanks.

Well, maybe I should go into more detail. As much as I'd like to think that this entire book came to me in a flash, many people contributed their knowledge and were quite generous with their time and expertise. If you've learned anything at all of value after reading this book, thank (in no particular order) these swingin' music lovers: Tom Leadon, Stan Lynch, Mike Lull of Guitar Works, Steve Davies of Stephens Stringed Instruments, Steve Hill, Malcolm Griffith, Veronika Kalmar, Bart Day, Freddie Patterson, Dillys Jones, Brendan Mullen, Bill Branvold, Chris Eckman, Gary Heffern, Pip McAslin, Jim DeVito, Dennis Turner, Liz Garo, Barbara Dollarhide, Peter Laird, Chris Hanszek, Ted Smith, Benmont Tench, Bob Welch, Mary Klauzer, Pete Anderson, Carl Petosa, Danny Amis, Jeff Jourard, and Fritz Wavecrest.

FOREWORD

by Tom Petty

think for this foreword, we'll go backwards...way backwards to Gainesville, Florida, in the mid-1960s, a northern Florida college town bit very hard by the British Invasion.

Rock 'n' roll bands were forming as fast and plentiful as spores on the swamp ferns.

It was somewhere in this confusion that I first met Marty Jourard, our author. Actually, I first ran into his brother Jeff at Chandler's 15-cent Burgers having a large lemonade. Jeff was odd for Gainesville: He wore a polka-dot shirt, Beatle boots, and owned a Gibson Firebird guitar. I went with him to watch his band, The Odds, rehearse. I there discovered his younger bro, Marty. The experience was, well, psychedelic.

It was no real challenge to start a group then. All you needed was four guys, some guitars and drums, and a garage.

I for one joined a group (one that actually worked!), showing no particular talent for anything musical. My position was secured by maintaining just the right haircut.

I learned to play because I had to, because I loved rock 'n' roll, and I especially loved being in a band. I was fourteen years old and found a social structure that would sustain me to this writing at the age of, um, 45.

As time flew by and gigs came and went, I saw more of Marty J. He was a bass player, then a piano man, then a sax man, a singer, or whatever got him off and by.

Our friendship remained intact to the days of the mid-'70s, when many of us relocated to Los Angeles (Mecca) to find recording contracts and avoid adult work. I formed the Heartbreakers and a few years later, Marty and Jeff would create The Motels. We both worked steady and even had hits. Marty would visit me at my house when we were off the road. We would laugh, play, smoke, and marvel at how we were getting away with this immaculate scheme of being paid for what we'd have done anyway.

This is not to give you the impression we found this place in life without our share of hustle and scuffle and awful gigs and beer in our amplifiers. But those things later became stories that bring hoarse laughs on tour buses and in dressing rooms and on down to the hotel bar.

We loaded the van, broke strings, wrote out lyrics from records, printed up business cards, dealt with the occasional asshole band member, hung out at Lipham's Music Store, drove home from gigs with no pay, lost girlfriends, and, more than anything, practiced, practiced...well, you know.

These years of discovery were among the best in my life and I'm sure, Marty's.

If you've bought this book, you've not only given Marty J. some money, you probably want to be in a band. You've come to the right place. I'd have been constantly referring to the following pages in the 1960s. But now, it's the '90s, which are really the '60s upside down.

I wish you a happy read and I wish I could go with you to your first gig, because no matter how bad or good it goes, I'd like a little of that feeling you'll get to rub off on me. It's a good feeling down deep and, at the worst, high adventure.

I'd like to be with you when you drive home feeling like a musician.

—Tom Petty
Los Angeles, July 1996

PREFACE

Can you learn something useful from a book? Of course. What do you expect me to say—I'm the author! If nothing else, this book includes a large body of information that can be used by all musicians currently involved in popular music of any kind.

Here was my approach to creating the text: First, I reviewed what I have learned from my experiences as a musician, songwriter, producer, recording engineer and general music lover. I wrote down everything I knew about anything. Then, using state-of-the-art research methods (extensive reading, phone interviews, in-person interviews), I gathered expert opinions and facts galore, attempting to weave everything into an easy to read, yet info-packed narrative. At the end of appropriate chapters, I've written a personal reminiscence, reflecting on some of my real-life adventures in The Music Business. If this kind of potentially self-indulgent narrative makes you blanch, simply skip it and move on to the next chapter. I won't be offended but my mom might. She finds it all fascinating.

Feel free to randomly move from section to section, reading what you want in whatever order you choose. However, I have presented the information in a fairly linear fashion, so you can read it in the order presented and get a feel for how important it is to know basic information before moving into specific details. Or something like that.

I truly enjoyed doing the research for this book. Metaphorically speaking, the music business is much like an amoeba, constantly changing shape. The best one can do is describe how it looks and feels at the time it is being studied. I tried to look under every rock. If this book helps even one reader, I'll be happy. If it helps a million readers, I'll be happy and in a higher tax bracket. May the information within teach you something new and truly useful.

CHAPTER ONE

THE BASICS

All great artists are amateurs.
—Erik Satie (1866–1925)

S o you want to start a band! What do you need to know? Plenty of stuff: how to get together with other musicians, how to audition for a band, how to choose a name, how to get gigs, how to promote the band with merchandise, and lots more. This chapter will provide you with an overview of all these subjects. The rest of the book will go into detail on each of these topics and other areas you may not even know about yet.

Let's begin by defining what a band is: two or more people playing music together. Although the traditional view of a band is usually at least three people (for instance drums, bass, guitar), this definition has broadened in recent years, partly due to sophisticated musical technology allowing two people (or one person) to sound like many more musicians. So, by our definition, a band is any group of two or more musicians.

If you're a musician who is eager to play with others but hasn't made connections yet, you will soon discover that there's a lot more to musical collaboration than simple musical technique. Social skills are at least if not more important than how you play. Why? Because you gotta be able to get along with people! If you are a great musician but you lack social interaction skills, you're gonna have a much harder time joining or forming a band compared to a less-talented musician who has superior social skills. Or to put it another way: A musician of average skill with a pleasing personality can always learn how to play better, but a musically gifted jerk will probably be, to put it politely, "moving" from band to band. There's one exception to this rule: If you're a genius, you can get away with almost anything. If you're not a genius, and you want to meet players to form a band, there are certain things you can do.

MEETING OTHER PLAYERS

You've taken lessons, practiced for thousands of hours, played along with your favorite CDs—and now you're ready to hook up with other musicians. How do you meet them? Maybe fate will hand you a partner, like when Paul McCartney met John Lennon in elementary school, or Mick Jagger bumped into Keith Richards at a playground when they were both five years old. But if you haven't grown up with someone else who loves to play, or managed by chance encounter to find like-minded players, there are several options you can explore.

First and foremost, ask your friends if they know of any musicians looking to form a band, or bands looking for musicians. Check out the bulletin boards at music stores, rehearsal facilities, and places where music lessons are given. If you take music lessons, ask your instructor if he or she knows any opportunities to play with other musicians. Listen in on conversations at live gigs in clubs; sometimes people talking to bands are musicians too, asking questions about equipment or songs, trying to figure out how a player gets a particular sound. Another way to meet musicians and songwriters is by going to an "open mike" night at a club or coffeehouse. Listen to other players at these events, and when you hear someone whose musical style seems compatible, go up and introduce yourself. Be brave; you have nothing to lose but your solo status. If you're naturally shy, and many talented people are, stretch a little. Get up the nerve to put yourself out there a little bit at at time. Frankly, the music world could use a few more shy people! Please trust me on this one, wherever and whoever you are: Nobody makes it in the music business alone.

Music stores are good places to become known to the staff as someone looking for fellow players. If the store doesn't have a bulletin board where bands and players can connect, politely suggest they put one up. Music store employees constantly deal with customers already in bands, and are often quite up-to-date on the ebb and flow of a band's musical style, personnel shifts, and its relative status in the musical community, and so are another useful source of information.

Another approach is to run a classified ad in the local paper (if there is no separate category, put it under Musical Merchandise), or respond to ads looking for players. Large cities usually have an "alternative" paper that covers music or pop culture. Check the "Gigs Wanted/Musician Wanted" listings. You've seen the ads: "Progressive Hardcore Thrash Trio seeks dedicated vegetarian nonsmoking bass player into Pavement, early Wham!, and Boy George. No flakes, no drugs, no college graduates." Call 'em up!

AUDITIONS

When a band is forming and looking for players, or has lost a player and is looking for a replacement, new musicians usually are recruited through an audition. The missing link to a band's success is often that final member, like when Ringo joined The Beatles or when Eddie Vedder joined Pearl Jam.

When established bands reminisce about their early, pre-success days, it often sounds like this: "We had this member who was a total ———, and he [either] a) left of his own accord, b) heard a voice and left per instructions, c) OD'ed, or d) got fired. We auditioned 37 ——— players and had just about given up when (your name here) shows up for an audition. We started playing together and suddenly *everything clicked*. That's when we realized something special was happening."

> Great players can and will inspire you to play better.

At auditions, just show up with your instrument and try to be totally incredible. Then again, what if the band you're auditioning for is terrible? Sometimes auditions reveal that you are a much better player than the members of the band you are auditioning for, and you may not want to join. Auditions are always a two-way street in this regard. Contrariwise, you may audition for a band whose members are much better players than you are. Don't be crushed. Let the experience motivate you. Stretching your comfort level is good for your soul as well as your career. Great players can and will inspire you to play better. Joining a band with experience (and gigs already booked) is a big plus; just ask Sammy Hagar (who joined Van Halen after they had sold millions of records), or better yet, Ron Wood, who started out playing bass for Jeff Beck, switched to guitar with Rod Stewart, and finally joined The Rolling Stones, demonstrating how upwardly mobile the music business can be.

Do your homework before showing up for an audition: Ask what **3** tunes you should know if it's a "cover" band (one that does other people's songs) and learn a few. Never forget: You are auditioning for them, but also they are auditioning for you. They might suck; you might be in over your head. Put yourself out there.

Be professional, and be aware that personality plays a larger part in the selection process than you might suspect. Auditions are tough but that's how the game works.

FINDING A PLACE TO REHEARSE

Bands need a place to practice. Two big aspects of rehearsal space you must deal with are sound insulation and security. You don't want to disturb other people when you practice, and you definitely don't want your equipment stolen. A basement can be an ideal place to rehearse because you are playing underground, out of sight, and out of hearing range. Sound travels in all directions, and a band in full swing puts out plenty of sonic information. While recording studios spend hundreds of thousands of dollars on sound insulation, a basement with carpet on the floor and sound-absorbing material on the walls could be a good choice for you. We will cover ways to sound-proof your practice space without going broke in Chapter 4.

Another choice is renting space by the hour in a rehearsal facility, a possibility available in most larger cities. Having your own permanent rehearsal space *not* in someone's home is a more expensive option but nicer, because you can leave everything set up and create a kind of "clubhouse" effect. If you can find another band that you could trust you can share rented rehearsal space and cut your overhead in half.

GIGS

Gigs are a necessity. Unless you're the rare sort who plays music just to feel the vibrations, eventually you're gonna want to play in front of people. Usually there is someone in the band who has a head for business and a special talent for talking to club owners. Until you get a booking agent, this person can be the one who helps the band get gigs. If this someone is not you, that's fine, but whoever it is, that person will be acting as a kind of surrogate manager/booking agent. If that member is not getting an extra share of the band's income for doing this work, you should at least be very nice to them for helping everyone out.

Successful bands seem to have a built-in division of labor: One member writes music, another writes lyrics, someone else is good at arranging, one member doesn't say a word and just follows suggestions, and so on. It all comes down to teamwork. We'll discuss various ways of getting gigs in Chapter 6.

NAMING YOUR BAND

One of the most fun (and maddening) aspects of forming a band is deciding what to name it. Bands can be named after continents (Asia), countries (America), states (Kansas, Idaho), cities (Chicago), neighborhoods (the E Street Band)—or better yet, diseases (Brucellosis, Tourette's Syndrome, Head Cold), creatures (Byrds, Beatles, Black Crowes, Eagles, Skinny Puppy), or nothing (INXS, Mott the Hoople, Let's Active, Gwar). There's no rhyme or reason to names now, and there never was. Trends change: Today's trend seems to be single words (Oasis, Blur, Pavement, Acetone, Sebadoh) or neo-Dada absurdity (Bob's Too Short, God Street Wine, Ben Folds Five, Archers of Loaf, Sunny Day Real Estate).

What seems trivial at first can often evolve into a devilishly frustrating and time-consuming process. Should you call your band Sally Hates Toast or does Allergen more accurately describe your particular sound? Ultimately your band name has absolutely no meaning until the public associates it with your songs, music, and image. Think about it—"The Beatles" is a very average name, a play on the word "beetles" with the spelling changed to get across the idea of a heavy "beat." But through their massive success the name is now associated with everything you think of when you think of the Fab Four. Ponder another name that has been around for so long that no one really thinks about the image it describes: The Rolling Stones. Do you visualize stones rolling down a hill? No! What do you think of? Keith! Mick! Charlie! "Start Me Up"!

For your comparison, amusement—and further education—on page 7 are some typical names of pop acts from the last 40 years.

HOW TO CHOOSE A NAME

The cleverest name of all time, The Who, has unfortunately already been taken. However, there are several ways to generate new, impossibly hip names. Here's a few techniques to get you started:

1. Get some darts and a newspaper. Open the paper up and tack it

to a wall you don't mind throwing darts at. Take turns throwing the darts and make a list of the words they hit. Mix 'n' match. One possible result: O. J. Clinton.

2. You and your bandmates make lists of words, and randomly combine them to make phrases or images. For instance: Make a list of descriptive words (morning, bored, purple, comatose, spiral, astroglide, chrome, God's, etc.) and a list of proper nouns (wood, potato, weekend, bedpan, air freshener). Combine until satisfied: Morning Wood, Chrome Potato, God's Air Freshener, Astroglide Weekend, Spiral Bedpan...there are literally dozens of possible word combinations.

3. Write down the first word that pops into your mind the moment you wake up in the morning (or afternoon). Collect a bunch and stare at these words; they come from deep within. Use them to create a band name.

4. Go to the dictionary (or thesaurus) and browse until you can't stand it any more. You'll eventually find something. "Eurythmics" is a word in the dictionary meaning "the art of performing various bodily movements in rhythm, usually to musical accompaniment." What a great word for a band name! Too bad it's already been taken.

5. Ask your parents to come up with suggestions for band names. Guaranteed to provide endless amusement.

WHAT NOT TO CALL YOUR BAND

Generally speaking, you can't name your band after a band that already exists. Calling your band The Beatles, Pearl Jam, or Kiss is a bad choice and automatically guarantees a cease-and-desist order if you use it. There are some exceptions to this rule that involve regional use. For instance, a band called Three Hits & A Miss performing solely in San Diego can share that name with a band that performs solely in Maine—they would probably never be mistaken for each other because of the geographic separation. The trouble begins when a band begins playing out of its region—something every band should strive to do! There are specific ways to check if a name you want is already being used, and methods of protecting your right to use a name once you find a good, original one. You'll need to contact an attorney who specializes in trademark law. He or she will search to see if your band name has already been registered,

A Band by Any Other Name...

'50s

Bill Haley and the Comets
Champs
Cheers
Chords
Coasters
Crests
Crickets
Danny and The Juniors
Diamonds
Drifters
Elegants
Four Lads
Four Preps
Hilltoppers
Impalas
Intruders
Johnny Ray
Platters
Rays
Royal Teens
Silhouettes

'60s

The Animals
The Association
The Beach Boys
The Beatles
Blood, Sweat & Tears
The Box Tops
The Buckinghams
The Byrds
The Classics IV
The Contours
Creedence Clearwater Revival
The Easybeats
The Electric Prunes
The Fifth Dimension
The Four Seasons
The Happenings
The Jefferson Airplane
The Lemon Pipers
The Music Explosion
The Newbeats
The Rolling Stones
The Searchers
The Supremes
The Surfaris
The Temptations
The Troggs
The Turtles
The Who
The Young Rascals
The Zombies

'70s

America
Bread
Chic
Chicago
The Commodores
The Eagles
Exile
Fleetwood Mac
Grand Funk Railroad
Lobo
Ocean
Stories
Styx
Sugarloaf
Three Dog Night
War

'80s

Ambrosia
Asia
Aztec Camera
The Cars
Foreigner
The Go-Go's
Journey
Loverboy
Motels
Night Ranger
The Police
Queen
Survivor
Toto

'90s

Indie Bands
(signed and unsigned)

Acetone
Acetylene
Bent
Birdy
Blink
Blister
Block
Braniac
Catpower
Cling
Clouded
Clutch
Crapshoot
Crow
Denim
Edsel
Fuzzy
Glue
Godplow
Gomez
Goodness
Granddaddy
Grover
Hall
Hollowbody
Hugh
Hush
Idaho
Inch
Laundry
Laurels
Low
Mensclub
Mumbleskinny
Nectarine
Perfect
Placebo
Please
Plum
Pond
Pur
Rail
Raw
Rise
Roxie
Ruby
Sammy
Seaweed
Seed
Self
Selig
Shiner
Silkworm
Skiploader
Softy
Spoon
Starbilly
Starfish
Stella
Sunflower
Superego
Tanner
Throw
Torcher
Tweaker
Vaudeville
Woolce
Wormhole

CHAPTER ONE

Origins of Some Band Names

Band Name	Origin	Previous Incarnation(s)
THE BEATLES	Influenced by Buddy Holly naming his band the Crickets	Silver Beatles, Quarry Men, Johnny and the Moondogs
MEN AT WORK	Sign on side of road	
POGUES	Gaelic for "kiss my ass"	Pogue Mahone
THE ROLLING STONES	Muddy Waters song	Rollin' Stones
TALKING HEADS	TV-camera jargon for head-and-shoulders shot	Vogue Dots
THE BYRDS	Named around Thanksgiving, misspelled like The Beatles who were a huge influence	Beefeaters, The Jet Set
CIRCLE JERKS	Never mind	Plastic Hippies, Runs
SONIC YOUTH	From Fred "Sonic" Smith, guitarist for the MC5, and Big Youth, an early Reggae Dub artist	
BUTTHOLE SURFERS	Named after song by Gibby Haynes (lead singer)	Nine Foot Worm Makes Own Food
STEELY DAN	Sexual device in William S. Burroughs' *Naked Lunch*	

and if it hasn't, he or she will register it on your behalf. You should probably avoid names that will hinder your ability to get bookings, unless you're a punk act that wants to offend everybody by calling yourself something like, uh, Shit. For instance, a band named Dipped In Puke may never get gigs at a Holiday Inn, which may be fine for all concerned. Similarly, a band called Elvis Hitler will probably get a lot of laughs but few Bar Mitzvah gigs and '50s sock hop engagements. Choose carefully.

MERCHANDISING

One of the best ways to increase awareness of your band is through promotional items like T-shirts, buttons, stickers—almost anything that your band name or logo can be put on. People love "stuff," and if you can get people to wear your band name, or drive around with your group logo affixed to their car bumper or window, you have created an advertising campaign for very little money. Plus, you can make a profit if you sell these items, as anyone who has ever bought a T-shirt at a major rock concert will attest. Matches, lighters, bumper stickers, key chains, even rulers (you know—"Braindead Rules!") are all different ways to promote your group. Look in the Yellow Pages under categories like Advertising Specialties, Decals, and Screen Printing.

Chapter Two
The Wonderful World of Equipment

**Players who chase the bleeding edge
of technology are destined to either die of
exhaustion or go blind from reading manuals.**
—Anonymous

t would be much easier if musicians could simply open their mouths and produce the sound of a guitar, drum, saxophone, or keyboard. With the notable exception of Bobby McFerrin, this is clearly not the case. We need equipment of all sorts to make music: P.A.'s, drums, guitars and other stringed instruments, synthesizers, woodwinds and brass, and nowadays digital samplers. Thirty years ago, when I started hanging out in music stores (always playing the guitars but never buying—I was twelve), equipment selection was limited to a few quality brands in each field. Today there is a truly bewildering array of guitars, drums, amplifiers, electronic keyboards, and other devices to choose from.

Before we dive in, let me share a couple of observations: First of all, many players, with the best of intentions, gradually become equipment junkies. I'm sure you've met someone like this: They are constantly talking about their gear, buying, selling, modifying and "upgrading" it, and slowly but inevitably drawing the focus of their energy away from playing music and toward music technology. Try not to make this mistake! Get the best equipment you can afford, then spend your time really learning how to control it; don't let it control you. If you buy a guitar or other musical instrument, play it enough so that you really get used to it. The same goes for amplifiers, effects pedals, signal processors—any link in your musical chain. In most cases, if you have chosen wisely, the ability to create a sound is already inherent in your instrument—if you have put in the time to explore what the instrument can do. Don't let equipment distract you from the music.

Second, try to maintain what I call a "healthy cynicism" toward all the claims made in the advertisements. Equipment manufacturers (instruments and electronic gear) have one goal: selling their product. They want you to believe that yesterday's equipment, even the stuff they manufactured last year, is old and not "cutting edge." Most of the time this is a load of crap. People have been making beautiful music for thousands of years with the simplest of instruments: piano, violin, drums, the human voice. Furthermore, the world of musical equipment is slightly schizophrenic. On the one hand, manufacturers emphasize their latest "state of the art" designs in digital sound synthesis, and sound processing and recording equipment, while on the other, musicians crave vintage gear—so "retro" style equipment is making a comeback. Many manufacturers (Fender, Gibson, Ampeg) have taken notice of the high price their earlier models command, and are reissuing these designs to an eager public. New stuff, old stuff, and new "old" stuff; it's all out there awaiting your consideration.

Try not to be seduced into switching your gear all the time. Resisting this urge won't please the equipment manufacturers but will save you money and time, allowing you to focus your energy on what your equipment was designed for—playing music.

The following information isn't offered as the Gospel Truth on equipment but more as an overview and a guide, with the occasional technique and suggestion thrown in.

GUITARS

Buying a guitar in today's market can be similar to buying a computer: many choices, many claims, and many price ranges. Despite the bewildering array of models and options, if you're armed with a little knowledge these are good times to go shopping. To know what's out there, a little background information can help.

The early years of electric guitar—the '50s—were dominated by two big names: Fender and Gibson. Fender was known for three famous guitar models: the Stratocaster, the Telecaster, and the Precision Bass guitar. Gibson made a much wider variety of acoustic guitars and solid and hollow body electrics, the most popular being the Les Paul, designed by the inventor of multitrack recording, Les Paul. The other big names in electric guitars from the '50s to the early '70s were Gretsch and Rickenbacker, while acoustic players picked (literally) Gibson, Martin, and Guild. There were a few other brands, English-, Italian-, and Japanese-made, but the ones listed above were the main choices available to musicians until the mid-'70s.

Then came the Great Asian manufacturing explosion. Boom! The guitar market became flooded with *exact* copies of American guitars made in Japan, then later on in Korea—brands like Ibanez, Yamaha, Takamine, and offerings from other lesser-known companies. The first wave of guitars from Japan were identical in design to their American counterparts except they were cheaper and of relatively low quality. After a few shipments of these Fender and Gibson clones were returned to Japan with the headstocks sawed off by irate American guitar makers and their patent lawyers, Japan took the hint and started modifying existing styles and then inventing their own.

> Despite the bewildering array of models and options, if you're armed with a little knowledge these are good times to go shopping.

Strictly speaking, all guitars, whether electric or acoustic, are an assembly of wood, metal, paint, plastic, and labor. The quality of each of these components determines the overall quality of the instrument. The good news is that today's massive global market for guitars has lured many manufacturers into competition with one another for your hard-earned bucks.

Although primarily designed in the U.S., the majority of new guitars (with the exception of Martin, Guild, Rickenbacker, Gibson, and certain Fenders) are manufactured overseas. And they bang them suckers out, folks. A guitar with a list price of $1,000 costs the manufacturer around $100 to make. It is sold to a distributor or store for around $500, and then to you for as much as the salesperson can get. Unsentimental but true. And what does your money buy? Believe it or not, on the manufacturer's end the most expensive part of a guitar to produce is the finish, or "paint job." Today's typical buyer believes that "shiny and flashy is better," so manufacturers spray on very thick, glossy finishes that actually tend to deaden the sound of a guitar, especially for the first six months to a year as the paint continues to dry out.

Once you decide what is visually appealing, the basic choice comes down to this: Do you want a solid-body or hollow-body electric? Hollow bodies can sound warm and "natural," and blues and jazz players sometimes prefer these traits. Solid-body guitars have a simpler, more straightforward tone, don't feed back (squeal) as much when played loud, and seem to be the choice for today's hard-rocking youth.

Many factors influence the sound of a guitar. For electric guitars, the most noticeable variable is the type of pickup—the rectangular things on the body under the strings that amplify the sound. Guitar pickups are essentially long flat magnets surrounded by a couple thousand wraps of wire, which create a small electric current when the string is plucked. This tiny current goes to your amp and is modified according to your amp design and settings. There are two basic types of pickups: single-coil and "humbucking." Single-coil pickups have a brighter, sweeter, cleaner sound. Unfortunately, they pick up stray electrical impulses too, such as 60-cycle hum from the wall current and local radio stations. That's why someone invented "humbucking" pickups—they don't hum. Humbuckers have more power and sound "fatter," but have less high-end. Acoustic guitars can also have pickups, usually mounted inside the body, under the bridge.

Enough technical crud. What brands and models are the best so I can run out and get one? Hold on. Focusing on brand names is not necessarily the proper approach. It doesn't necessarily matter what brand guitar you buy, it matters what actual guitar you buy, because every maker manufactures better or worse copies of each model.

A row of identical make and model electric guitars can sound quite different from one another, for many reasons. One reason is that wood, as you might suspect, varies a lot in quality and how long it has aged. Various copies of a specific acoustic guitar model exhibit even more variance in sound quality—their tone depends almost exclusively on wood rather than electronics. Which of several guitars sounds "better" is a matter of taste. You can get a real bargain in a used guitar by being in the right place at the right time (i.e., luck), but the general consensus is that a new, decent-sounding acoustic will cost at least $200. Because wood is so critical to the sound, the better-sounding acoustics have a solid one-piece top (often spruce) as opposed to a laminate (alternating layers of cheap wood and glue). As acoustic guitars age, the ones with a solid top start sounding sweeter and mellower. The laminated top ones. . .well, they just get older. Costlier acoustics (such as Martins, Guilds, and Taylors) have solid wood sides and backs, and these age with even better results.

To start your guitar search, here's a great unscientific test to perform. Go into a music store with lots of guitars hanging on the racks. If you're trying out acoustic guitars, walk by them and strum each one quickly. Several of them will sound pleasing to your ears, no matter the price or brand or whether they are old or new. Begin your selection from these. Remember, if you like the tone, that's the guitar for you.

If you're shopping for an electric, start by playing it without plugging it into an amp. Really good-sounding electric guitars tend to sound good unamplified. Strum a few times with your ear crammed up hard against the top of the body so the sound goes right into your skull. Do this with a lot of electrics and you'll hear plenty of variety.

After you select from the good-sounding guitars which you can actually afford, focus on the heart of the guitar: the neck. It should be straight, with low action and smooth, even frets. Is the action easy to play? Can you push down the strings without heroic effort? The height of the action can be adjusted, within certain limits. Next, play bar chords up and down the neck. Do you hear fret buzz when you strum? Any used guitar may have fret wear, which can either be uneven fret height or little dents in the first few frets from extensive chord playing.

Here's how to check a guitar neck for straightness. Push down the high E string (the thinnest one) on the first fret and the twelfth fret at the same time and look at the distance between the string and the neck at around the sixth fret. Ideally, this space should be about the thickness of the string. If it's not, the neck may be bowed; it can be straightened by adjusting a metal rod running the length of the neck called a truss rod.

Used instruments should be checked carefully for cracks in the body (they don't affect the tone as much as you think and are usually repairable) and also for splits in the neck (sometimes the entire head has broken off and been reglued on: be careful, and ask questions).

Price is probably the controlling factor in your choice of an acoustic or electric. If you can't afford a brand new Martin D-35 or Gibson Les Paul, take heart; how you play, not the quality of the instrument, has the biggest influence on your sound. Nirvana's Kurt Cobain seemed to actually prefer truly cheesy guitars and he got a unique sound out of them. Getting a great sound out of a cheap guitar is probably one of life's greatest thrills. Go Hondo! Go Univox! Go Teisco!

Electric guitars come in a maddening range of styles and prices. To a certain extent you get what you pay for. For instance, a new Gibson Les Paul can cost between $800 and $5,000, but a guitar like this can actually appreciate in value. Certain cheaper guitars hold their value better than others. By way of example: Korean-made Fender Squiers usually go for $249 and are occasionally "blown out" at stores for $199. Although not a masterpiece of craftsmanship, the Fender name will help you sell it later on when you want to trade up. If you're serious about guitar playing you will probably change guitars several times, so it's important to consider this "front-end/back-end" equation. Buying a used guitar with a recognizable brand name such as Fender and Gibson instead of a brand new and less expensive copy is often a better deal in the long run. It holds or even increases its value while you own it.

> *Really good-sounding electric guitars tend to sound good unamplified.*

New guitars are available at music stores and also from mail-order catalogs like *Musician's Friend*, *American Musical Supply*, and *Interstate Musician Supply*. However, one advantage of buying locally is that stores usually "set up" your guitar, adjusting the action and neck several times during the break-in period, to your satisfaction. Guitars aren't set up at the factory—it costs too much, and changes in climate from factory to you puts wood through heavy changes; also, the neck and frets settle slightly as you play. So, when you get a guitar, the best $50 to $100 you can spend is to have it "set up" by a guitar shop. Typically this tune-up will include truss rod adjustment, which straightens the neck, setting the nut and bridge saddle to the proper height (this adjusts the action), cleaning and tightening the tuners, choosing the appropriate string gauge, and setting the intonation so the guitar plays in tune with itself. Performing these adjustments all at once can make a remarkable and noticeable improvement in how your guitar feels and plays, and if done at a reputable shop is definitely money well spent.

A lot of lower-end "flash guitars" with wild paint jobs and bizarre angular body styles can look impressive, but the paint can be masking cheap plywood bodies, the frets can be of marginal quality, and the electronics and hardware can be crudola.

Before you buy anything, play some guitars out of your price range to help you get a feel for what money buys, or sometimes doesn't buy.

In the long run, it's hard to blow it by buying a new or used Fender or Gibson anything. Both of these companies have started reissuing versions of the guitar models they first produced in the '50s and '60s, with the same specs as the highly collectible originals. Used American-made Strats sell for $400 to $500, and Strats manufactured in Mexico can be bought used for around $200. Older (made in USA) Epiphone electrics are good buys too. Other recognizable names to look for are Ibanez, G&L, Yamaha (they make everything), and Music Man. To find used guitars, look in your local paper under Musical Equipment, ask your musician friends if they are selling gear or know of any deals, and check bulletin boards at music schools and rehearsal facilities—anywhere that musicians meet. The following brand acoustics are good values in used acoustic guitars: 10- to 12-year-old Yamahas ($200 to $250), Seagull (around $200), mid- to late-'70s Washburns (especially Prairie Songs and Festivals), and most Takamines (copies of Martin designs).

BASSES

The standard classic electric bass was, still is, and probably always will be, the Fender Precision. They look and sound great! Although older ones sell for many dollars, the new ones are relatively affordable and excellent. Basses come in short-scale or long-scale designs, with a string length of either 30" or 34". Although most basses are four-stringed instruments, tuned E–A–D–G one octave below a guitar, many other configurations exist. Fender, among others, makes a five-string bass, adding a high B string. Hagstrom used to make an eight-string bass by adding an extra string tuned an octave higher next to each regular string (E–E', A–A', D–D', G–G'). Fender and Danelectro used to make a six-string bass model, essentially a specially reinforced guitar with thick strings tuned an octave below normal. This style has been reintroduced by Ibanez, Fender, Jerry Jones (identical to Danelectro), and others.

Hollow-body basses are more costly to manufacture but have a warm, "round," almost acoustic bass tone. If you're lucky you might find an old Framus, Epiphone, or Eko hollowbody. Good hunting. A few easy-to-find good used brands to check out for solid-body basses are Fender and Gibson (of course), Ibanez, Yamaha, and G&L. Find a bass that fits the size of your hand, the style of music you play, and your budget. Strings come in different styles too: flat-wound, round-wound, and half-round.

Take the time to try out a lot of guitars before you buy, and realize that it's easy to get caught up in the details and lose sight of the reason you want a guitar—to play music.

DRUMS

Q: What's the difference between a
drummer and a mutual fund?
A: Mutual funds mature and make money.

Where was I? Oh yeah. Drums are relatively expensive: A guitarist can purchase a reasonable instrument for a couple hundred dollars; a singer only has to open his or her mouth to create music; but even a decent, name-brand used drum kit will cost between $750 and $2,000. It sounds pricey, but if you combine the cost of at least four drums (bass drum, floor tom, rack tom, snare), hardware, cymbals, and cases, you can easily understand how a premium quality new kit can range from $4,000 to $9,000. Read it and weep! Drums, unlike electronic gear which is mostly software programming trapped inside a box, are entirely acoustic instruments and require a tremendous amount of labor to manufacture.

The original big names of Ludwig, Rodgers (now defunct), and Slingerland are augmented today by Sonor (made in Germany), Pearl, Yamaha, and Tama. According to some top players, the best drums are custom manufactured by relatively new companies like DW (Drum Workshop), Noble & Cooley, and GMS. When it comes time to buy, often a drum instructor or other professional can help you choose a setup that is appropriate for your style.

A well-balanced drum set, or kit, is a matched set of drums that sound good together, with no one component louder than the other. If one of your toms is a lot louder than the rest of your kit this will sound weird when you play live. This balance is achieved through trial and error and careful attention to choice of drumheads, size of each drum, and head tension. One way to get a big sound from smaller drums, which, incidentally cost less than larger diameter shells, is by tuning the heads lower than normal. The great rock drummer Jeff Porcaro played with small diameter tom toms, but they sounded absolutely huge because he tuned them lower than usual. A big drum with a tightly tuned drumhead will actually sound smaller than a little drum with a loosely tuned head. This overtightening is a common mistake.

No way am I going to recommend the "correct" kit! Having said that, here is a "typical" rock kit as a basic description:

16" x 22" kick
9" x 12" rack tom
16" x 16" floor tom
5" x 14" snare
20" ride, medium thin
17" crash, medium thin
14" matched hi-hat cymbals

A few comments. All things being equal, the sound of the snare drum defines the style of the drummer. Piccolo snares are thinner, smaller in diameter, and have a higher, tighter, brighter sound. The Ludwig Black Beauty was a very popular snare drum that has now been reissued. Careful adjustment of the batter, and choice of drumheads and tuning, can radically affect the sound of the snare—something to be aware of when trying out drums. Hi-hats come in different sizes, with 14" being the standard and 13" gaining popularity with jazz and jazz-rock players. Fifteen-inch hi-hat cymbals are bigger and darker, a favorite with "metal" and hard rock players. Ah, categories!

Drumheads: Remo is the most popular drumhead manufacturer, followed by Evans and Aquarian. Remo's white-coated drumheads come in three basic thicknesses: Diplomat, for a light, thin, jazz-style sound, easily dented and from then on hard to tune; Ambassador, mid-thickness, for a loud, noisy, wide-open English sound, like Led Zep and The Who; and Emperor, the thickest head, designed for heavy hitters. Oddly enough, the thinner heads can be loudest if tuned and struck with proper technique. CS ("Controlled Spot")

heads have a thick-coated spot in the middle of the head designed to eliminate overtones, and are often used in studio situations for a more compact, controlled sound. Pinstripe heads have a built-in muffler around the edge of the head that acts as a sound deadener, eliminating ringing sounds. Also available are natural calf-skin heads and their synthetic equivalent, hydraulic heads, that are actually a double head with oil suspended between them, and so on. Different drumheads create different sounds and are a critical component of your gear—more critical than you may believe at first. New heads bring out the natural sound of the drum, just as new guitar strings bring out the natural sound of the guitar.

> *All things being equal, the sound of the snare drum defines the style of the drummer.*

TUNING DRUMS

Part of your gig as a drummer is to tune the drums, just as a guitarist is expected to tune the guitar. Every time a guitarist takes a moment to tune up, you can do the same. Drums are musical instruments too! They produce a pitch, but one low enough not to interfere with the sonic range of the other instruments.

Every drum has a resonant pitch, even the bass drum. If you've ever sung in the shower, you may have noticed how certain notes seem to fill up the space; this note is the resonant frequency of your bathroom. Well, every drum has a resonant frequency that fills up its space and makes it "sing." Finding this frequency range for each drum is your goal. More expensive manufacturers such as Drum Workshop actually write the pitch on the drum shell as a guide for tuning. In reality, when a drum is struck it produces several, shifting frequencies as it rings, so a general frequency range is what we are shooting for. The method used to tune the drums is called tympanic tuning, which is similar to the way tympani are tuned in a symphony orchestra.

This statement bears repeating: *Tuning is not an option, but is part of your job as a drummer.* Tuning is definitely a pain in the butt; it's not fun, it's a hassle, you probably won't dig it, but if you take the time you will end up with a great-sounding kit. It's hard work, but who said being a legend was going to be easy? Besides, guitarists never claimed that tuning their guitars was fun, but they do it. OK—Here's how it's done.

Each drum has equally spaced lugs (also known as tension rods) surrounding the rim. The tighter these are screwed down, the higher the tension on the head, which produces a higher pitch. You begin by tightening these lugs evenly to the lowest possible setting that produces tension on the head. Then, while deadening the center of the head with the index finger of one hand, tap a spot in front of each lug with the index finger of your other hand, listening for the pitch. Your goal is to turn the lug with the drum key until the pitch of this spot matches the pitch you have chosen for the drum. Repeat this process on the other lugs. Remember to muffle the head in the middle with a fingertip while tuning, or the entire head will cross-resonate and you won't hear a distinct pitch.

When you've tuned the top head, repeat the process with the bottom head, tuning it to the same pitch, or a pitch slightly above or below it. If a drum has two heads (some drummers don't use two heads on tom toms or bass drum) you gotta tune them both. Like I said, it can be a hassle, but oh! what a sound you're gonna get.

Tuning drums is more of an art than a science, and it's best to tune with no interruptions from the other band members. Painstaking work, but you will definitely hear the difference! Once you've experimented and found out what works with your drums and your style, replacing worn heads and tuning them will be much quicker and easier.

Unless you are into the big band jazz sound, you should cut a perfectly round, centered hole in the front head of the bass drum. This hole aims and focuses the sound of the drum, and allows the head being struck to produce the only pitch. This hole also permits easy microphone placement for recording and live performance situations. For a 22" drum, a centered 9" hole is appropriate. Use a 9" cymbal or a pie plate as a template, and cut it out very carefully with a sharp blade so it doesn't eventually tear from a ragged edge. Don't be afraid to experiment with the size and placement of the hole that produces the sound you're looking for. Experiment.

If this all seems like too much trouble, it's important to understand something about the drums you hear on recordings. The engi- neer, producer, and drummer may have spent days tuning them in **21** the studio before cutting the basic tracks. In five years of running a recording studio, I can count on my thumbs how many drummers I recorded that brought in a set of well-maintained, tuned drums. Take the time—you will be pleased with the results.

ELECTRONIC PRODUCTS AND MIDI GEAR

Describing and commenting specifically on all of the available electronic gear is futile—there's so much out there, even just the stuff with memorable names like the i1, XP-10, G800, X2, DA-88, and JV-1080—and the product lines change almost monthly as new models are released and old products are discontinued. In the short time between the writing of this book and the publication date, a vast array of newer/faster/cheaper/more powerful products will be released. Entire books, workshops, and technical libraries are dedicated to explaining how these products work. With the advent of digital technology, the boundaries between instruments and recording devices are blurring and in many cases disappearing altogether. This being said, it helps to know what is out there these days.

By surveying electronic gear that is most appropriate for live performance we simplify the subject considerably.

KEYBOARDS AND MIDI

Generally speaking, in the old days (pre-'70s) the following keyboards were available to the musician: a real piano, the Wurlitzer electric piano, the Fender Rhodes electric piano, the Hohner Clavinet, and the Hammond B3 organ. With few exceptions, these were the instruments producing the keyboard sounds of pop/jazz/blues. Then along came synthesizers. The early greats (by name and most popular model) were Oberheim (OBX), Moog (Minimoog), Roland (Jupiter), Arp (2600), and Sequential Circuits (Prophet). In the early '80s, Yamaha introduced the truly revolutionary DX7 keyboard featuring clean FM *digital synthesis*, and MIDI. By plugging one keyboard into another via a MIDI (Musical Instrument Digital Interface) cable, playing the first keyboard would trigger the other one. Because the second keyboard didn't need keys to produce sound, those clever manufacturers found a way to save money and space by inventing the *sound module*, a rack-mountable box containing the electronic circuitry of a keyboard synthesizer—without the keys. *Sound modules* are triggered by either a keyboard or sequencing software. As a keyboard player in a band, the most practical setup probably would be a self-contained keyboard synthesizer with the built-in sounds appropriate for your style of music. Most electronic keyboard manufacturers offer a model designed for live performance, featuring the most practical sounds that bands use—piano, Fender Rhodes, Wurlitzer, brass, string, and orchestral samples.

Another way to go is using a MIDI performance controller, a keyboard with weighted piano action designed to trigger the above-mentioned sound modules. The keys feel a lot better than the cheap plastic ones on most synthesizers, and the keyboard usually has more of them—77 or 88, compared to 64 or less on other synths. Check out these keyboard models and also the selection of sound modules that have good usable sounds—strings, piano, organ—or (if you're into different music) explosions, Star Trek beeps, and hip-hop scratching. Yo!

Most of the big firms (Yamaha, Roland, Korg, Peavey, Kurzweil, Ensoniq) make what is known as a *Digital Audio Workstation*, or DAW. These megadevices combine a keyboard, sampler, sequencer, effects section and hard disk storage all in one expensive and remarkably complicated package. As bitchin' as they are, the DAW is happier being used at home or in a recording or production studio and isn't really appropriate or necessary for live music.

EFFECTS

Additional gear for band use includes rack-mounted effects processors with a zillion programs (distortion, reverb, delay, chorus, flanger phaser, tremolo, harmonization), giant pedal boards that offer much of the same, and individual effect "stomp boxes" plugged in between your instrument and your amp that are controlled by a footswitch mounted on the top. Try 'em all out, but remember this: If everybody else has the same "special effects" at their fingertips, they aren't special any more. Getting an individual sound takes two things: practice and experimentation.

SAXOPHONES

This is pretty simple. Instruments come in three levels of quality: student, intermediate, and professional, and they are priced accordingly. The standard for saxophones has been set, probably forever, by the

Selmer Mk VI, or "Mark 6," which of course is no longer manufactured. A prime condition used Mk VI alto or tenor sax currently sells
for $4,000 to $4,500. Yamaha copied the Mk VI design and offers its
version of it in the above-listed quality levels, as do other Japanese
manufacturers. Kielworth are top-quality horns that are expensive.
Selmer, now merged with Bach, makes a line of saxes under the
Bundy name that are good beginner instruments. Bundy, Conn,
Yamaha, Vito, and Jupiter are all reputable names to check out when
shopping for a new or used saxophone. Other used models that are
good to seek out but which may be considered "collectible" (and
therefore expensive) are: Conn 10M, Buescher Aristocrat and 400,
King Super 20, Martin, and Couf.

Unfortunately, many used saxes—especially used ones owned and
played by amateurs—have leaks. These are tiny spaces between the
pad and tone hole that let air escape when the key is pressed down
and that make producing a full, clear tone difficult or impossible. This
is easily remedied by adjustment or pad replacement, but a leaky
horn is hard to judge when you're trying to decide how it sounds.
If purchasing from a store you should insist that it is in perfect working order before you buy.

The mouthpiece is a critical (some say the critical) part of the
instrument, and as your technique improves you can move away
from a student mouthpiece that produces a kind of wimpy tone and
up to a more open, full-chambered model. Many players think that
a metal mouthpiece is the only way to get a cutting sound, but this
simply isn't true. The equipment on the other side of the reed—
you—is the biggest factor in tone production. The more expensive
reeds are more consistent and last longer than the cheaper variety.
Players often have to try out a whole box of 25 mid-price reeds to
find two or three that sound good. Artificial reeds—such as
Fibracell—and plastic-dipped reeds (Plasticover) last longer and have
a brighter sound that really cuts through when playing live gigs.

AMPLIFIERS

Choosing an amp is strictly a matter of taste, so the following is simply a description of what is currently available.

Amplifiers serve two purposes: to increase the volume of your
instrument, and to color the sound. The preamp section, power amp
section, tone circuitry, and speakers are all critical factors influencing

the volume and tone. As with guitars, the retro scene is alive and well in the amplifier world: Vintage amps go for thousands of dollars more than they ever cost new. However, Fender and Ampeg are both reissuing popular vintage designs that are worth trying out. Tube amps are known for their warm, musical tone, even when purposely overdriven to achieve distortion. Solid-state amps are more economical and create a very clean distortion-free signal appropriate for instruments that need to be amplified but not significantly altered in tone, like the sound of the piano, bass, or acoustic guitar.

Amp manufacturers have made real advances in approximating the sound of tube distortion with solid-state transistorized circuitry, but the key word is approximating. Nothing sounds quite like real tube distortion! Tube amps are back in a big way. Guitarists should bring their own guitar along when trying out amps, and spend as much time as possible messing around with the tone controls, starting out with all of them in the minimum position and turning them up one at a time to check the individual effect. Bass amps need plenty of clean, distortion-free watts to accurately amplify the power-hungry low end generated by the bass guitar. Your budget as well as your ears will probably be your guide when shopping for an amp. It also helps to be realistic when shopping for an amp. If you'll be playing mostly small clubs, do you really need that Marshall stack? Jimmy Page recorded his guitar through small amps like the Vox AC30 or the Fender Champ on those Led Zeppelin records. Volume and tone aren't necessarily related. Be aware that tube amps sound great but will in time need replacement tubes, so spare tubes are a must when gigging.

> Amplifiers serve two purposes: to increase the volume of your instrument, and to color the sound.

SOUND REINFORCEMENT— P.A.'S AND MICROPHONES

If you are in a band that intends to play mostly clubs that have their own systems, for better or worse, you may not need a complete P.A. system. However, you will probably need some combination of microphones, amplification, and speaker cabinets for rehearsals unless you strictly play instrumentals. Sound systems, whether elaborate or simple, are made up of microphones and mike stands, cables, a mixing board, and an amplifier (sometimes combined in one console called a *powered mixer*), speaker cabinets (for the audience), and monitors (for you). Regular mixers will need a separate power amp (made by Crown, Soundtech, Alesis, QSC, Carvin, Carver, and many more) that is almost always rack-mountable. A 19" wide rack mounting is a standard spec used by all electronic equipment manufacturers, allowing equipment made by different companies to fit together in equipment racks, available in many sizes and styles.

The main speaker boxes ("mains") usually have a woofer (15" or 12" low-end speaker) and a tweeter (a tiny transducer that delivers high frequencies). A three-way system will add a third component, often an 8" mid-range speaker for greater clarity and vocal presence. Monitors are smaller speaker boxes with slanted backs, so that when you place them in front of you on the floor they aim at your ear, not the ceiling. For vocalists who want to sing on key, a monitor is a must, especially in loud rock bands. Each channel on the mixing board has a knob (or fader) to adjust the volume of each input (instrument or microphone) going to the mains, and another knob ("monitor send") to adjust how much signal is sent to the monitor. More sophisticated consoles allow several separate monitor mixes: The drummer might need more guitar or bass in her mix, the vocalist might need more keyboard in his.

There are many microphones to choose from, ranging from cheap Radio Shack models up to pricey German mikes like Beyer, AKG, and Sennheiser. Microphones come and microphones go, but for years the "workhorse" mikes for live sound reinforcement (as well as recording use) have been the Shure SM-57 and SM-58. The SM-57 is rugged, reliable, and sounds great for vocals and miking snare drum and guitar cabinets. The SM-58 is designed specifically for vocals, but either one of these models will work fine for almost any live application. They are available for around $100 through various mail-order sources.

CHAPTER THREE
MUSIC BASICS—A LITTLE GOES A LONG WAY

I know that the twelve notes in each octave and the varieties of rhythm offer me opportunities that all of human genius will never exhaust.
—Igor Stravinsky (1882–1971)

very musician should know at least a little about music theory. We're going to cover only three things: the keyboard, major scales, and chords. If you can grasp these concepts, you will have a good basic working knowledge of the structure of music.

Music, like English, is a language, and has a grammar of its own. Instead of 26 letters, music has 12 notes. If you combine these notes vertically (up and down) you create *chords*. If you combine the notes horizontally (left to right) you have *melody*. Add *rhythm* to chords and melody and you have a song! Of these three components, we will be focusing on *chords*, the musical framework of every song you are likely to learn in a band context.

Warning: Some of these concepts are hard to grasp, as well as hard to explain without the benefit of hearing the sounds we are describing. Because of this you may have to read a sentence (or section) several times to fully grasp the concept. This is normal.

Please don't mistake this chapter for a comprehensive treatise on music theory. This is purposely just the basics—where chords come from and how they are used in songs. If you already know this stuff, good—it won't take long to skim over. If you don't have any musical training and you "play by ear," learning some basic theory will make you an even a better player.

This chapter will teach you:

- How to play a major scale in every key, by learning the pattern of the spaces between the notes.
- The family of seven chords (three major, three minor, one diminished) built from, and based on, every major scale. Knowing this family of chords will help you to understand the harmonic structure of most of the songs you will play.

- What the key of a song is and why a key signature has a certain number of sharps or flats in it. This is directly related to musical scales.

- How to assign each chord in a song a number (1, 2, 3, 4, 5, 6, or 7) in order to show every chord's relationship to the key of the song. When you understand why musicians often use numbers in describing chord progressions (i.e., "play a 1–4–5 progression in C" instead of "play a C chord, an F chord, and a G chord") you'll learn to "hear" the chord progression of a song without actually knowing the names of the chords. Understanding the architecture of chord progressions is something worth knowing.

- How to write chord symbols for lead sheets the simple way, so everyone in the band can learn and show songs to each other quickly.

KEYBOARDS, MAJOR SCALES, AND KEY SIGNATURES

A chord is a combination of three or more notes sounded together in harmony. The majority of pop tunes use chords based on (and built from) the notes in a major scale. Because these chords are built strictly from scale notes, they are called *diatonic* chords, which is what we'll learn. Using the C-major scale is the easiest way to demonstrate this because it has no sharps or flats.

First, we'll look at how musical pitches are named on the keyboard. If you can, get hold of a small, cheap, battery-operated Casio keyboard or similar portable model. It will increase your understanding of music theory and song structure tremendously. The visual layout of a keyboard is helpful in explaining many abstract musical concepts.

Take a look at this rather alarming-looking keyboard visual aid and refer to it as you read the section below:

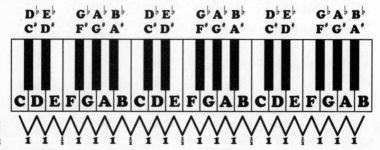

- The distance between each key and its neighbor is called a *half step*, the smallest musical interval our Western ears are accustomed to. Look at the keyboard and notice that most of the white keys are separated by a black key, so these white keys are a whole step apart. Some of the white keys do not have a black key between them—the B and C keys, and the E and F keys. These pairs of white keys (B–C and E–F) are *a half-step apart. Remember this important fact.* The other pairs of white keys (C–D, D–E, F–G, G–A, A–B) are a *whole step* apart—because they have a black key between them. Gaze at the keyboard till this starts making sense.
- The white keys are named after the letters A, B, C, D, E, F, G. When you get to G, you start the alphabet over again. The black keys are the flats (♭) and sharps (#) of these white keys, and are named accordingly.
- A black key directly to the *right* of a white key (go ahead and look) is the white key's sharp, and is pitched a half-step higher. This same black key is also directly to the *left* of a white key, and is that key's *flat*, and is pitched a half-step lower. Accordingly, a black key is simultaneously the sharp of one note and the flat of another.

Knowing these facts will help you understand the structure of a major scale.

In the key of C, a major scale is C–D–E–F–G–A–B–C. This happens to be every white key in a row, starting on one C, and ending on the next C on the keyboard. By studying how far apart each note is from the next in the scale, we can determine the major scale pattern, and this leads us to a thrilling conclusion: the C-major scale is a series of pitches with intervals in this order:

whole step, whole step, **half step**, whole step, whole step, whole step, **half step**

⬇ ⬇ ⬇ ⬇ ⬇ ⬇ ⬇ ⬇
C D E F G A B C

or, using numbers instead of words:

scale step	1	2	3	4	5	6	7	8
scale note	C	D	E	F	G	A	B	C
interval		1 ·	1 ·	½ ·	1 ·	1 ·	1 ·	½

There are 12 different major scales, each one starting on a different key of the keyboard—that is, every note from C to B. Take a moment to count them. Go ahead. There are 12. Each of these major scales:

- Starts on a particular note (this note is called the *key* of the scale)
- Ends on the next highest note with the same name (this interval is called an *octave*)
- Has a half-step between notes 3–4 and 7–8, and
- Has a whole step between all other notes.

Since every major scale follows these rules, you can build any major scale by knowing the pattern. Look! Here's an F-major scale:

scale step	1	2	3	4	5	6	7	8
scale note		F	G	A	B♭	C	D	E	F
interval			1	1	½	1	1	1	½

It would be easier if all these notes were a whole step apart. However, if you remember that these **half-step intervals are between 3 and 4, 7 and 8**, you've got major scales figured out.

When you start building a major scale on a note other than C, such as the F-major scale shown above, you'll need to use some black keys to play the scale with the correct half-step intervals when they come up in the sequence. The F-major scale uses one black key, a B♭. The G-major scale uses one black key, an F#. Other major scales use more.

Can you write out a G scale? By looking at the keyboard and knowing the major scale pattern, you can build a G-major scale using these notes: G A B C D E F# G. Work with me, now: the G to A is a whole step, the A to B is a whole step, the B to C is a *half step* (between 3 and 4), the C to D is a whole step, the E to F is *not* a whole step so we sharp the F to make it a whole step, the F# to G is a *half step* (between 7 and 8), and we're done.

LEARNING THE BASIC CHORD FAMILY

The musical staff consists of five lines and four spaces. Each line or space has a letter assigned to it, and these letters correspond to the notes on the keyboard:

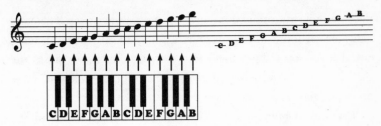

A C-major scale is shown at right.

Enough about scales: We're interested in chords, so we can learn songs, play songs, and maybe even write songs. The simplest chord is called a *triad* (from the Greek word for "three"), and is built from a root note, plus the third and fifth notes following it in the scale. It's easier to understand if we put the notes of a C-major scale in a circle and build the chords by starting on one note and using every other letter:

Let's use the wheel to build the three-note chords generated from a C-major scale. We'll number these chords and label them as either major or minor : C–E–G (C major), D–F–A (D minor), E–G–B (E minor), F–A–C (F major), G–B–D (G major), A–C–E (A minor), and B–D–F (B diminished). Notice that each chord takes its name from the first note in the triad, or root.

No matter which major scale you choose to build these chords, these truths are self-evident:

- The *first*, *fourth*, and *fifth* chords are always *major*.
- The *second*, *third*, and *sixth* chords are always *minor* (m).
- The *seventh* chord is always *diminished* (o).

This is important, so consider these chords for a moment. These major, minor, and diminished triads are called *diatonic chords*, because **31** they are built from scale notes only. Don't get me wrong. There are many other, more interesting, nondiatonic chords used in music, especially in pop and jazz tunes and Steely Dan songs, but our Music Basics chapter is purposely limited to these simple triads and how they are built.

The chords built from the first, fourth and fifth notes in the scale—all *major* chords—are what we will call The Big Three, used in countless (seriously) rock, folk, blues, and jazz tunes. The chords built from the second, third, and sixth notes in the scale—all *minor* chords—are commonly used to enhance the harmonic movement of the song. They play a smaller role in songs than that of The Big Three, but are almost as common. The chord built from the seventh note in the scale—a *diminished* chord—is not as common as The Big Three, but is used as a connecting chord and also by many moody songwriters.

USING NUMBER NOTATION ("NASHVILLE NUMBER SYSTEM")

In the figure on the bottom of page 31, we numbered the chords to help keep track of which ones were major (1, 4, and 5), minor (2, 3, and 6), and diminished (7). Take a quick look to verify this.

Because the 1 chord is built from the first note in the scale, it is the root or "home" chord, the key of the song. Numbers (instead of specific chord names) are used to show you the relationship of the other chords to this home chord. All the other chords are defined by how far away they are from this "home base."

Once you memorize the type of chord (major, minor, or diminished) associated with each number—and this should take you no longer than five minutes (go ahead—I'll wait)—you can name and play a chord by simply knowing the key of the song and the chord's number. Huh? I'll show you. In the key of F major the scale notes are F, G, A, B♭, C, D, E, and F:

F	Gᵐ	Aᵐ	B♭	C	Dᵐ	E°	(F)
1	2	3	4	5	6	7	(8)

Just like the figure on page 32 (based on a C scale), the chords based on an F scale have the same qualities: the 1, 4, and 5 are major; the 2, 3, and 6 are minor; and the poor old 7 chord is still diminished, and probably a little lonely. So, if I asked you to play a "2–5–1" progression in the key of F (the scale notes of which are F–G–A–B♭–C–D–E–F), would you know what to play? G minor, C major, and F major. How about a "2–5–1" progression in C? That's right, D minor, G major, C major. Congratulations! You've just accidentally learned how to use numbers to represent chords.

This idea of assigning numbers to chords is the essence of the famous Nashville Number System, used by all the session players in Nashville. For example, in the key of C, we have the major scale—C, D, E, F, G, A, and B—and the chords associated with these scale notes: C major, D minor, E minor, F major, G major, A minor, B diminished. These become chords 1 through 7 in the key of C. It may seem way too simple, but once you get the hang of it, it makes great sense. All it requires is that you remember what quality each chord has—major, minor, or diminished—and know your scales. If you want to be a professional musican, this is essential information, and more importantly, learnable.

Why do Nashville session players use this system? Two reasons. One, you can write a chart very quickly. Two, since the essence of country music is still the lyrics and vocals, the musicians must always cater to the needs of vocalists; that is, play in the key that best suits the vocalist's range. With a musical chart written using numbers instead of actual chord names, a song can be played *in any key* and the players will know which chords to play—good players, that is. In addition, this simplified chart method allows each player the flexibility to exercise his or her own style and taste in how he or she plays each chord or background fill, without complicated notated instructions.

Another reason to use numbers is not so obvious; except for A and F, all the names of the chords sound the same: B, C, D, E, and G. They all have an "eee" sound, and misunderstandings often occur when learning songs under high volume. If you're playing a song in the key of D, someone shouting out "Go to the five!" is clearer than shouting "G," as the other players wonder, "Did he say E?… B?…C?…D?"

A wonderful side effect of learning songs by using chord *numbers* instead of names is this: You'll start recognizing the same number **33** patterns (2–5–1, 1–5–4, 1–4–5, etc.) in many seemingly dissimilar songs. Learning these patterns and how they are combined can give you a true understanding of song structure. This knowledge will help you in all aspects of songs—learning them, writing, them, transposing them. Give this notation method a try. A great book to check out is the aptly named *The Nashville Number System* by Chas Williams, listed in the Information Sources in the back of this book.

WHAT KEY IS IT IN?

A song can be played in any of 12 keys. But what is a "key"?

We've learned that a family of chords lives in every major scale, and these chords are used together in many songs. The "key" of a song is the name of the major scale that the chords and melody are built from. It may help to think of the key of a song as an actual key on a keyboard that is the first note of this particular major scale.

Here's an example. If you wrote out the melody of the first line of the Christmas carol "Joy to the World," you would have a descending major scale: "Joy to the world, the Lord is come . . ." The name of that major scale is the key of the song. Another example: The various notes in the melody of "Twinkle, Twinkle, Little Star" are the first six notes of a major scale. The name of that major scale is the key of the song.

If you tried to sing and play "Old McDonald" on guitar, using C and G as the two chords, and it was out of your vocal range, you might choose to sing it in a lower key, such as B♭ (the two chords would now be B♭ and F), or you might choose the key of A (the two chords would now be A and E). Changing the chords of a song so they are in a more appropriate performance key is called *transposing*.

In reality you will use only a few scales and keys in pop music, unless you're Brian Wilson (many chords) or Public Enemy (almost no chords), but you should know *how* to build a scale in any key. If not, reread the previous section until it makes sense.

TWO COMMON CHORD PROGRESSIONS

If you've followed along this far, you'll know that chords are built from scales. You also know about **The Big Three**: They are the **1** chord (root chord of the song), the **4** chord, and the **5** chord. From these three chords were born rock 'n' roll. A blues progression is probably the most obvious example of these three chords in action. Here they are, hidden in a C scale:

C	D	E	F	G	A	B	C
1	2	3	**4**	**5**	6	7	1

Here's an example of a "blues" progression, with the numeral notation above the lyrics, showing when the chords change. This song can be performed in any key. Simply pick a key; determine the first, fourth, and fifth notes of the scale that starts on the key note; build major chords from these scale pitches; and use them as your 1–4–5 chords. Here's an example in C:

Beverly Hills Blues (in C)
© 1996 Marty Jourard

```
(1)              (4)              (1)
C                F                C
```
My Cadillac's in the shop/and my Rolls is leaking oil,

```
   (4)                             (1)
   F                               C
```
Lord my Cadillac's in the shop/and my Rolls is leaking oil

```
(5)              (4)              (1)
G                F                C
```
My fridge is on the blink/I guess my caviar will spoil

To give you an idea of the variety of songs that have these three chords as their primary structure, look at this list:

Song	_Artist or Writer_
"Twinkle, Twinkle, Little Star"	Traditional
"Camptown Races (DooDah, DooDah")"	Stephen Foster
"God Bless America"	Irving Berlin
"This Land Is Your Land"	Woodie Guthrie
"Rock Around the Clock"	Bill Haley & the Comets
"Kansas City"	Wilbert Harrison

Continued

<u>Song</u>	<u>Artist or Writer</u>
"Jailhouse Rock"	Elvis Presley
"Johnny B. Goode"	Chuck Berry
"Wild Thing"	The Troggs
"Louie, Louie"	The Kingsmen
"Birthday"	The Beatles
"19th Nervous Breakdown"	The Rolling Stones
"Start Me Up"	The Rolling Stones
"Diamonds on the Soles of Her Shoes"	Paul Simon
"Stand"	R.E.M.

Although these are not blues tunes, they all feature the 1, the 4, and the 5.

If you choose to spend one afternoon playing these three chords in every key (C–F–G, C#–F#–G#, D–G–A, etc.), by evening you'll already know the chords to hundreds of songs.

Another chord progression that was born of the Tin Pan Alley era of songwriting (late 19th century through the 1950s) is the **1–6–4–5** sequence. Remember that the **6** chord is a minor (m) chord when built from a major scale. You probably won't use this progression if you play hardcore punk, but it helps to be familiar with it. To show how useful this sequence has been to songwriters, here is a very brief list of songs using these chords:

<u>Song</u>	<u>Artist or Writer</u>	<u>Year</u>
"Blue Moon"	Richard Rodgers	1932
"All I Have to Do Is Dream"	The Everly Brothers	1958
"Silhouettes"	Herman's Hermits	1964
"Tell Me Why"	The Beatles	1964
"Every Breath You Take"	Police	1983
"Slave to Love"	Bryan Ferry	1985
"I Will Always Love You"	Whitney Houston	1992

As you can see, this old chestnut of a chord progression has served popular music well, and for a long time. The **4** chord is often replaced with a (minor) **2** chord, making it a **1–6–2–5** progression. Replacing one chord with another to change the feel of a progression slightly is called *chord substitution*.

LEAD SHEETS

A lead sheet is nothing more than a very simple notation of a song—sometimes just the chords, other times with lyrics included. Symbols for chords vary considerably throughout the music world, but simplicity and accuracy should be your guide. Here are some suggestions for notating chords, in this case different types of simple C chords:

C major	**C**	**C dominant 7**	**C7**
C major 7	**CΔ**	**C diminished**	**C°**
C minor	**Cm**	**C augmented**	**C⁺**

The simplest lead sheet might be nothing more than chords written above lyrics, showing where the chord changes occur:

Martian Love Song
© 1996 Marty Jourard

C   Am   F   G
I love you and you love me, that spells trouble, can't you see?
C   Am   Dm   G
I'm a Martian, you're from Earth, on my planet men give birth
    F   Fm   G   CΔ
But come on girl, don't be blue, we're gonna have a little barbecue

Another way to do it is to skip the lyrics (I don't mind), but show the places the chords change by representing each beat in the measure by either a chord symbol or a slash mark /:

| Cm / Am / | F / G /| F /Am / | Dm / G / |F / Fm / |G / CΔ /|

This type of lead sheet is easily written on a three-by-five note card for easy storage in a guitar case.

Find a notation style for lead sheets that works for you and use it to document all your songs. It's a fast, efficient, tapeless way to record your ideas and repertoire.

PERSONAL REMINISCENCE: JUST ENOUGH TO GET BY

My interest in music led me to be mostly self-taught, picking up just enough theory on the way to give me a basic framework that helped me understand the structure of the music I liked.

I did myself a big favor one afternoon when I was about 14 years old. I sat at the piano and figured out every major and minor triad: C major, C minor, C# major, C# minor, etc. I noticed that a lot of them looked the same; they had similar shapes. This primitive self-induced music lesson served me well. I never got lost in the worlds of jazz and classical piano theory, so my approach to playing and writing rock music was fairly simple: major and minor chords, with an occasional dominant 7th or minor 9th for "crunch."

When I was 15 years old, I wanted to get in a rock band so I could play all those cool songs on the AM radio. I figured out the quickest way was to learn how to play bass. Drums cost too much and guitar was too hard to learn (too many of those pesky "licks" and "riffs"). Bass only had four strings and I figured that when in doubt, you played the root note of each chord over and over while smiling. It seemed to work. Yet I did want to improve, so I took bass lessons from a local musician named Don Felder, who later joined the Eagles and cowrote "Hotel California." This was in 1969, and each half-hour lesson cost $2. That was a lot of Spiderman comic books, but I plugged away at arpeggiated scales and struggled with the bass clef notation. Soon I joined a band with the fabulous name of The Airmont Classic, and the first song I ever learned was Steppenwolf's "Sookie Sookie." I just listened to the record and copied the bass part. So much for arpeggiated scales. My favorite songs were by Creedence Clearwater, not only because they were so great but because the bass parts were ultrasimple, hanging out on one note for almost an entire verse. My kind of part! Airmont Classic led to Uncle Funnel led to Road Turkey. Yes, folks, I'm not making this up. I should have read Chapter 1, the section on Naming Your Band.

In my freshman year at college I took some basic music theory classes but these were mostly notebook exercises and didn't seem to relate to the real world of rock music. I returned to Florida from Massachusetts (too cold) ready to rejoin my band but they had found a new bass player, so I switched to keyboard and sax. I needed to learn a few more chords and scales and I was ready to rock once again.

Keyboard knowledge was very helpful with my saxophone playing. I would visualize key transpositions (the tenor sax was pitched one step higher than piano notation) and sax riffs on the keyboard. I also began to play along with jazz albums, searching out different chords for piano and riffs and scales for the saxophone—anything to increase my limited harmonic vocabulary. By borrowing little things that appealed to me from the world of jazz I found I could spice up my keyboard and sax playing in a rock band without sounding too "jazzy."

Because I never got very good at reading music, I had to develop my ear to learn songs off records, and this helped me throughout my music career.

CHAPTER FOUR
REHEARSALS AND REHEARSAL SPACE

Practice is the best of all instructors.
—Publilius Syrus, first century B.C.

t first glance, rehearsals seem easy to describe: The band members show up, plug in, play their hearts out, and then go home, satisfied in the knowledge of time well spent.

I've played in at least eight bands (early details are sketchy) and spent thousands of hours in inefficient rehearsals, doing it wrong. These rehearsals could be summed up as Big Egos in a Room Making Loud Sounds. Unfortunately, most rock band rehearsals are unorganized and inefficient. At many rehearsals the unwritten rule seems to be that anyone can play whatever they want whenever they want as loud as they want. At these sonic free-for-alls, musicians often play with little or no interest in what the other band members are playing; endless instrumental noodling occurs between songs, making discussion impossible; amp volumes are invariably raised because another player turned up, and all the while the singer is going hoarse trying to be heard over all the noise. Does any of this sound familiar? I'm not speaking to you from above: In my band I was known for many years as "El Rey de La Pasta" (the Noodle King). I know the temptations of an instrument plugged into a loud amplifier.

So I'm going to discuss rehearsing. After that we'll turn our attention toward how to set up a rehearsal studio for maximum effectiveness. We will also discuss soundproofing techniques.

REHEARSAL STYLES, TECHNIQUES, AND SUGGESTIONS

There are many different band lineups and styles of music, so there isn't one "correct" approach to rehearsing. A 12-piece jazz band reading charts may need a highly structured rehearsal to get anything accomplished. A bass/drums/guitar band specializing in extended blues jams may only need a six-pack, a few key signatures, and four uninterrupted hours to accomplish their goal. A cover band seeking work in a hotel lounge or bar might need to spend their rehearsal time carefully learning songs from records or sheet music, trying to match the original arrangements as closely as possible. And an avant-garde, post-neo-urban noise ensemble may need to free-associate their way through a rehearsal, taking care to record everything so they can repeat cool sonic events.

The idea is to figure out the most efficient way to spend your rehearsal time, and then stick to the particular approach. Try to bring this topic up in an early meeting so there is a mutual agreement as to what form your rehearsal will take.

This raises a touchy question: Who will "run" the rehearsals? If the band is a vehicle for one writer's songs, this person will probably be the leader. If the band has more than one writer, the leader may change as each member introduces their song to the group. No matter who writes what, most bands have a member with a knack for organization, and this person may be your best choice to keep rehearsals going in the right direction. In fact, having someone simply keep track of the *time* might be all that's needed. A little structure can go a long way.

The following tips, suggestions, and techniques are meant to expose you to ideas you may not have considered. Some of them may rub up against your personal philosophy of musical self-expression. Good! One of the goals of this book is to stretch your ideas about music and musical collaboration.

YOU ARE NOT ALONE

This seems so obvious I'm almost embarrassed to bring it up, but hey: If each musician in a band really listens to what the others are playing, you'll begin to sound like a "group" instead of just a bunch of musicians playing music near each other. Each instrument is part of the overall musical ensemble. By concentrating on the entire sound of the band, you become aware of how *your* musical contribution fits in (or doesn't fit in) with the overall musical arrangement. Without this awareness, instrumental parts can clash, especially two rhythm guitar parts, or keyboard and guitar parts. Even if the guitar parts are fine by themselves their combined output may bear no relation to what the drums and bass are playing—the lead guitar might be stepping all over the vocals, etc. The concept of *really* listening—not only to the other players, but to the entire arrangement—requires that you focus your attention outward instead of inward. Believe me, this is an acquired art and requires a close inspection of your IGN (Immediate Gratification Needs). You also need to be good enough on your instrument that you can listen to others and still play well. As you become a better player, you'll be able to focus more on finding the perfect part to play, the one that best serves the song. Unless you're a genius, this "perfect part" may not be the very first idea that pops into your head and therefore out of your instrument!

DEALING WITH YOUR WONDERFUL EGO

There really is at least one truly great arrangement that best serves a song, that brings the song to life. Your goal as a musician and a band member is to help create this arrangement. Truly professional musicians, when considering what to play, tend to focus on what the song needs in contrast to what their own *ego* might need for gratification. This focus on the Song rather than the Self is a giant conceptual leap for many players. Once you have made this leap you'll begin listening to music with different ears. A song is a living entity that deserves your attention as much as your ego! The main theme

> To love the song more than the sound of your instrument will lead your playing down a more selective path.

throughout this book can be summed up by this mantra: Worship the Song—Place No Other Gods Before It, Including Your Ego. Ultimately, the song is why we're all here. To love the song more than the sound of your instrument will lead your playing down a more selective path. Don't think that this means playing without passion! It means playing with insight into the effect that your playing has on a song. Does the part you choose to play on your instrument "hide" the song under a barrage of note production or does your restraint and thoughtful playing help bring the song into clearer view? This rarely discussed concept of serving the song's needs rather than those of your ego is guaranteed to generate lively band discussion.

SHOWING ORIGINAL SONGS
TO THE BAND

There are several ways to show an original song to a band for the first time. Some writers make an elaborate demo tape of their songs with each instrument represented, play the demo for the band, and say "Do it just like this." This method, although certainly efficient, eliminates any possibility of experimentation or creative input from the other musicians. Just because you made a demo of a song doesn't automatically mean the band should try to copy the arrangement.

Another approach is to show songs to the band in a minimalist performance, perhaps only guitar (or whatever instrument the composer plays) and vocals. This open approach can lead to a much more interesting and natural sounding arrangement than your demo. Handing out simple lead sheets with the chords and lyrics written out is another good way to provide just enough information to allow experimentation and a creative atmosphere. Specific songs may require one approach or the other.

Sometimes after playing around with an arrangement for a while it is helpful to deliberately try a completely different approach. This strategy often brings forth a new idea that may provide a better feel, a new "hook," a more appropriate tempo, and so on. Although a certain amount of structure is necessary in running a rehearsal, remember this: *Experimentation is the key to creativity*. One of the concepts to practice at rehearsals is simply being open-minded. This includes a willingness to try ideas by *playing* them instead of *discussing* them to death. Play the idea first and *then* offer an opinion! Saying "no" before trying out ideas is a quick way to stifle all creativity. Don't make this common mistake—be willing to experiment.

LEARNING FROM THE BEATLES

Once upon a time (1962–1970) there were The Beatles, inarguably the most successful and significant rock group in history. Impossible to hype, this band was willing to try anything and in fact invented and presented to the world new forms of pop music with every album. You don't have to be from the age group that grew up listening to the Fab Four to learn from their music. Check out the *Beatles Anthology* CDs, particularly Volume 2. These collections of

Beatles demos, alternate takes, and song-arrangements-in-progress brilliantly illustrate their open-minded approach to writing and arranging. Many classic Beatles songs are barely recognizable in their earlier, experimental forms. In the course of working out the final arrangement of a song they might change the basic rhythmic feel several times, duplicate a catchy guitar lick in the solo and put it at the beginning, try lyrics in different combinations and order, or vary the instrumental lineup—in short, they were constantly "messing around." You can do the same when you rehearse. Remember, songs aren't "made" out of anything except ideas, and ideas are free. A hit record may have gone through many musical arrangements before the band found the one arrangement that worked. Experiment.

OVERPLAYING

Generally speaking, most players tend to overplay, especially after performing a song many times. Although drummers are no more guilty of this than other players, overplaying seems more obvious when the drummer is playing more drum breaks in a song than straight time. Overplaying is often the result of boredom and the mistaken belief that playing many notes (or beats) proves that you are a dedicated and hardworking musician. Nothing could be further from the truth. It takes a certain amount of courage to play less and then consider what might be added instead of overplay and wonder what you should leave out. This is true no matter what instrument you play. Although personal taste is the final judge of what constitutes "overplaying," it helps to be aware of how important this self-editing process is to the overall band sound. Often, the hardest songs to play well are the simple ones with just a few chords.

TAPE THEM REHEARSALS

Recording your rehearsals is a great idea. At the very least you should use a cassette recorder with a built-in mike, preferably one with *Automatic Level Control* (ALC) which automatically adjusts the input level so it doesn't distort. Unfortunately most of today's boomboxes have crummy mikes that distort easily. A better approach is to use a quality cassette deck with a decent mike on a stand positioned to pick up the most balanced sound. If you need a spare mike to do this, check out your local Radio Shack. I mention them because they are everywhere and some of their stuff is fine. They have a wide selection of microphones to choose from including the totally cool **45**

PZM (Pressure Zone Microphone) model. This $60 mike looks like a metal rectangle with a cable coming out of one side and is designed to be mounted on a flat surface. You can tape it discreetly to a wall, plug it into the deck, and forget about it.

> *Taping rehearsals is also a great way to prepare for studio recording; becoming comfortable with playing when you're being recorded is a good skill to develop if you intend to make records.*

Recording your rehearsals will help you remember all of the brilliant musical ideas you had played and promptly forgotten, aid you in solving arguments regarding how many verses there are before the second chorus and who played the wrong chord, and enable you to hear your songs objectively as opposed to while you are playing them. If a player is having trouble with a song, they can take the tape home and practice. If you spend the time to experiment with microphone placement, you can make acceptable demo tapes for almost nothing—literally the cost of the tape. Demo tapes like these are effective for getting club dates because club bookers will know how the band sounds live as opposed to in the studio.

Taping rehearsals is also a great way to prepare for studio recording; becoming comfortable with playing when you're being recorded is a good skill to develop if you intend to make records. Try to use brand-name 90-minute high-bias Type II cassette tapes like TDK SA or Maxell XL-II: Bought in bulk they aren't too expensive and they really do sound better.

On the subject of cassette decks: If you can afford it (around $400), buy a Marantz PMD222 portable cassette recorder. It's a three-head mono (yes, mono) deck with a balanced XLR input for a pro mic, and many other useful features: speaker, VU meter, pitch control, built-in mic, two speeds (normal and half), cue and review, memory rewind/replay, and a quarter-inch headphone jack. It also has a switchable limiter, automatic noise-control switch, metal tape capability, and runs on three "D" cells. Use it to record rehearsals and songwriting sessions, to slow down tapes for figuring out speedy guitar riffs, and for tuning prerecorded tapes to your instrument for learning songs. A real workhorse of a deck. Available through Bradley Broadcast (see Information Sources at the back of the book), and many other places.

A USEFUL EXERCISE

A highly educational (and possibly humiliating) experiment worth trying is this: Take a song your band already has played for a while, and break it down to its components. I mean all the way down. First, have only the bass player and the drummer play their parts together. Listen to the bass drum pattern and the bass guitar part. Do they sound like they're on the same planet? If they do, move on. If they don't, DO SOMETHING ABOUT IT! Next, add one guitar (or other instrument) and play the song again, listening to these three parts together. Keep running through the song, adding an instrument each time. Experience the raging battle between your musical common sense and your ego.

This exercise can lead to some thrilling revelations regarding what you thought the other musicians were playing, as well as what they thought you were playing, not to mention what you thought they thought you were playing, and so on.

If you want to hear a brilliantly arranged, rhythmically complex song that illustrates true ensemble playing, check out "Everybody's Got Something to Hide Except Me and My Monkey" from The Beatles' *White Album.*

SECTION REHEARSALS

An effective technique that will improve your overall band sound is letting different parts of the band get together apart from regular band practice to work on their parts. Two guitarists can meet at the rehearsal space early or stay after in order to work on their parts together. Try playing the songs at a slower tempo to really zero in on how the guitars interconnect—or don't. Separate bass player/drummer rehearsals are extremely useful in clarifying the rhythm section parts. Vocal rehearsals, without all those loud amps blaring away, are extremely effective in perfecting harmony and background vocal parts. Sing along with an acoustic guitar, low-volume electric guitar, or keyboard to keep everyone on pitch.

I KNOW YOUR AMP GOES TO 11, BUT . . .

I'll come right out and say it: Most bands rehearse too damn loudly. Rehearsal spaces are almost always smaller than live music venues, and normal gig volume can be deafening as well as counterproductive when rehearsing.

If the only math equation you learned is Instrument + Amplifier = Loud, let me introduce you to *dynamics*, the effect of varying degrees of loudness or softness in the performance of music. For many musicians this is unexplored territory.

Varying the volume is an important aspect of music, and exploring the different sounds your instrument produces at the various volume levels is a valuable addition to your musical knowledge. For many musicians, including drummers, this is a hard concept to grasp. Playing drums with dynamics takes practice and a musical approach that goes beyond adrenaline and "hitting" the drums. I'm not picking on drummers, it's just that drumkits don't have volume knobs; they actually have to be struck quieter to lower the volume.

There are of course an infinite number of gradations between Death-of-the-Universe Loud and I-Can't-Hear-You! Soft. Your band will be remarkably sophisticated if you can identify and play three distinct levels: soft, medium, and loud. Using dynamics greatly

Keeping Your Ears

The word "deafening" is not an expression but a real possibility. If your ears ring for a while (tinnitus) after rehearsals, concerts, or any exposure to loud music or sounds, the volume was definitely too loud and can cause permanent damage. There are special earplugs available for musicians that give a flat response (called ER-15 or ER-25) available at local hearing aid dispensers. High frequencies are the first to go when you start to damage your eardrums, and a sure sign of this is having to always boost your treble knob on your amp. Two of the greatest rock guitarists of them all, Jeff Beck and Pete Townshend, admit to hearing loss from extended exposure to high sound levels. For a free set of earplugs and more information about protecting your hearing (and therefore your career) write to HIP (Hearing Is Priceless) Campaign, House Ear Institute, 2100 West Third Street, 5th Floor, Los Angeles, CA 90057.

increases the drama in an arrangement and can vary the listener's focus as attention is drawn toward the lyrics during a quieter passage or toward the guitar lead during a louder one.

Unfortunately, most bands never know how a well-balanced, medium-volume rehearsal sounds and feels. It feels good! At lower volumes you can hear the other players, and this gives you a chance to *play with them*, not just near them. Bringing instruments in and out of the arrangement during a song is a simple and effective dynamic variation. For instance, a song may start with bass, drums, and vocals, with guitar added at the second half of the first verse, followed by a second guitar and keyboard for the first chorus. The flip side of this trick is the "breakdown," usually near the end of a song, where you pull out everything except the drums, bass, and vocals, then bring the other instruments back in for a stunning and climactic ending. This arrangement trick always seems to work.

WHEN NOT TO REHEARSE

You must obviously rehearse at least to the point where every player knows their part to every song. But there comes a time when rehearsing is actually counterproductive. Why? Because the only thing worse than a band not knowing how to play a song is a band that is already sick of their material before they ever hit the stage. You want to play with a certain energy and edge to your performance, and rehearsing six days a week will definitely dull this edge.

If you're lucky, someone in your band has a basement available for rehearsals.

If possible, don't rehearse the day before a gig for two reasons. First, the players will be more alert and attentive when they do play because it feels fresh, and second, a day off for the singer will give vocal chords a rest. Any really troublesome songs that the band feels massively insecure about can be played during the soundcheck at your gig.

YOUR REHEARSAL SPACE

If you want to set up your own rehearsal room in a residential area (a room or garage) you'll have to deal with sound control. It's hard to exaggerate the difficulty of insulating enough so that your neighbors don't keep calling the cops. Drums are unbelievably difficult to shield from the rest of the world. The alternative is either to turn it down or to practice in a commercial rehearsal facility that rents by the hour.

If you're lucky, someone in your band has a basement available for rehearsals. A basement is an ideal choice: It is secure, private, and has a natural advantage in sound insulation—being underground with a house on top of it. Garages of course are more commonly available, as the term "garage band" tells us, but they require sound insulation to some degree. Unfortunately they often come with irate neighbors, especially at night and on weekends, the usual time for rehearsals. Soundproofing is a very difficult job due to two factors: the nature of sound and the amazing amount of this sound a band produces.

THE TROUBLE WITH SOUND

We all love sound for the wonderful things it can do, such as come together in forms known as "songs." But, just as a weed is nothing more than a plant in the wrong place, "music" becomes "noise" when someone else hears it and doesn't want to. Let's discuss sound.

Sound travels in the direction it started in until it hits something solid, and then it is either reflected or absorbed. Absorption is our goal. A blank wall reflects around 95% of the sound that hits it; porous (and therefore acoustically absorbent) material such as carpet, foam, or heavy drapes can absorb 50% of the sound; acoustic tile will absorb up to 80%.

Most bands put out a wide range of frequencies, from the 40 Hz of the bass drum and bass guitar up to and beyond the 2500 Hz of the cymbals. These frequency ranges have their own absorption characteristics: High frequencies are easy to absorb (scream into a pillow to demonstrate this), but low frequencies are almost impossible to contain. Low-frequency sounds tend to radiate in all directions, and need truly massive amounts of insulation or solid mass (thick concrete walls) to trap them. This is why you hear the deep rumblings from those monster car sound systems when you pull up next to one at a traffic light, even with the windows of both cars rolled up.

SOUND INSULATION

There are two possible solutions to this problem: building a concrete bunker (highly impractical and expensive), or the "room-within-a-room" approach. This double-wall design—putting a wall in front of each existing wall with an airspace between them—is the only truly effective way to isolate the sounds made by a band in full swing. The dead air between the two walls stops low frequency transmission effectively. If you think an extra layer of Sheetrock or fiberboard on the walls of your room will soundproof it you're living in a fantasy world.

To build a wall you'll need 2 x 4 lumber and 12d nails, dense fiberglass insulation, 5/8" Sheetrock and fiberboard, time, and patience. You'll need to seal all cracks and spaces with caulk or expanding foam sealant—the amount of sound that can pass through a small crack or hole in an otherwise solid wall is absolutely astounding. For maximum sound isolation, build the new wall using staggered-stud construction. This effectively isolates one side of the wall from the other.

If this all sounds like a pain in the butt, that's because it is. For details on how to actually do all this contact your local carpenter or pick up a handyman book. This kind of work qualifies as major construction and is not a project for the fainthearted.

SOUND ABSORPTION

The previous example was an example of sound insulation—preventing sound from going any further than your rehearsal space. What about what goes on inside your rehearsal room? The walls, floor, and ceiling might be so "live" that everything sounds like a train wreck when you play. This is where sound *absorption* materials can help you.

There are many brands of acoustic foam panels available, such as Azonic, Sonex, and Cutting Wedge, designed for wall-mounting in recording studios or theaters. These invariably cost too much and are overkill for a rehearsal space. The best bang for the buck is Owens Corning 703 series fiberglass insulation. Look under Insulation Materials in the Yellow Pages. These stiff rectangles of acoustic deadening fiberglass measure 2 x 4 feet, vary in thickness from one to four inches, and cost between $6 to $10 each. Four of them combined are the same size as a 4 x 8 sheet of plywood. Frame them in **51** cheap wood strips, cover the assembly with cloth, and hang them in various places around the rehearsal space. If you cover the whole room with them the place will sound like a head cold, so don't go overboard.

OTHER SOUNDPROOFING TIPS

- No matter how else you choose to soundproof or deaden your rehearsal space, be sure to carpet the floor, preferably including a carpet pad. Carpet absorbs a tremendous amount of sound, especially from floor-level amplifiers. Try to get free used carpet. Carpet installers routinely take away the old carpet from residences and businesses, and often leave it in the trash behind the carpet store. Fascinating color combinations can result from multiple finds. After carpeting the floor, staple extra carpet up the walls with a heavy-duty staple gun.

- Hang heavy cloth in folds from the ceiling (above the drums if nowhere else) to break up the flat surface and trap some low frequencies.

- In basements, attach acoustic tile to the exposed ceiling joists after you have filled the spaces between them with fiberglass insulation. Seal any spaces between walls and pipes with aerosol foam sealant.

- Replace hollow doors with solid-core doors and weatherstrip all around the doorframe. Remember, sound waves leak through holes and cracks like water through a sieve.

- If your rehearsal room sounds kind of "woofy," you can trap some of this bass resonance by using "bass traps." These are columns of carpet approximately a foot in diameter and around six feet tall standing upright in every corner. You can just roll a piece of carpet up and tie it with string for a low-cost solution to this type of acoustic problem.

PERSONAL REMINISCENCE: REHEARSING AT THE MASQUE

For a couple of years during the late '70s (July 1977 to October 1979) the nerve center of the punk scene in Los Angeles was the Masque, a combination venue/rehearsal space in a basement underneath a porno theater near the corner of Hollywood Boulevard and Cherokee Avenue. I was there, and I remember it well.

Scottish entrepreneur Brendan Mullen was the proprietor of the place, which was originally intended as a live music venue but was quickly shut down by the fire department. It was, however, considered safe enough for punk rock bands to rehearse in. Go figure.

Entrance to the place was through an industrial-looking metal door on the side of a very dark and dangerous-looking alley just south of Hollywood Boulevard's star-lined sidewalks. The poorly lit staircase that descended to the bowels of the building was challenging and intimidating to first-time users. Even street people avoided the place. For a while, we were scared to rehearse there at night until it dawned on us that, as punky rock musicians, *we* were the ones that people were scared of. And no wonder. Some of the bands whose sweet and gentle music wafted through the halls included early punkers The Skulls, The Controllers, The Screamers (featuring Tomato du Plenty), The Berlin Brats, The Secrets, Hal Negro and the Satintones, and, in one rehearsal room, The Go-Go's and The Motels. After we got a record deal, a band called X took over our share of the room.

The Masque was a typical commercial basement space—a huge central area (with support pillars) surrounded by six small rent-by-the-month rehearsal rooms with exceedingly thin walls. Copious graffiti was everywhere ("Spike your hair—how trendy. Rip your T-shirt—how trendy." "Sid [Vicious] is dead and I want to die too"). You could always hear other bands rehearse through the walls, so Martha, our sensitive and demure singer/songwriter, spent one afternoon mixing plaster by hand and jamming it in the space between the wall and ceiling. We found some heavy black theater curtains in a corner of the basement (probably from the Pussycat Theater up above) that we nailed to the walls, thus completing our state-of-the-art sound insulation. We split the space with The Go-Go's, each band paying half of the $250-a-month rental fee.

The room itself was long and rectangular, with one P.A. speaker next to the entry door at one end and the other P.A. cabinet in the

> *For a while, we were scared to rehearse there at night until it dawned on us that, as punky rock musicians, we were the ones that people were scared of.*

adjacent far corner. Each band set up their equipment alongside opposite long walls, with the microphones on stands in the middle of the room. Each band could leave their equipment set up, and just turn the mike stands around when it was their turn to practice.

The Go-Go's would rehearse from 4 to 8 p.m. (after school) and we would rehearse from 8 p.m. to 1 or 2 a.m. Two mikes suspended from the ceiling fed into a cassette deck, and we recorded every rehearsal to help us continually refine the musical arrangements. The Go-Go's wore so much Day-Glo lipstick and lipped the mikes so much that after a few weeks the P.A. began sounding more and more distant. My brother Jeff, guitarist and technical whiz, took the mikes home, removed the metal windscreens and boiled them clean. We bought foam windscreens and installed them, thus solving a pesky technical problem.

Although the Masque was technically a rehearsal space with an occasional live gig thrown in, it was also a punk hangout because of its close proximity to the Canterbury, the only cheap apartment building in Hollywood willing to rent to the spike-haired dog-collar set. Darby Crash of The Germs was a frequent Masque visitor. The constantly trashed and always fragrant restroom featured my favorite graffito: I Stink, Therefore I Am.

It was my brother who asked me to come down to the rehearsal space one fateful night to play sax on a song. I wasn't officially in the band yet. After proving that I could play a simple three-note sax part when prodded, I was asked if I knew how to play keyboard, more specifically the dusty Polymoog in the corner. I casually said, "Sure." I had never played a synth in my life, but it had keys, just like a piano. We plugged it into the P.A., since I didn't have an amp. In fact, I played our first three gigs in the same manner, although I couldn't really hear what I was playing. During the third live performance, I looked down at one of the sliders on the synth marked "pitch trans-pose." It was on and pushed way up, something I'd never noticed. It suddenly dawned on me that I'd been playing in a different key from the rest of the band for our first three gigs. I bought an amp the next day and our sound improved considerably.

The Masque finally closed in October 1979 and the entrance was sealed up by the landlord, who never succeeded in renting it again. The door was unsealed recently (July 1996) by an interested party wanting to reopen the space as a rehearsal hall, and everything was perfectly preserved: All the graffiti and residue from 17 years ago was still there, a true punk music time capsule. Perhaps it has reopened by the time you read these words. No matter. The Masque was the real thing.

CHAPTER FIVE

WRITING SONGS

After silence, that which comes nearest to
expressing the inexpressible is music.
—Aldous Huxley (1894–1963)

Q: How do you get a songwriter off your front porch?
A: Pay him for the pizza.

One of the most fascinating aspects of songwriting is the inherent paradox of creating something that literally doesn't exist. Songs are made up of nothing more than vibrating air molecules, a commonplace and cost-free medium. Set those molecules in the right patterns and you've got a hit record! Another trait that makes songs unique among the art forms: They can be performed in widely differing styles yet still retain their basic structure and identity—as in Frank Sinatra and Sid Vicious both covering Paul Anka's "My Way."

Yes, songs by design have an inherently mysterious power about them, and this may explain their emotional impact on the listener as well as their vast earning potential. To put it plainly, the money generated by songs allows the entire music business to function. Without songs, pop culture would probably scream to a halt: no music on the radio, no MTV, no Friday nights in the mosh pits, and no waiting in line at Ticketmaster outlets.

No one can actually *teach* you how to write songs. Just as important, no one can make you *need* to write songs. Either way, you learn how to write songs by writing. This chapter's goal (and chapters, like people, need goals) is twofold: to show you the general framework used by many songwriters to create an environment conducive to writing, and to give you some tools to help you get started.

Pete Droge, a Seattle-based songwriter, said it best when, in an interview in the local music paper *The Rocket*, he described the force that drives him to songwriting as "a philosophy to write *all* the songs. Write the bad ones, write the mediocre ones, and that would get me to the few good ones." Sound like a lot of work? It is. But getting to those good songs—that's what all the fuss is about.

LEARN LOTS OF SONGS

First off, as a songwriter/musician, you should learn as many songs as possible. Learn them from songbooks, recordings, the radio, and other musicians. Songs contain the musical grammar you will use to write your own music. By knowing the chords and words to lots of songs you will gain access to a vast library of musical ideas that will be at your disposal when you begin composing. Much of the musical information you absorb will eventually resurface, but in a modified form. Your goal is to "front-load" your musical memory banks so that when you begin the creative process you have a wealth of musical material from which to draw. Write chords and lyrics down on index cards and carry them around with you, bring them to your day job—but don't get fired staring at them! Memorizing songs is easier for some musicians than others, but oddly enough, the more you memorize the easier it becomes.

INFLUENCE AS INSPIRATION

Just as painters study the great artists of yesteryear as a guide to their efforts, songwriters learn from and are influenced by the songs and writers they admire.

Woody Guthrie's music had a huge impact on the songwriting of Bob Dylan, who in turn influenced Jimi Hendrix, John Lennon, Bruce Springsteen, and Mark Knopfler, to name just a few. Early Beatles songs drew heavily from the music of Little Richard, Carl Perkins, Elvis, the Everly Brothers, and others. John Lennon admitted in an interview that his song "Please Please Me" from 1964 was an attempt to emulate Roy Orbison. The Rolling Stones began their career by covering American blues and R&B tunes. The first full-length record to feature all Jagger–Richards originals was their *sixth* album, *Aftermath*.

Clearly, original music grows from deep roots.

As you continue to write songs, your style will begin to evolve away from your influences and toward something uniquely your own. Even if you flat out copy the style of another writer/artist, the result won't sound exactly the same because you are not that person. *Don't*

be afraid to mimic and emulate the players and writers you admire, but *do* try to figure out exactly what it is you like about a songwriter's style. Then you can develop your own version of these qualities.

WARMING UP TO WRITE

As part of your musical education as a writer, you should actively listen to songs, and this doesn't mean casually listen as a consumer. I mean take them apart and study them! Find a song you really like. Analyze the chord movement. Write out the arrangement by counting the number of bars in the intro, each verse and chorus, bridge, etc. I'm not just saying this. You can learn an immense amount from getting absolutely specific. Determine the relationship of the melody to the notes of the accompanying chords. Listen to the rhythm of the syllables in the words as the song moves from verse to chorus to bridge. Do these rhythms vary widely? If so, how does the change affect the "feel" of the song? Study the details.

After concentrating on general aspects, focus on the instrumentation. Listen to the same song you analyzed above. Concentrate on the drum part the first time through. Then listen again, but this time check out the bass guitar part and how it fits with the drums. Every time you listen, focus on a different instrument and how it fits in with the arrangement. Knowing what you like about a song arrangement will help you in your songwriting.

> Every time you listen, focus on a different instrument and how it fits in with the arrangement.

This seemingly dry analysis of something warm and fuzzy like a song can be very enlightening. You may even notice how musicians play very simple parts to help focus attention on the tune. This is more of a "pop song" approach—letting the song structure and melody do all the work. However, the line between arranging and writing has been blurred in recent times. The song standards of the past relied solely on the chord structure and melody to communicate the emotional core of the song. Many of today's youth-oriented songs (a broad enough category, don't you think?) depend heavily on the interplay between the instruments and the vocals to deliver the song's "message." If you don't know what I'm getting at, try to imagine Nirvana's guitar-onslaught album *In Utero* as an E-Z piano arrangement. Basically, you need to study all aspects of songs—content and form—to learn how the music you like is put together. Think of this approach as attending a tuition-free music school where you only study what appeals to you, and you always get an *"A."*

PATIENCE REALLY IS A VIRTUE

We've all heard stories about songs that were written in ten minutes while waiting for a bus; the truth is few people are willing to brag about how a song took two weeks to write. Songwriting is hard work and revision. People often underestimate just how much time a songwriter spends on each song. Why? Because a well-written song has a certain internal structural grace—it seems like it must have sprung forth from the composer in one stream of inspiration. This is rarely the case. Not only can a song take many days, even weeks of concentrated effort to compose, but it may consist of parts that were written at various times and then assembled later. Example: A writer has been toying with a chord progression and melody on and off for years but can't come up with a decent lyric. One day, while browsing newspaper headlines, he spots: "Rotating Blackouts Temporarily Solve Regional Power Shortage." "Rotating blackouts" is weirdly catchy, reminding the writer of his college fraternity days. The rhythm of the lyric phrase brings up the memory of an old guitar riff. It fits with the lyric phrase as well as the chord progression. A song idea is born! Songs are often written by assembling and modifying previously existing musical ideas. Document these ideas and you'll create a library of song parts at your disposal.

COLLECT YOUR THOUGHTS

Professional songwriters are hunters and collectors, constantly accumulating raw material for songs—ideas, song titles, musical motifs, chord progressions, riffs, and the like, stored in a notebook or on cassettes. Storing your ideas is vital! A forgotten idea is an idea that will never be used. Fewer feelings are worse than a great idea lost forever. I personally have written four Number One hits that I forgot before ever committing them to tape or paper. Honest!

Develop the habit of carrying a pen and a pocket-sized notebook (or some three-by-five index cards) with you at all times. Whenever you leave the house, fold one in half lengthwise and stick it in your back pocket along with a pen. Don't ask me why you should fold it in half, just do it; it feels better. Leave more of the same in your car, instrument case, in the bathroom, on your nightstand next to your bed. Some of your best song titles or ideas may appear as you drift off to sleep. Reach over and write them down because chances are you won't remember them in the morning. It's very difficult to hang an idea on a mental hook and remember it after a full night's sleep. I speak from experience.

Another indispensable tool is a Walkman-style cassette (or micro-cassette) recorder. They are quite affordable and are useful because the recording quality only has to be good enough to understand what you have sung or played. I also recommend the pricey but extremely versatile Marantz PMD222 portable cassette recorder for general all-around musician/songwriter use. Use it to write one hit song and it will pay for itself.

GENERATING SONG IDEAS

Where do ideas come from? Everywhere! Once you decide you are a songwriter you'll start to see everything as potential song material. Talking to people, listening to people, watching television, over-hearing conversations, reading TV movie guides (movie titles can make great song titles), book titles, dreams, misinterpreting lyrics from others' songs (I always thought Missing Persons' "Walking In L.A." was "walking in a lake"), and—well, you get the idea.

The key is learning how to tune in. Learn how to really listen, observe, and remember when a slang phrase or odd headline catch-es your ear or eye and causes a creative spark. If you combine your knowledge of music and musical structure with a key idea, lyric hook, or any other source of inspiration, you can create a song. Need some real-life examples?

Back in 1965 the great soul singer Otis Redding was griping to his drummer about life's ups and downs. Drummer Al Jackson decided Otis was feeling a little sorry for himself and commented, "What are you griping about, you're on the road all the time. All you can look for is a little respect when you come home." Otis thought about this for a moment, then based on his conversation he wrote "Respect," which was a Number One hit for Aretha Franklin in 1967.

John Lennon found most of the lyrical inspiration for the Beatles' **61** song "Being for the Benefit of Mr. Kite!" by lifting phrases from an old circus poster purchased at an antique shop.

Isaac Hayes and Dave Porter wrote and produced songs for Memphis-based Stax Records in the '60s. During one fateful song-writing session Porter left for a minute. Hayes waited. Time passed, and still no Porter. After a lengthy search, Hayes finally found him in the men's room takin' care of business. Porter was taking his time and Hayes yelled through the door at him to hurry up. Porter irritably replied: "Hey man, hold on. I'm comin'." Bingo! The duo wrote "Hold On, I'm Comin,'" a huge hit for Sam and Dave in 1966. Inspiration really does come from the strangest places.

> *Here's one experiment worth trying: Set aside 30 minutes to an hour each day for songwriting.*

Paul Simon came up with the idea and title for 1972's "Mother and Child Reunion" from the description of a chicken and egg dish on a menu in a Chinese restaurant.

The Police had their first chart success in 1979 with "Roxanne," the story of a prostitute and her rather distraught boyfriend. No, Sting wasn't going with a hooker. The Police had traveled to Paris to open for a punk band in 1977 only to find no headliner and practically no audience. After the gig, their van broke down, and Sting, being Sting, decided to walk through the red-light district. The experience, coupled with his imagination, led him to write "Roxanne," the first "new wave" hit single. Sting chose the name "Roxanne" because it sounded great when you sung it.

SELF-DISCIPLINE AND SELF-CRITICISM

Having trouble getting started? Here's one experiment worth trying: Set aside 30 minutes to an hour each day for songwriting. Do so at the same time and place each day. Here are the rules: You can either write music or do nothing at all. There is no third choice. You have to stay in the room during the allotted period, even if you just stare at the walls or at your instrument. Out of sheer desperation and/or boredom, you will eventually begin to write songs.

Aside from self-discipline, another important songwriting technique you must learn to master can be summed up in this phrase: "withhold judgment." Constant analysis can stifle creativity. Scientists tell us that the right hemisphere of your brain contains the productive and creative centers, while the left hemisphere is the area that edits, refines, and revises what the right side has produced. For instance, the creative side may come up with a phrase like "bologna soufflé" or "amazing disgrace" and the critical side will say "Impossible! No such thing! And whaddaya mean, 'Smells like teen spirit'? Don't be ridiculous!" You need both sides of your brain to write songs, but the trick is to turn off the critical side while you are creating, then apply it at the appropriate time: *after* you have created something/anything. Unless you are a Mozart and music just pours out of you directly from God, you need to consciously separate these creative and critical processes. To help you remember this and other concepts we've discussed so far, here's a summary—Document, Experiment, Analyze, and Finish, or, to be cutesy about it, D.E.A.F.

GO D.E.A.F.!

Document every musical idea you come up with—phrases, melodies, riffs, lyric lines. You always should have a cassette recorder running when you are writing, for artistic "insurance" and objectivity. It may help to keep chord progressions, lyrics, and other song ideas in a notebook rather than on a random collection of napkins, matchbook covers, and other paper scraps. A single storage location often leads to ideas combining with others quite easily. A melody you wrote two years ago may work beautifully with a partially completed lyric you came up with last week.

Experimenting is the central focus when crafting a song; you need to turn off your critical faculties so your imagination can run free. This is an acquired skill. You must give yourself permission to try anything and everything, knowing that all ideas, good and bad, will be available for your next step: Analysis.

Analysis: When you rewind the tape and hit "play," kick in the critical part of your mind. Listening to a taped performance gives you the necessary sense of detachment you need to view the song as an object instead of the deeply sensitive and absolutely flawless outpourings of your soul. Take notes while listening, reading along with the lyric sheet. Should the second verse really be the first verse? Is there too much musical filler between verses? Does the bridge make musical sense or should it be in another song? Do you have *too many* chords in the verse? Could the chord progression be simplified? This begs an important question: Do you have too many ideas going on? A good song is often similar to a short story, with one general idea or theme, even if this idea is hard to describe in words.

Finishing a song occurs when you have analyzed your experimental ideas and arrangements to the point where you understand what to change and you change it. This process may occur only after repeated sessions of experimentation and analysis, so this final stage may take longer than you think. Knowing when you're "finished" is an art in itself. It may take a relatively short time to firm up a melody and chord progression, but you may get stuck on the lyrics. If so, sing dummy lyrics with the right rhythmic pattern. Sometimes by not caring what you sing you can accidentally come up with cool lyrics since they don't "count."

If you get hung up on a song that isn't responding to your care and attention, let it "rest" for a few days on the tape. When you get back to it you'll probably work on it with a fresh perspective.

WAKE UP YOUR GUITAR

If you write songs on guitar, here's two things you can do that may help you generate ideas: Learn some new chords and new tunings.

Learning new positions and shapes for workhorse chords is always helpful. Try a few of those listed below. Some of these chords are labeled "noncommittal," not because they haven't decided to become chords, but because they purposely lack the third. Without a third, a chord is neither major or minor, and this can free you up to sing a much wider range of notes when you are trying to develop a melody. Removing the third in any chord gives it more of a "power chord" feel.

Even a small difference in a chord voicing can lead to a fresh writing approach. Adding a thumb is a bit of a hand stretch but can give you a whole new sound. Check these out:

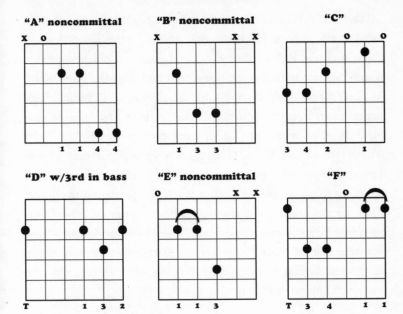

6 ways to play a G chord

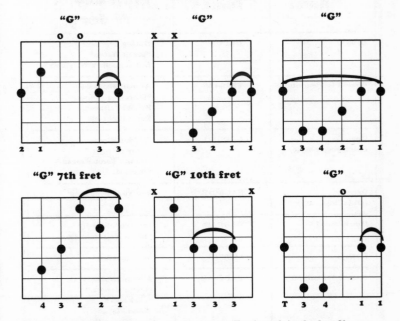

X=don't play string/O=open string/T=thumb/1=index finger
2=middle finger/3=ring finger/4=little finger

Have you ever tried to figure out how certain guitarists played a chord or riff, only to become exasperated and bitter, figuring it was studio trickery? Relax—they may be playing in a different tuning. Jimmy Page often used exotic tunings for Led Zeppelin songs. Keith Richards wrote many classic Stones songs in open-G tuning. Pearl Jam, Soundgarden, Joni Mitchell, Sonic Youth, and blues-based slide guitarists all write and play in alternate tunings. The B-52's Ricky Wilson removed the D and G strings from his guitar to help achieve their first album's wacky party sound. Trying different tunings is a great way to get a new perspective when composing on the guitar. If you are the music half of a songwriting collaboration, a new tuning might help you come up with that irresistible instrumental track that inspires great lyrics. If you have an extra guitar, try leaving it in an alternate tuning. Here's a chart showing some hip tunings, who used them and on what song:

Name	Tuning	Artist and/or Song
Drop D	DADGBE	Doobie Brothers' "Black Water," Led Zeppelin's "Kashmir"
Open E (slide guitar)	EBEG#BE	Allman Brothers' "Statesboro Blues," Robert Johnson, Keith Richards
Open G (slide/finger style)	DGDGBD	Rolling Stones' "Brown Sugar," "Honky Tonk Woman," "Start Me Up"
Open A (slide/finger style)	EAEAC#E	You/your next song
D suspended	DADGAD	Led Zeppelin's "Black Mountain Side"
E 5th	EEBBBE	Soundgarden
Open D (cross note)	DADF#AD	Allman Brothers' "Little Martha," Pearl Jam's "Even Flow," Joni Mitchell's "Free Man In Paris"
Double DAD	DADDAD	Crosby, Stills & Nash's "Suite: Judy Blue Eyes"

Tuning your guitar down a half-step isn't technically an alternate tuning but can give you a half-step more upper vocal range when singing. Another trick is to tune your guitar down a whole step, so the strings are D–G–C–F–A–D. Loud metal rockers do this because the open chords sound real big. Songs using open chords in this tuning sound great, especially if you play along with a standard-tuned guitar. To accompany a standard-tuned guitar playing an open G, you play an open A. The notes in both chords are similar but the different open chord positions create an interesting sonority. Translation: It sounds cool, try it.

For a fascinating insight into the role that tuning can play in one composer's craft, read the Joni Mitchell interview in *Acoustic Guitar Magazine*, August 1996. Mitchell has used 51 different tunings in her prolific career, and recorded only two songs on her 17 albums in standard E–A–D–G–B–E!

THE WORLD OF COLLABORATION

If you are brave, vulnerable, self-confident, and have good enough social skills, you may be able to take your craft to a much higher level by collaborating with another songwriter. It takes a special type of personality to collaborate. Not everyone can do it. When a collaboration is productive it really is a case where 1 + 1 = 5.

All initial collaborations are huge leaps of faith. You need to start by giving your partner the benefit of the doubt as you begin to work together. You shouldn't work with someone you don't trust, but the only way to find out if you trust them is to work with them. This sounds like a paradox, but it leads to this conclusion: The way you find out if someone is compatible is to give them a try. To collaborate you must be willing to try, try, try. Collaboration will put you in a place of deliberate artistic "unsafety," and from this risk can come great songs—if you have the guts to be open and vulnerable.

The most common collaborative effort is a split between words and music. This allows each person to concentrate solely on what they do best, and has worked out just fine for the songwriting teams of Jagger–Richards, (Elton) John–Taupin, Bacharach–David, Petty–Campbell, and Page–Plant. Each of these teams has been remarkably successful and it's due to a couple of things: the actual musical and lyric talent of the individuals and their ability to work together. Having both talents obviously pays off.

Some bands (The Doors, Van Halen) agree that all their songs are collaborative efforts, and for arrangement-driven tunes this makes practical as well as philosophic sense. Almost all the songs on Jackson Browne's 1995 album *Looking East* were credited to the entire band because they grew out of jam sessions at rehearsals.

> Songs are still pretty much made out of two components: words and music.

As you can see, there is no standard method of dividing up writing credit. When you're in a band, musical arrangements sometimes cross over into the golden world of compositions. If you come up with an inarguably killer guitar riff like the intro to "(I Can't Get No) Satisfaction" or "Whole Lotta Love," then you may rightfully deserve writing credit. A good test is this: Would the song have essentially the same feel if you removed your instrumental "hook"? Generally speaking, though, a cool riff does not make you a songwriter. Songs are still pretty much made out of two components: words and music. A song title, however, if used as the inspiration for a song, may be a legitimate part of the tune and deserve a cut of the songwriting credit. This may not be the case if you come up with "I Love You" as a concept for a song, but a title like "Strong Enough to Bend" may tell a tale by itself.

There are many ways to collaborate, only one of which is sitting in a room with a couple guitars and a thermos of coffee. Bernie Taupin sends Elton John neatly typed lyrics and Elton sets them to music. Guitarist Mike Campbell creates complete instrumental song demos and sends them to Tom Petty for lyric consideration. Often an instrumental track that doesn't grab one lyricist will go the rounds of other writers until something groovy happens. Don Henley took separate instrumental tracks by two different writers (Mike Campbell and Bruce Hornsby), added lyrics, and voilà—two hits, 1984's "The Boys of Summer" and 1989's "The End of the Innocence." This type of collaboration is relatively painless because one writer is simply presenting his contribution to the other and in essence saying "Here, I'm done, see if you can run with it." Of course you need to be very good at writing music or lyrics to inspire the other half of the songwriting team. But that's why we're all here—to work.

 If you do plan on collaborating with someone, you need to reach an agreement for a general plan, even if your plan is to try anything and everything. Collaboration is a team sport. To do your part you must be open-hearted, open-minded, not afraid to speak your artistic mind. At the same time you can't be a jerk and act like you are the one with all the answers. A good mental exercise is to ask yourself: Would you like to work with yourself as a partner?

To collaborate you must put your ego aside and focus strictly on the needs of the song, not your immediate personal gratification. Your best friend the ego usually kicks in the first time your partner suggests a musical or lyrical idea you don't particularly like. This is your first chance to test a potential long-term writing partnership.

To keep the creative juices flowing, don't let the division of imaginary songwriting royalties interfere with the subject at hand: the song. A secure collaborator will not be keeping track of which line or chord was contributed by whom. In fact, when a collaboration is working, the two (or more) parties may not recall at a later time who contributed what, because the creative feeling carried the songwriting session along. Do all that you can to let it flow.

So how do you split a song? This can be an exceedingly delicate matter. You should certainly never start a collaboration agreeing on a split before you begin working together, otherwise the other person may simply cough and say "There's my 50%." The best attitude is for everyone involved to be generous and focus on the big picture. Another way to put it would be this: Don't be greedy, and think long-term. Greed will kill a creative environment instantly. This often takes the shape of the dreaded affliction known as Post–Writing Hindsight. You know, "That was easy...I could have written that song all by myself...why did I split it?" Well, the song may have been written with ease precisely because you spent time and energy working with someone else. You won't be able to go back in time, write the song yourself, and compare versions!

Thinking long-term is closely tied to the greed issue. If you like the results of a collaboration and you can imagine working long-term with your writing partner, try to be loose and generous with how you divide up each song and look to the future. Don't use a microscope, use binoculars.

Be generous of spirit; songwriting at its best can be a spiritual give-and-take of deeply felt opinions ideas and emotions. It also helps if you can work with someone more skilled at songwriting than yourself. If you collaborate with someone higher up in the songwriting world, the business version of the Golden Rule usually applies: He who has the gold makes the rules. If you are getting valuable insights into songwriting by working with this writer, you may have to settle for how they want to divide up the songwriting credit. You only have as much clout as you actually have, not what you think you have.

Some people are more generous than others in an arranging/songwriting situation. It helps to work with someone who believes in sharing the joy: Roy Orbison gave the drummer on "Oh! Pretty Woman" songwriting credit because of the signature drumbeat. Hard to imagine the song without it, and Roy felt the same way.

It takes a lot to collaborate with another writer. Give it a try, it could lead to a relationship that is artistically and financially gratifying.

PERSONAL REMINISCENCE: MY BRILLIANT SONGWRITING CAREER

The most satisfying money I've made in the music business (aside from playing live gigs) has been from songwriting royalties. Yes, folks, just like the product that cleans your oven while you sleep, you can earn money as you sleep, knowing that somewhere in the world your song is being played on the radio or sold in a record store. I didn't consider myself a professional songwriter while writing the songs I'm about to describe, it was more of a fun thing to do while playing my instrument and toying with lyrics. A sense of playfulness helps.

While still in high school, I began my band career as the bassist in a power-trio with the unbelievable name of Road Turkey. In 1971 we were asked to contribute a song for a compilation album put out by Atlanta's Emory University. These were the hippie days, so something like this could actually happen. Our musical offering (with lyrics by yours truly) was "Out on the Shreds," the title of which was inspired by Led Zeppelin's "Out on the Tiles." Believe me, that was the only relationship our song had with Led Zep. Opening lyric: "People tell me things are great, fun all day/All those games just bring me down if I can't play." We drove from North Florida to Atlanta to cut the track at what turned out to be a small jingle studio. As we were setting up our equipment a Creomulsion laxative commercial was playing back over the studio monitors: "Creomulsion works naturally, so naturally it works..."

It was at that moment that I knew I wanted to write and record songs forever.

We cut the track, briefly felt like rock stars, then drove back to Florida. When the album came out we bought a whole bunch (probably 50% of total sales) and played it for all of our friends. Strangely, no one from a major label tried to contact us.

I moved to L.A. and eventually joined The Motels (1978–1986), a band blessed with the writing and performing talents of vocalist Martha Davis. I considered myself a sax and keyboard player, nothing more. I mostly contributed little instrumental hooks and quirky synth squiggles as well as some fab sax solos, yet I did end up writing and co-writing four songs that made it to vinyl.

> *I'm as amazed as you are that a few weeks of work in 1980 can generate income today.*

The first collaboration was in 1980 with Michael Goodroe, the bassist. While the producer was mixing the first half of our 1980 album *Careful* in the control room, he suggested we go in the back of the studio and write some songs for the second half of the album and in a hurry. We set up keyboard and bass gear, then noodled. Relying heavily on current musical influences to inspire us, we prayed that Influence plus Noodling would eventually equal Song. It soon did.

(Note: In this era of songs that integrate digital samples of previously recorded tracks—mostly hip-hop and rap music—I have no shame in telling you exactly what music was floating around in my head when I wrote the following tunes.)

Our debut composition was "Bonjour Baby," the piano intro of which had been inspired by an Elvis Costello tune, "Oliver's Army." The rest of the song featured soundbite lyric imagery, although to this day neither of us are sure what the song is about. Still, nothing beats the thrill of that first song, the one that makes it on an album.

The next collaboration was "Crybaby," musically influenced by two seemingly unrelated sources: Marianne Faithfull's "The Ballad of Lucy Jordan" (from *Broken English*) and Thin Lizzy's "Old Flame" (from *Johnny the Fox*). I loved Steve Winwood's brilliant keyboard part on the Faithfull tune, so I came up with a synth part that seemed to emulate Winwood, whom I admired greatly. The Thin Lizzy song had an arrangement that alternated instrumental licks with vocal passages, a concept I borrowed from freely. We roughed out an arrangement with keyboard, bass, and drums and showed it to the producer and other band members, who went for it. Then we wrote lyrics for Martha concerning a girl who needs to cry, baby. Boom! Now we had two. Next stop, the Grammys.

The final song, "Careful," became the title track of the album. I thought it would be funny to write a song with three stepwise major chords in a row, in this case F major, G major, A major. Don't ask me why. General surrealism along with fragmented lyric phrasing were artistic highlights. Sample lyric: "I need/you need/Listen/I understand that." My Prophet 5 synthesizer had a sound that reminded me of a cuckoo clock, so for the bridge I wrote a cuckoo clock part.

Of these three album tracks from our 1980 album *Careful*, two of them ended up on our *No Vacancy—Best of The Motels* CD that earns royalties like clockwork every three months. I'm as amazed as you are that a few weeks of work in 1980 can generate income today.

My final example encompasses many of the topics covered in this chapter. I was on the phone to our producer John Carter bewailing my current love problems with my girlfriend. Carter, deeply moved, said, "Well, you know what they say…take the 'L' out of 'Lover' and it's 'Over.' Hey, that would be a good title for a song." Once I got the pun, I thought it was the corniest thing I'd ever heard, like an old country weeper, but it stuck in my head. During this time, I had been listening to a song by The Hollies called "Pay You Back with Interest," featuring a cool four-note piano intro that was a definite pop hook. I wrote my own version of it, in the same rhythm but with different notes. I took my four notes (F–A–E–G) and wrote chords for them (F, Am7, C/E bass, G). The lyrics I wrote came from a genuine emotion, as I thought of how love doesn't always work out, of how "good intentions are never good enough." As clever as the wordplay was, I was still one bummed dude and the song was born of strong personal feelings, as the best songs usually are. I liked what I had so far but knew the structure of the chorus wasn't quite there, so I asked for help from Martha Davis, who moved some chords in the chorus around. The two minutes she spent on the chorus solidified the entire structure of the song. Spot-collaboration to the rescue!

Although most of the lyrics came quickly, the few lines I needed for the second verse took days to decide upon. Finally, we rehearsed the song extensively and recorded it in one take. I gave both Carter and Martha a percentage of the song for their contributions: a great title and a chorus that made musical sense.

The combination of a genuine emotion, a phone call, a keyboard hook inspired by a favorite oldie, and a bit of welcome collaboration all came together to create what has been my most successful song-writing experience. Songs are remarkable items.

CHAPTER SIX
WRITE SONGS!
EARN MONEY!

*People compose for many reasons: to become immor-
tal; because the pianoforte happens to be open;
because they want to become a millionaire; because
of the praise of friends; because they have looked into
a pair of beautiful eyes; for no reason whatsoever.*
—Robert Schumann (1810–1856)

*But the overriding thing is, if you don't got
the fucking music, you don't got anything.
You could go up there dressed as a fucking flower
and you ain't gonna get anywhere
if you don't have good songs.*
**—Ozzy Osbourne (1948–),
quoted in Pulse!, April 1996**

Not everyone reading these words wants to be a Big
Rock Star, but it's safe to assume that no one would
be upset if they wrote a song that made money. The
music business is a multibillion-dollar industry. What
is the driving force behind all this money? Quite simply, songs. It is not an exaggeration to say that one hit
recording can make the writer a million dollars. If you'd written
"White Christmas" or "Yesterday," you'd know what I'm talking
about.

Unlike other art forms, songs have a particular chameleon-like
magic to them: They can be expressed in as many ways as there are
different performances. Some of these ways may lack artistic merit,
such as a lounge act butchering your favorite band's hits. But it's possible to write a song with such universal appeal that it can be recorded successfully by Frank Sinatra, Alice in Chains, Michael Bolton,
and Muzak. Although it's hard to imagine what this song would
sound like, each one of these interpretations would produce income
for the writer and the publisher of the song.

Because of the large earning potential inherent in every tune you write, it makes sense to learn how songs make money, and just as importantly, where this money comes from.

If we discuss songs and song income, the logical place to start is with the way our society defines ownership of a song, and that is through the *copyright*.

COPYRIGHT

A copyright is the right to copy something—for our purposes, a song. As author of a song you automatically own the copyright; you have the exclusive right to make and sell copies (sheet music, tapes, CDs) and the right to perform the song, which is also a form of copying. This concept is part of a body of law that recognizes that the creative output of your mind (for better or for worse), if in a tangible form, has a value that should be protected. The key phrase is *tangible*, meaning something that has actual form or substance. You can think up a song in your head, hum it, or play it for your friends at parties, but the first step in protecting your ownership is putting it in tangible form. What this means in street talk is recording it, either by a sound recording or by writing out the melody in musical notation, along with the lyrics—commonly called a "lead sheet" (see Chapter 3). In this world of cassettes and cheap recording studios, making a sound recording is usually the easiest and most common method of storing your song in "tangible" form. It doesn't have to be slick: just the words, the melody, and a basic rhythm accompaniment on a cassette. Once your song is fixed in a storage medium, you are the "author" of the song.

To prove this, the key is to *register* this copyright with a recognizable authority; in this case, your friend the Federal Government, more specifically the Copyright Office of the Library of Congress. There are alternative methods, but let's start with the safest and most recognizable form of registering.

To begin the registration process, write to: Copyright Office, Library of Congress, Washington, DC 20559, and ask for Form PA (Performing Arts) and Form SR (Sound Recording) and Packet #105, which contains copyright information, or, now that you know what to ask for, call the Copyright Hotline at (202) 707-9100. The Copyright Office's main number is (202) 707-3000. You can request as many forms as you need (they're free)—but you also can photocopy a blank form for additional copies. When they arrive, read the attached line-by-line instructions carefully; the Library of Congress will return any form not filled out *exactly right*.

Which form should you use? Form PA is for registering works of the performing arts, including music. This is what you use to register your song. It's the *musical work* you are interested in protecting, not the musical performance, unless you feel strongly that someone is going to make millions bootlegging a tape of you singing your song in a room with a guitar. Form SR is used to register copyright ownership of the *sound recording,* something record companies do routinely because they own the

> It's the musical work you are interested in protecting, not the musical performance...

recordings. Owning the rights to a *song* and the rights to a *performance* are two separate entities. For example, if your band, God forbid, recorded a tribute album to Milli Vanilli, the unique recording of those songs would be your property (or the record company's) but the songs wouldn't be; you didn't write them. For protecting your songs, the Copyright Office suggests you use Form PA. Now, the fee for each song submitted is $20, no biggy. But if you want to protect your ten latest demos, there goes the rent! Solution: Put all the songs on one tape as a "collection" and give it a name (it can even be "Songs"). If a copyright dispute comes up this could lead to difficulties in identifying a particular song, but if your budget won't permit separate registration, this is the way to go. Fill out the form carefully and return it with the fee and a copy of the song (tape/CD/lead sheet) and in about six weeks you'll get back a photocopy of the form you submitted with lots of bar codes and rubber stamped dates and stuff. This is proof that somewhere, in a huge warehouse in Landover, Maryland, your song rests snugly in a special plastic envelope, stored as a national artistic treasure of the Library of Congress. It's a great feeling.

What about alternative ways of protecting your songs? There are really two other methods, neither of which provides the same protection as the Copyright Office, but which in essence can provide proof that your song existed on a particular day. The cheapest way is the so-called "poor person's copyright." You send a copy of your song to yourself via registered mail, and when you receive it, store the unopened package in a safe place. The postmark in this case is considered proof that your song was created on or before a certain date. Another method is a service offered by the National Academy of Songwriters called Songbank. You submit a copy of your song (either tape or lead sheet) along with their registration form and $10 for the first song, $6 for each additional, and they send back a receipt acknowledging your submission. For further info write or call: NAS, 6381 Hollywood Boulevard, Suite 780, Hollywood, CA 90028; 1-800-826-7287 (outside California) or (213) 463-7178.

Do you really need to do any of this stuff? Statistically, the odds are against your song being plagiarized, and financial considerations may play a large part in what you do to protect your songs. You have to decide whether or not you feel the need to copyright or otherwise protect your musical creations.

SONG LICENSING

As mentioned before, if you write a song, you automatically and exclusively own the copyright. This gives you certain rights according to copyright law, most importantly the exclusive right to perform the work publicly. "Public performance" isn't just playing the song live. The legal definition includes the playing of the song on radio. To stay within the law, a radio station must be licensed by the copyright owner (you). This "license" is also needed by people who run local, network, and cable TV; clubs; hotels; aerobics classes; malls; theaters; restaurants; elevators; corner bars—in short, just about anywhere recorded music is performed publicly.

Since it would be impractical for you to locate and grant permission ("licensing") to every music user, and a similar pain for each of these places to locate you, there is a better way: *performing rights organizations.*

Performing rights organizations license the public performance rights of songs to users—all the places listed above. There are three organizations of this type in the U.S.: ASCAP, BMI, and SESAC. They were formed to serve as clearinghouses for music copyright owners and music users to solve the hassles associated with licensing. When you join one of these organizations and give them permission to license your song by filling out a form, they issue "blanket licenses" to businesses (radio and TV stations, bars, restaurants, etc.) that use music. This blanket license allows the businesses to play all of the music in that performing rights organization's catalog. They also take legal action against those who don't pay for licenses, and devise methods of monitoring airplay that determine how many times a song is played.

Here's the reason you should join: The businesses that use these songs pay a fee (which varies according to many factors) to get the license. Every three months, the sum of these fees (known as performance income) is divided up and distributed to you and the other organization members in proportion to the amount of airplay your song(s) received. Although radio stations generate the majority of this income, newer ways of distributing (and therefore licensing) music are constantly evolving. The health club I belong to has a service called Digital Music Express, which offers 61 channels of digital cable audio in various formats: Channel 1 is Gospel, 2 is alternative, 3 is McJazz, etc. Each performance on Digital Music Express generates money for the writer and the publisher of the song.

TWO SOURCES OF SONG INCOME: WRITING AND PUBLISHING

As you may have guessed, songs are both written by someone and "published" by someone. The "writer" is the creator of the song and the "publisher" is the party who owns or controls the copyright of the song. This is a very important distinction.

The word "publishing" is misleading because it originated during a time in history when the chief source of income from songs came from the printing and selling of sheet music. Back in those days, you might go to a music store and hear an employee pounding out a song on the piano, in the hope that you'd like the tune enough to buy the sheet music, thus generating a song royalty for the writer, and a sheet music sale for (literally) the publisher. Today, music publishing is still a major source of income from songs and a very important part of the music business. If you, the writer, also create your own publishing company, you'll earn money from your songs both as the writer *and* the publisher.

Let me illustrate with a real life example. Back in 1982, as a member of The Motels, I wrote a song called "Take the L." In addition to writing it (and thanks to a good lawyer), I also created a publishing company, Excessive Music, which published the song. Since the song received airplay and was on an album that went gold (500,000 copies sold), I got paid, as the writer of the song and as the publisher. This is a good thing!

Music publishing is a separate part of the music business. It is directly tied to songs, yet is separate from the act of creating a song. Confused? This is where my famous "Theory of Two Pies" may be helpful.

Think of each song as two pies: One pie is the writer's share, and the other is the publisher's share. Each of these parts earns money.

> On album sales and performance royalties, this publishing income is equal in size to the writer's income.

The author (or authors) of a song receive money generated by the writer's pie. Ownership of this part can't change—no one else can write a song after it's been written. The publisher(s) of a song receive income from the publisher's pie. The ownership of this part can be bought and sold independently of the writer's share. A perfect example is Michael Jackson's purchase of The Beatles' publishing for very big bucks. "Buying the publishing" really means buying the right to receive the stream of income that the publishing generates. On album sales and performance royalties, this publishing income is equal in size to the writer's income. Jackson paid plenty for this right because The Beatles' songs earn, well, a considerable sum—"Yesterday" is still one of the most covered songs in pop music.

We'd all love to get a song placed on an album or in a movie. If you're a songwriter with a record deal, chances are you have an inside track on getting your songs on a record—your record. But what if you're a songwriter without this advantage? Does it ever make sense career-wise to have someone else publish your song? It does indeed. Large publishing companies (such as Almo–Irving, EMI Music, Polygram Music, Sony–Tree, and Warner–Chappel) will sign various types of publishing deals with songwriters who they feel have the potential to write successful tunes.

FOUR KINDS OF PUBLISHING DEALS

There are four basic kinds of deals you can sign.

The first is a *Single Song Agreement*. If you have a song a publishing firm feels they can place with a recording artist, or in a TV or movie soundtrack, they will sign you to this type of deal in exchange for the publishing. This means you wrote it and they publish it. Why give them half your income? Because they have the connections, the time and the staff to get your song in the marketplace. If splitting the money still seems unfair, remember this basic math equation: 50% of something is always more than 100% of nothing.

A second type of publishing deal is the *Term Exclusive Songwriter's Agreement*. In this one, the publisher you sign with keeps the publisher's share of income on every song you write during a given period of time, usually a year with options for two to four more years. In exchange, you get cash advances from the publisher based on how much they think they'll earn from the publishing income of your song. This publishing advance is typically from $7,500 to $30,000 per year for first-time writers, $25,000 to $100,000 for established writers and even higher for writers with a super track record.

The third type of deal is the *Administration Agreement*. In this agreement the publisher (or "administrating publisher") handles the collection and distribution of all your songwriting income for a relatively low "administration fee" of up to 20% of the publisher's share. This is a good setup when you have songs already generating income on various records, especially if there are significant record sales outside the U.S. Although nearly every publishing company offers this kind of deal, Bug Music Group, based in Los Angeles, specializes in it.

The fourth kind, the *Co-publishing Agreement,* is just that: The songwriter not only receives the writer's share of the performance income (as in all these deals) but also retains 50% of the publisher's share. It's the most common deal these days if you have a recording contract and your songs will be on a commercially released album. The publisher, of course, offers the songwriter a tempting cash advance in exchange for part interest in the song. In turn, the publisher is reasonably assured of receiving at least some publishing income from future record sales, since the song has already been "placed."

Now that you know a little about songs and copyrights, performing rights organizations and publishing, you're ready for the exciting part: the four main sources of song income.

FOUR SOURCES OF INCOME

First, the *public performance income*. This is radio airplay, TV music, etc. income collected by ASCAP, BMI or SESAC. The money they collect and distribute every three months ("quarterly") for each song is split 50/50 between the publisher and the writer. They actually write two separate checks. And of course, the more times your song is played, the more money it earns.

Another source of song income is *mechanical royalties*, from the sale of sound recordings—CDs, cassettes, and vinyl. Every three months the record company writes a check to the publisher of the song at the current "statutory rate" of 6.6 cents per song per recording sold. The publisher splits the money 50/50 with the songwriter. Example: You have a song on an album that went platinum (1,000,000 sold) and you were able to keep your own publishing. If you get paid at the full statutory rate, your share of the mechanical royalties for that one song would be $66,000. If you wrote all ten songs (the maximum number of songs per album record companies will pay on) you'd get a cool $660,000. However, most record labels will only pay 75% of the "statutory rate" of songs written by the artist. Why? After extensive research, I've determined that it's because they can, claiming it's "standard industry practice." Welcome to the music business!

Publishing can be a serious negotiating point with an artist interested in covering your song. Example: Madonna calls you up one evening to say she wants your song "Never So Deep" for her next album and video, and she'll record it—if you give her the publishing. Would you say no? Well, at least sleep on it.

Sheet music royalties come from those glossy songbooks you see in music stores. Usually a deal is cut with one of the major print companies that specialize in printing sheet music, and the writer's share is about 10% to 12% of wholesale, prorated among all songs. Big hit records generate big songbook sales, and although some songs don't translate well into sheet music, nothing beats the thrill of hearing your little sister pounding out R.E.M.'s "Losing My Religion" on the family piano.

Synchronization income refers to money you receive from movie and television production companies for the right to use your song in their movie, TV show, or commercial. The bigger the act and the better the lawyer, the more money you can get. $25,000 is not uncommon for a song in a movie. Examples: The large number of youth-oriented movies with sound-tracks by today's "alternative" acts. The soundtrack to *Singles* is a perfect example. A very lucrative aspect of featured music in a movie is the inevitable soundtrack album. In this era of MTV it's not much of a stretch to consider the actual movie as noth-

> A very lucrative aspect of featured music in a movie is the inevitable soundtrack album.

ing more than a long promotional tool for the accompanying sound-track CD. Other examples of sync income in action: Nike's use of The Beatles' "Revolution" to help sell running shoes, Chevrolet using Bob Seger's "Like a Rock," and the licensing of The Rolling Stones' 1981 song "Start Me Up" to help promote Windows 95. The license fee was reportedly $1 million. As they say, nice work if you can get it.

So how much money can a big hit song make? Oodles. Theoretically there's no limit. Songs can and do earn income years after they're released. If you write a standard that other artists want to record, like George Harrison's "Something," or Billy Joel's "I Love You Just the Way You Are," you could live quite comfortably off the income of one song. Mel Torme cowrote "The Christmas Song" ("Chestnuts roasting on an open fire") back in the '40s and this makes money *every year,* so don't forget to write a Christmas standard if you can.

REACHING CRITICAL MASS

An interesting aspect of pop culture is the fact that success breeds success breeds success. When someone is already famous, putting their face on the cover of a magazine boosts that magazine's circulation dramatically—giving the magazine more profit and making that someone a little more famous, a living example of that old phrase "you scratch my back and I'll scratch yours." Reaching this kind of "critical mass" is desirable and can happen with a hit song, too. Airplay momentum, which begins to build as stations start adding a song to their playlists, causes more and more stations to play a song, until stations have to play the song in order to reflect what's currently "popular." This increased airplay, which record labels encourage in many ways, leads to increased album sales, which generate mechanical royalties. And of course, hit albums cause music publishers to cut lucrative songbook deals, and then Hollywood desperately needs you to write a sitcom theme, at which point Ford wants your song for a Thunderbird commercial. Only in America!

It takes some serious study to fully understand the money side of the music business. For those of you utterly fascinated with this part of the trade, the Information Sources section in the back of the book will be of interest.

PERSONAL REMINISCENCE: SONGS HAVE LIVES OF THEIR OWN

Songs can have a life separate from a band's repertoire, as the following tale will illustrate. My brother Jeff kindly loaned me his reminiscences regarding a song he cowrote as a member of The Motels. Since I was in the band from start to finish he's given me permission to chime in if I'm polite about it. Big brothers can be strict.

Back in 1978 Martha Davis, founder of The Motels and chief songwriter, wrote a punky Lou Reed–like song called "Complete Control," with a beat similar to Reed's "Waiting for My Man." Jeff, who was working with Martha to arrange songs and help form the version of The Motels that finally got a record deal, was enthralled at the time with a slow, hypnotic Be Bop Deluxe track called "Panic in the World." Jeff suggested changing the song title to "Total Control" and slowing the tune down—way, way down. "The slower it got, the cooler it sounded," he recalls. "Total Control" became a centerpiece of The Motels' live show and was a huge hit single in Australia in 1979, giving the band their first commercial success, and earning The Motels an Australian Gold single and album down under. Jeff left the band in 1980, but the song he cowrote continued with a life of its own.

First, in 1980, Italian pop singer Anna Oxa released a version in her native tongue called "Controlle Totale" which was a minor hit. Her version had a note-for-note copy of my original sax solo on it, and I was amused and flattered to hear another sax player copy what had come out of my imagination—a real turnaround for me after playing other sax players' parts in copy bands for so many years.

In 1986, the director of the movie *Something Wild* chose "Total Control" as background music for one scene, and as cowriter Jeff received $2,250—50% of the synchronization license fee. Not bad! But the story gets better.

Because the song was a huge hit in Australia, it ended up being featured in a—get this—Australian Cheezles television commercial—the Australian equivalent of Cheetos, the popular snack food. The commercial consisted of a woman singing "Total Control" to a bag of Cheezles on a pedestal, in reference to how hard it was to "eat just one." The sync license fee for this "featured use" of the song was $15,000, so Jeff's share was $7,500.

In 1992, Capitol Records reissued the first Motels album (with "Total Control") in CD format as a "mid-line" product, meaning it had a lower list price and would pay out royalties at 75% of the normal rate. Since the album was now back in print, the lower royalty rate was fine with Jeff, since, and you've heard this before, 75% of something is more than 100% of nothing.

Tina Turner had cut a version of "Total Control" as well, and although it was never released on her albums, it did make it on a Tina Turner compilation "boxed set" that came out in December 1994, generating more royalty income.

A good song takes on a life of its own. And you never know which song it will be.

**Q: Could you tell me how to get
to Carnegie Hall?
A: Practice.
(World's oldest musician joke)**

Believe it or not, there are plenty of places your band can play: concert halls, bars, taverns, lounges, restaurants, juice bars, coffeehouses, bookstores, even shopping malls. No matter what style of music you play, chances are you can get a gig. It's just a matter of the band, the venue and the audience getting together. Let's agree to call all types of venues that offer live music "clubs," and the people who book the music "bookers," whether they work exclusively for a club or as indies.

How do you get a gig? First, the simple answer: Have enough material to play at least one set, put together a promo pack (essentially a tape/CD, photo, and bio), mail it to or drop it off at various clubs, and wait to hear from the booker. Easy, huh? Now the fine print…There's more to it. There are so many variables in a club's booking policy that the details are worth discussing.

THE BOOKER'S VIEW

For starters, how do clubs choose bands? In several ways. Smaller venues may be booked by the owner, who is also the bartender, dishwasher, and bouncer. However, many clubs hire a person whose sole job is booking the talent. They listen to hundreds of tapes each month and choose from these the acts they feel are of a style and level of professionalism that will suit the club they're booking. Let's divide these clubs into three broad categories.

Concert-style clubs that book national acts may hire the opening act solely through word of mouth or recommendations from other booking agents. These are good gigs if you can get them. Opening for a well-known act can be a turning point in a band's career. National acts attract many music-biz types in the audience (radio **87** station people, record company reps, music writers from the local paper) who can help your career—particularly if they like what they hear.

Most live-music venues book recognized local and regional talent. If they primarily book acts that already have a strong local following, these clubs often reserve a particular night of the week for "New Talent Night." If you've been on the club circuit a while, these are the clubs you'll play most.

The third type of club you can play offers what can be called an "entry-level" performance situation. They often have a wide-open booking policy and you get paid either in drink tickets or by splitting the cover charge receipts with four other bands. Everyone starts somewhere, and this is where many bands begin their careers. You probably know which club in your town fits this description. The positive side of starting at this kind of venue is that you have nowhere to go but up. I used to watch Van Halen play at a go-go club in L.A. called Gazarri's for a $3 cover. Whatever happened to them?

Bookers usually keep tabs on who's playing at other clubs. So, to increase your visibility when starting out, don't be too picky about where and when you play. Try to think of the gigs where you go on at 1 a.m. and play to five people as paid rehearsals. As Thelonious Monk once said, you practice every time you pick up your instrument and play. Your early strategy should be to get your name in the club calendars as often as possible. After a while you will become a known quantity to Those Who Book.

PROMO STUFF:
JUST THE ESSENTIALS

Promoting your band is a never-ending process, and one important device is the inevitable "**promo pack**." This is an important tool in getting work; still, there's no need to go overboard with expensive printing and glossy folders. Club bookers are busy and rarely in the mood to read the life history and food faves of each band member. Skip it. Something better than a handwritten bio and not as slick as a major printing job is fine. The essentials, however, never change.

A **tape** or **CD** is a must—they gotta hear a band before they will consider booking them. Bookers form opinions quickly when listening to a recording, so put your best song first with no more than three songs total. Haven't gone in the studio yet? As mentioned in

Chapter 4, a clean, well-balanced live rehearsal tape will be just as good if not better for judging how you will sound in a club setting. And always, always put your phone number on the cassette or CD. Really. If the rest of the promo gets misplaced you can still be reached.

Supplying a **group photo** is optional but highly recommended. Band photos give the booker an idea of, well, how your band looks, and whether or not the visual presentation is in keeping with the music. Of course, if you're a skinhead-vegetarian-polka band a brief explanatory note should be attached. When your budget won't allow a pro photo shoot, get a friend to take some black and white photos of everyone huddled together (it looks more band-like), choose the best one and get professional copies made.

A **brief bio** (including any or all reviews or interviews) can be assembled and photocopied. Drop the tape/photo/bio package into a manila envelope (glossy folders are unnecessary). Then call the club(s), ask where to send the material, and either mail it in or drop it off. Do this at a lot of places. Meanwhile, talk to other bands about places to play, and meet as many people on the music scene as you

Playing the Part While Playing Your Part

Without having to play dressup every time you play, it is important that your band look like a band and not several people on completely different fashion trips thrown together. You've probably seen bands like this—the singer wants to be in Bon Jovi and the guitarist wants to be in The Grateful Dead. Bands are essentially little tribes. Finding common fashion ground is challenging but possible. A real life example: During the late '60s when I was growing up in Gainesville, Florida, I remember seeing a phenomenally gifted guitarist named Don Felder play in local bands. As a reflection of his incredible and technically flawless guitar playing, Felder always favored nicely tailored, expensive shirts and slacks. By 1976 Don had moved to L.A. and joined The Eagles (he wrote the music to "Hotel California") and I had moved to L.A. and was working at a music store. He came into the store one day (with Joe Walsh) looking for rare, expensive guitars (I couldn't help him) and I still remember what Don Felder was wearing: A very Eagles-like outfit of jeans and a plaid work shirt...both of them neatly pressed and starched.

can. If you've just begun playing live, don't despair if your first gig is the last set on a Monday night at the Crawl On Inn, and your remuneration is five drink tickets. This is called "paying your dues" and it will help you examine how dedicated you are to playing your music.

NOBODY WILL BOOK AN ASSHOLE

Say you've done all this, and still…nothing. Is it possible to be too anxious and pushy with club bookers, causing them to lose interest in you and your band? I must tell you the answer is yes. Why? Well, if we look at the typical day of someone who books a club we'll get some insight. They show up at the office, check about a dozen phone messages, then open and look through promo packs—sometimes 60 to 70 every ten days. They listen to tapes, either in the office, their car, or at home, then continue working on the bookings for the next month. They proofread and approve the club's print ads in the local magazines, phone in or fax the calendar listings for various other media outlets, arrange the printing of posters and gig calendars for the club, and in the evening act as liaison between the club and the bands playing that night. No need for violins and hankies, but generally speaking, bookers are usually busy people, so here are some

---

Mailing lists

If you put in the time, effort, and postage, mailing lists can be a great tool in helping to build a loyal following. When playing a club, leave cards on each table with your band's name on it and space for each person interested to leave their name and address. Periodically send out info to your ever-expanding following, either on postcards or tri-fold paper.

To make your own postcard mailers: Crease a sheet of 8 1/2" x 11" paper into four rectangles, then take four correctly sized (4 1/4" by 5 1/2") copies of your upcoming gig info and paste each one into a quarter section of the creased paper. Photocopy this on colored card stock, then cut each sheet into four postcards. Postcards are more work than flyers but cost less to mail.

To mail flyers simply fold them into thirds (with info side in) and seal with 3/4" circular self-adhesive labels. For maximum convenience keep your mailing list on a computer database and print your addresses on laser-printer labels.

etiquette suggestions. First, some no-no's: Don't drop by unannounced and talk to bookers during business hours or when they are at the club working the show. Don't call more than once a week or actually more than once a month when asking about a gig. Never promise a club you can bring in 500 people unless you really can. Don't call the day after you drop off a tape and ask if it's been listened to; chances are it hasn't.

It's OK to be persistent in a polite way, but don't be abusive. In short, nobody will book an asshole. *Memorize these last five words.*

Remember that a club owner or booker doesn't owe you anything just because you sent in a promo kit and called a few times. Try different approaches. For example: Let's say the band you're in, Dullärd, is friends with another band, Speed Bump, and the musical styles are compatible. Package the bands as a double bill, hit up a club for a booking, then help promote the gig. Put up posters. It will always start to rain when you begin stapling these posters to telephone poles. Do it anyway. Hand out flyers. Send out mailers to all your pals and tell them to show up. Call up the local paper and add your gig to the club listings. If you have friends in bands that play certain clubs regularly, have them suggest your band to the club's booker.

The bottom line is this: Every venue has a different clientele, location, booking style, and person in charge. If you take the time to figure out how to best approach each venue, keep a positive attitude, stay on the scene, and never give up, you will get gigs and a following.

ACTUALLY PLAYING A GIG

So you've got a gig at a club! Great. The theory, of course, is to build a following while you get better at playing live. I don't have to tell you the obvious stuff so I won't: Show up on time, start on time, end on time, don't destroy any club equipment (mikes, cables, monitors, dressing room walls, employees), be nice to the waitresses, etc. You know, real Golden Rule stuff. If part of your image includes being rude and obnoxious, destroying club gear and behaving like a total putz, fine, but YOU BETTER BE AN AWESOME MUSICIAN or you will have the very briefest of careers.

What about your set list? How do you decide what order to play your songs? The correct order may seem obvious at first but there is a true art to building a set list that presents your music in the most appealing manner. Even if you knew only three songs there are six **91** different orders they could be played in (1-2-3, 1-3-2, 2-1-3, 2-3-1, 3-1-2, 3-2-1). Ten songs can be played in 55 different orders! Which order is the "perfect set?" Plenty of experimentation will provide the answer. After you've learned the songs, you should practice running through the set at rehearsal in "real time," with no pause for discussion between songs. One way to

> After you've learned the songs, you should practice running through the set at rehearsal in "real time," with no pause for discussion between songs.

figure out the song order is by writing on an index card the name of each song, the general feel (fast, slow, hyper, coma), and the key. You can sequence the cards in various orders and experiment with your set list without constantly writing each order on paper. You should try to start your set with a bang (hello!), then build slowly up to another bang (thanks and bye!), which should be the climax of your set and, theoretically, your last song. This doesn't have to be your fastest most high-energy number, just your best song. Try not to

have several slow numbers in a row unless all your songs are slow. However, alternating slow/fast/slow/fast can drive the audience/ dancers—nuts. You should also avoid playing songs in the same key one after another, which can make you sound more boring than you really are. Some people believe you can actually lift the energy of your set by playing songs in higher keys as the set progresses. Give it a try, maybe it's true. Sequencing is extremely important but rarely given the attention it deserves.

MORE GIG TIPS

Here's some strictly practical info to make playing gigs as rewarding as possible:

1. If there's anything you just gotta have or the show can't go on without it, have TWO of them, or at least a plan-B substitute. Cord, spare guitar (tuned up and ready), fresh nine-volt battery, picks *everywhere* (in your pocket, in the back of the amp, in the guitar case, etc.).

 2. It may be louder than you think. Try putting your head at audi-

ence level and bashing an open A on your guitar to hear what the people hear. You might consider turning down your treble and volume a bit because most people in the room except for you aren't listening to the amp with the backs of their knees.

3. Most guitarists have a lot of similar gear. Put your name, your band name or some identifying mark on *everything* of yours—tuner, mike, mike stand, amp, cases, cords (everyone has a black cord with silver ends) and at gigs you will know what belongs to whom.

4. Sometimes the P.A. is grounded differently than your amp is and the mike can shock the hell out of your lip when you sing. No need! Instead of testing with your lip, touch the strings or metal tuning pegs of your guitar to the mike—if you see a spark you should change the grounding on your amp. *Always bring a ground lift plug.*

5. Ever pick up a radio station on your amp? Radio Shack sells an item called a "ferrite choke" that is mounted on your cable or power cord. These things eliminate the stray radio signals picked up by your cord, which is acting as an antenna—especially with longer cords. Put one on your cord and amp power cable and you won't have this problem.

6. If you have to load your gear offstage but can't leave the venue for a while, pile it all in a heap and throw a tarp or sheet over it to keep things from looking stealable. Put the little stuff in the middle where it's hard to get to.

7. Before you eat that chili cheese dog and fries, are you going to be able to wash and dry your hands somewhere before you put your hands on your guitar/bass/sticks/mike/keyboard/didgeridoo? Buy some disposable towelettes and stash them within easy reach.

8. You didn't read this here: To sneak your personal stash of beer/drink into a club, make sure they sell that same brand in that same bottle or you are b-u-s-t-e-d, homeperson.

9. Never leave anything in the car for a minute—equipment goes directly from club to car to rehearsal place or your living space. Plan on it. If your car or van is festooned with band and musical equipment stickers and you leave your gear in it unattended, you might as well have put a neon sign on the roof: ATTENTION! VALUABLE, PORTABLE, EASILY SOLD EQUIPMENT INSIDE! Think about it. If you must leave it, at least

carry your guitars into the restaurant for that post-gig 2 a.m. breakfast. In Liz Garo's *Book Your Own Tour* (see the Information Sources at the back of this book) there is a detailed description of how to build a van loft to help secure your equipment and slow down thieves.

10. If you want to give your singer an extra half step of vocal range and also get a slightly darker overall sound, tune all the instruments a half-step flat. You know, guitars to E♭, A♭, D♭, G♭, B♭, E♭; bass guitars to E♭, A♭, D♭, G♭. On electronic keyboards lower the overall pitch a half-step with the master tune. Your singer (and audience) will love you for it. You can also try lowering a whole step and using heavier-gauge strings on the guitar.

11. If you're walking with your guitar/sax/bass case, walk with the lid closest to your leg instead of the bottom of the case: If it isn't latched securely and your axe is about to fall out, you will instinctively hug the case close to your body, saving your instrument. If the lid is on the outside, it's adios axe and "why didn't I latch it?" I offer this as the voice of (sob) experience.

12. Unless every piece of equipment you play through or with has wheels, you will probably never regret buying a good-quality hand truck and using it to roll instead of lift. This saves wear and tear on your body and when you get bored you can wheel your fellow band members around on it.

13. One of the smartest things you can do when playing clubs is to be nice to the sound engineer (the person who runs the P.A.). If you are particularly pleased with how well they did their job, tip them, thank them, give them a free CD or cassette, anything to make them feel appreciated. After the first 423 bands, running the sound system at a club becomes routine, even downright boring. The last thing you want is a bored sound engineer who gets paid regardless of how much attention they pay to your band. If you are genuinely grateful and you communicate this fact, the next time you play the club you'll have an enthusiastic partner running the sound board instead of someone who is "sound bored." They can also help you by recording the P.A. inputs to a cassette for an instant gig tape. If the sound person is a talentless, underpaid jerk who would rather be watching VH-1, sorry; you're out of luck.

PERSONAL REMINISCENCE: THAT'S ENTERTAINMENT!

The worst gig I ever played? Years of therapy have almost obliterated the memory, but if hearing about it cheers you up I'll do my best. There were two specific week-long gigs in a row that still give me flop sweat and the heebie-jeebies.

The year: 1974. The place: Cocoa Beach, Florida. The band: Road Turkey, my first real "we-play-originals-and-danceable-cover-songs" van touring act. The first gig was one week at a venue called Tom's Pillow Talk Lounge, inside a crumbling beachside hotel I won't mention for fear of a lawsuit. We were offered free lodging in a hotel unit exclusively reserved for every band that played that gig. Let your imagination run wild visualizing the state of this room. We weren't the first band to stay there, I assure you. Always on a budget, we often traveled with a hot plate and cooking implements in order to create a cheap lentil-and-ham-hock concoction our bass player aptly named "botulism stew." However, at this particular stage in our culinary preference we favored "surfer packs," a prepackaged combo of bologna and fake cheese available in beachside grocery stores that, combined with a loaf of bread and a jar of Miracle Whip, was a dandy and nutritious food staple.

The venue was a surrealistic place to be. It was a cocktail lounge in a hotel built in the late '50s, with small satin pillows attached to the walls ("pillow talk"—get it?). The clientele, when anyone did show up, seemed to have drifted in by mistake, as if they were lost, which many of them were. The main rule stressed by the manager seemed to be: Play music as quietly as humanly possible, so the audience can whisper to each other and the waitresses can hear the all-important drink orders. We were asked to turn down so many times that finally the drummer, a very rock-oriented Stan Lynch, switched to playing with brushes and I eschewed singing through the P.A. altogether, preferring to croon au naturel. The guitarist, who could achieve his trademark tone only at a certain volume now unavailable, brooded, blanched, and basically bummed out big-time. This went on for a week, per our contract. On a break we went down the road to a place called George's Steakhouse, a 24-hour spot with a lounge and live music. The place was rocking and packed, with everyone dancing to a band consisting of five very pretty blond guys wearing white satin shirts and bell-bottoms, a real Florida showband.

Girls swooned. Desperate, we begged for a gig, and the owner gave us the available slot: 2 a.m. to 7 a.m., Monday through Saturday. Knowing what they say about beggars, we accepted. This gig, however, made the Pillow Talk feel like Carnegie Hall. After the Rock Star band finished their set at 1 a.m., they would collect a few new girlfriends and leave while their roadie dealt with the equipment. We would set up and play the graveyard shift to a very unique audience: night workers who had just finished their eight hours (6 p.m. to 2 a.m.), female impersonators who needed a few drinks to unwind before heading home, drug dealers who didn't need sleep anyway, and every weirdo in Cocoa Beach who wanted to go somewhere in the middle of the night. We would quit at 7 a.m., have breakfast, go to the hotel and close the curtains, sleep till 4 p.m., then eat breakfast. We ate a lot of breakfasts. I have no memory of what we did until 1 a.m. At the end of the week, the owner took us aside and shared his feelings: "You know how I judge a band? By this," he said, patting the cash register. "And you boys just don't have what it takes. We did lousy business last week. Let me give you a piece of advice. Quit the business, you're never going to make it."

We thanked the man and got the hell out of Cocoa Beach forever.

READY, SET, RECORD

The recording studio is a very unnatural place
to make music. It's dark, it's dead-sounding, and
someone is saying, "This is take 4, please be a genius."
—Jimmy Iovine, as quoted in
Musician Magazine, April 1983

S ooner or later you'll probably want to record your band in a studio, either for a demo tape to get gigs or to make your own cassette/CD release. Playing your music in a studio requires a different set of skills from those needed to play in front of a live audience. Making records and playing gigs are two separate worlds. Bands that put on a great, entertaining live show may find that, once in the studio, their live energy doesn't necessarily come across on tape. Other bands may be highly skilled at making hit recordings but don't know diddly about entertaining an audience. Still other groups, like The Rolling Stones, excel both as live performers and recording artists.

Your goal in the studio is to ignore the surroundings and play with all the heart, precision, and energy you can muster. This can be a real challenge, and frustration and tempers can run high when trying to "capture lightning in a bottle," which is one way of looking at the recording process. The tape recorder, like the camera, doesn't lie; if good music isn't coming out of your instrument (or vocal cords) it won't get on the tape. The upside to this brutal truth is that the studio can capture an inspired one-of-a-kind performance, allowing you to share it with the rest of the world.

CHOOSING A STUDIO: YOU BETTER SHOP AROUND

Studios differ widely in hourly rate, number of tracks, storage medium (analog or digital), staff experience and knowledge, and overall ambiance. All these variables should be considered before you choose. The least important is the hourly rate/number of tracks **97** combination. The *most* important thing is the person running the equipment. It all comes down to "the nut behind the knobs." A hip, heads-up engineer with good ears and real technical knowledge can perform magic with relatively cheap gear—and a lame engineer/producer won't get anywhere, even with expensive, high-quality "state-of-the-art" audio equipment. The key to your search is finding a qualified, talented person you feel *comfortable working with—someone you can trust*. More on that later.

Musicians, especially newcomers, often expect too much from the studio. Studios are not magic places, although magic can and does happen in them. Tracking at the top studio in town won't turn a dud song into a hit, won't tune your drummer's drums, won't give your singer voice lessons. Just making a clear, straightforward tape of how you really sound and finally being able to hear the vocals are useful goals for your first few sessions. So, with realistic expectations and an understanding of how important the recording studio staff is, begin searching for your studio. To help narrow your choices down at the start, think about two things: your *recording budget* and how many *tracks* you need.

First, the budget. Should you find the cheapest per hour studio? Not so fast. Here's an example. Studio A is only $15/hour, but the engineer just hooked up everything last week, shows up late, and works at what could charitably be called a very "relaxed" pace. Studio B is $25/hour. However, the engineer is alert, has many years of experience, the equipment is in perfect working order, and the guy (or girl) works very fast. The initial appeal of a low hourly rate can be very seductive—so it helps to be aware that you're paying for expertise (or lack of it) when you compare rates.

How many songs you want to record has a large effect on drawing up a realistic budget. Recording will *always* take longer than you think—a four minute tune doesn't take four minutes to record! And as time ticks away mercilessly, players get nervous, drummers speed up, equipment breaks, and you will suddenly get picky about things that didn't matter during rehearsals. Getting the right "take," overdubbing, mixing—each aspect takes time. Working hard on your two best songs might be a more productive goal than slamming through your entire set, but that depends on your needs.

 In terms of figuring out how many tracks you want, more isn't

necessarily better, or even needed. Eight might be fine for a duo or a three-piece band. For bands, 16 tracks usually give you more control over the final drum mix because each drum has its own track. Twenty-four tracks are very nice but could be overkill if you're cutting a demo or even an indie CD. Sixteen-track studios are probably the most common and offer the widest variety of machine formats, including reel-to-reel decks using half-inch or one-inch wide tape, and digital recorders, often two 8-track Alesis ADATs connected together, making a hybrid 16-track digital deck. Theoretically, the wider reel-to-reel tape format sounds fuller because there is more room to store sonic information, but so many other factors contribute to sound quality that further research is needed before making a choice.

DIGITAL VS. ANALOG RECORDING— DON'T WORRY ABOUT IT

Until recently, recording studios used 8-, 16-, and 24-track reel-to-reel analog audio recorders and recorded on magnetic tape in 1/2", 1", and 2" widths. *Analog recording* has been the method used to make virtually every record from the invention of the phonograph in 1877 until the 1980s. Analog recording works by taking the minute electrical currents that represent your music (the output of microphones and electronic gear), converting them to magnetic patterns, and storing them on tape. The magnetic patterns stored on the tape are *analogous* to the original audio waveform, hence the phrase *analog recording*. Playing the tape back reverses the process, converting the magnetic patterns back into electric current, which is then amplified and sent to the loudspeakers for your listening pleasure.

> The magnetic patterns stored on the tape are analogous to the original audio waveform, hence the phrase "analog recording."

Digital recording, however, converts the sound signals into digital information in binary form—literally, millions of electronically stored ones and zeros stored on the tape as on/off, or voltage/no voltage. How is this done? Well, if you can visualize a curved, up-and-down waveform on a graph, the image will help you understand. The wavy line (running from left to right) represents sound-waves (music) and any point on the wavy line is always a specific height above the bottom (horizontal) line of the graph paper. If, moving from left to right, you measured this height every inch and stored each number (in the order you measured it) on recording tape, you would be "sampling" the waveform (music) and this is what digital recording is: many—48,000 per second—"snapshots" of the music, stored in binary form on recording tape. Glad you asked? Digital is accurate, but not as "warm" sounding as analog. In fact, there is now a device that consists of eight vacuum tubes that you can run the outputs of an 8-track digital recorder through when mixing, to achieve a warmer, more "musical" sound. Talk about coming full circle!

In 1991 The Alesis Corporation came out with a small, relatively inexpensive 8-track digital recorder called the "ADAT," using economical VHS videocassettes as a storage medium. Because of the low price and high sonic quality of these decks, many studios sprang up overnight, offering low-cost "digital" recording. This low-cost format is both a blessing and a curse—because anyone can record you! For around $5,000 anyone—regardless of their engineering background—can buy an ADAT, a low-cost mixing board, some monitors, a few mikes, and a DAT mixdown deck and declare themselves a recording studio. Hence you must be particularly choosy about who is running the equipment—they may not have an extensive audio background. At any rate, don't worry about digital versus analog too much—your music should be the main focus.

Although studios with eight tracks are sometimes not taken seriously by some bands, the Alesis ADAT format (and a similar format offered by Tascam using 8-millimeter "camcorder" tape) sounds very good indeed. Recently great technical improvements in analog gear involving better electronics and noise reduction systems (dbx© and Dolby©) have made eight tracks appropriate for many projects. Nirvana's *Bleach* was cut on a 1/2" 8-track! *Led Zeppelin II* ("Whole Lotta Love") was an eight-track album. So think about your budget, number of songs, and how many tracks you realistically need.

Then, go to different studios, meet and talk to the owner and engineer (many times the same person), and ask to hear a few tracks that were recorded there. Can they play you material with a style similar to yours, or do they only record post-urban techno-jingles?

Many studios find little niche markets and become known for specializing in them. When listening, don't pay attention to the song or the performance; that was the responsibility of the band. Listen to the different instruments. Can you hear them clearly, or have they been drowned in reverb and electronic effects? Sometimes artists like their music overlaid with a lot of processing, but if *everything* coming from a studio seems to have the same layer of dubious "extra effect" then beware!—you may have an overeager engineer/producer. Such folks can force their ideas on unsuspecting artists who don't understand what is under their control.

Another good tip in helping you choose comes from Seattle-based producer Jack Endino: Bring in a CD or tape that you are familiar with from home and ask to hear it over the studio's monitors. It won't sound exactly the same, but if it sounds *really weird* you may not be happy with any of the mixes from that particular studio. Also, get a feel for the atmosphere of the facility. Does it seem too "high-tech" scientific, like a doctor's office? Or is it too funky—even worse than your rehearsal space? Whatever *you're* comfortable with, that's the bottom line. Personalities count too. If spending ten minutes in the room with a particular engineer makes you want to run screaming for the door, keep shopping—no matter how gifted he or she is.

After doing all this hard work you'll be ready to narrow your choice down to the appropriate lucky winner. If you have the time and the money, record a few songs at each of several studios before selecting one for your album-length project.

There is an immense amount to learn about the recording process, and choosing a studio wisely is a great start.

CUTTING TRACKS

As an individual and as a member of a band you have your own way of writing and playing music. Well, there are also many approaches to getting ready to record and actually recording. Some artists subscribe to the "go-in-and-see-what-happens" theory, and that's cool. However, with a few dreaded "organizational skills" you may get results that are closer to what you were aiming for when you booked the time. Some of the following may be self-evident, some of it you may already know, and some of it may be a pain in the ass. How true! Such is life.

The most obvious suggestion is: *Know the songs inside and out!* **101**

Many hours have been wasted as bands argue over how many verses there are before the bridge, how long the guitar solo is, etc. This should already be figured out at your rehearsals. Go ahead, break down, and write out the order; it's cheaper than discussing it as studio time ticks away. Singers should have the words written down clearly, or better yet, memorized.

Before you go in, talk to the engineer regarding how many tracks you will use for the "basics" and how many will be open for overdubs and various "takes" of vocals and leads. For a four-piece band (drums, bass, two guitars, vocals) recording at a 16-track studio, the drums might use six tracks (bass drum, snare, floor tom, rack tom, overhead left, overhead right), the guitars and bass three tracks, and the vocals one track. This leaves six open tracks. Knowing this will help you decide how many extra parts you'll be able to add to the basic recording. Some bands use these extra tracks to precisely double the guitar and vocal parts, creating a very "fat" and full sound without complicating the musical arrangement.

One aspect of songs that is often overlooked is finding the right tempo. Experimenting with the tempo can help you discover the

> Experimenting with the tempo can help you discover the "perfect feel" that makes each song settle into its true identity.

"perfect feel" that makes each song settle into its true identity. Trust me on this one. By figuring out this ideal tempo (with the help of an electronic metronome or a drum machine) and writing the number down in "beats per minute" (e.g., 68 bpm) you can make sure each song is counted off at the right tempo when you go into the studio. From either nervousness (impossible!) or sheer excitement, drummers often count off a song too fast directly after the engineer utters those three fateful words: "OK, we're rolling." When it's time to mix, the band is in shock as they listen to the speedy tempo at which they recorded the song—way faster than they ever played it at rehearsals or gigs. A difference of even 1 bpm can make or break the "feel" of a song.

Equipment, including the human voice, often breaks down in the studio. Bring spares, although bringing a spare singer might be a tough call. Realistically though, for guitarists and bass players this means extra sets of strings, spare picks, and by all means a fresh nine-volt battery for that DeathTone Megamuff effects pedal so crucial to your band's sound. If your amp hums hideously when you turn it on or when you plug in your instrument, get your equipment checked and fixed; you won't like all that hum in the mix and it's a lot more noticeable on a recording than at a live gig or a rehearsal. For drummers, putting new drumheads on your kit and tuning them before the session will noticeably improve your sound. Extra sticks—yes, even drum keys—are items drummers have forgotten at many sessions. Vocalists should remember to bring the special throat concoction that helps them relax and warms up their throat. Although for some singers this is a bottle of booze, be careful. If the vocal session isn't going well and a few shots of "liquid courage" seem to help at first, after repeated doses you can end up with a drunk and belligerent singer who has "self-medicated" past the point of singing anything the world will recognize as lyrics. Hot tea with lemon juice and honey is very good for a singer's throat. No, I'm not your mom, I'm just telling you what works for a lot of vocalists, especially smokers.

Once you are in the studio, set up the equipment so you can see each other when you play—especially the drummer and the bass player, who are the foundation of every band's sound. Guitarists might have to adjust their volume to adapt to the size of the room or use a smaller amp cranked up instead of their live gig amp. Amazing death-of-the-universe sound can be achieved with a small amp on "10" and careful miking. Get comfortable, adjust the lighting, do whatever you have to to make the studio—an unnatural place to begin with—a more relaxed setting in which to play. Spend some time getting a decent headphone mix; it makes tracking much easier when everyone can hear everyone else. An hour spent making these adjustments is an hour well spent. Skipping this critical step will make the recording session uncomfortable and frustrating. Take the time at the start, it's worth it.

Some songs, especially slow ones, benefit from giving the drummer a "click track" in his headphones to play along with when you record the basic track, but it can drive some people crazy. Once you get the hang of it, it works great. Playing to a click helps ensure a rock-steady drum track that keeps the song grooving and makes overdubbing a lot easier. It's harder than you think to play steady. Most drummers speed up during a drum break or when they play louder; it's just human nature. But you decide whether a click track will work for a song. Some people swear by them, others swear at them. Some songs need 'em, some don't.

Recording tape has imaginary, parallel stripes running lengthwise from one end to the other, and each stripe is a "track." Multitrack recording allows you to play along with previously recorded tracks and "overdub" new parts, or redo tracks with mistakes. Because each instrument is on a discrete track, one part can be changed without affecting the other parts. Before multitrack recording, every instrument had to be played perfectly or the song would have to be completely rerecorded. Now, individual players can go back and fix their parts after the fact.

The usual order for recording is: Cut the basic tracks (including a "scratch vocal" for reference only), rerecord any parts with mistakes in the basics, then overdub additional parts. Before overdubbing, the band listens to each take and decides if the rhythm section (drums/bass) is acceptable. This is crucial. Make sure it has a great feel. If the other instruments in the basic tracks need to be rerecorded, rerecord them first. Then you overdub additional parts and recut the vocals.

Finished recording? Great. Now it's time to mix. Sometimes, especially after a grueling tracking session, it helps to come back the next day to begin mixing. This gives the engineer and the band a fresh perspective on the music. Ear fatigue is a fact of nature and can distort your ability to perceive sound accurately.

MIXING

When it's time to mix, the band and the engineer should discuss the "sound" and feel the artist is aiming for. Bringing in CDs or tapes of songs whose production you like is helpful, but only to a point. Remember that your band will always sound like your band, not like the bands whose recordings you brought in for reference. However, a good engineer sometimes has a much-admired song available for "A–B comparison" during the mixing process to keep the mix "on course."

When mixing, the engineer usually starts with the drums. The volume and equalization (tone control) of each drum is adjusted separately: First the bass drum, then the snare, the toms, and finally the two overhead mikes, although the order can vary. This may take some time, but don't rush it: A good drum sound pumps up the whole mix.

After the drums are adjusted, the bass guitar is added and a good blend is achieved. Then the guitars (or keyboards and additional instruments) are tweaked for tone and volume. Also, the stereo position of each track is determined: left, right, or any point in between.

> **O**nly when the band sound is completed are the vocals added to the mix.

Only when the band sound is completed are the vocals added to the mix. Although each engineer will approach mixing a little differently, understanding the usual order will help you through what some artists consider the most boring part of the recording process.

Too many band members "helping" with the mix can be a frustrating situation for all. If possible, trust one band member to make suggestions to the engineer. Remember, each song can be mixed an infinite number of ways, so you may want to request several mixes of a tune, each with a slight variation—more or less bass guitar, vocals up front or further back, less reverb, and so on. The decision on which one to use can be made after you hear the cassette of the mixes on various sound systems—your car, a boombox, your home stereo gear.

Then choose the mixes you want, put them in order on a DAT or a 1/4" tape, and you're done—nothin' to it!

SIGNAL PROCESSORS

No discussion of recording would be complete without a brief survey of signal processors—electronic devices that modify and enhance the sound of your instrument, theoretically for the better. Knowing the names of these devices and what they do is extremely helpful and will allow you to ask for certain specific effects when you're in the studio.

Equalization is simply tone control, and equalizers are very sophisticated and sensitive devices that can boost or cut any frequency range. Through "eq" you can brighten the sound of your guitar ("instant new strings") or add low end to a wimpy bass guitar sound. The tone controls on your instrument amplifier or stereo are one example of equalizers, although recording studios usually have very sophisticated equalization devices. *Graphic equalizers* have a separate slider (up to 30) for each frequency range, from 20 Hertz (cycles per second) up to 20 kHz (20,000 cycles per second, audible only to dogs).

Sparkle and brilliance can be added to instruments that may sound great if recorded alone but tend to get lost in a band setting, such as an acoustic guitar overdub in a rock band. Drum kits benefit greatly from individual "eq" (equalization) of each drum. For instance, the fundamental tone of a bass drum head is around 60 to 80 Hz, in addition to the 2.5 kHz slap sound of the drum beater hitting the head. A knowledgeable recording engineer will boost these frequencies (during recording or mixdown) for more presence, to give the song a rock-solid bottom that grounds the whole arrangement. Often the combination of several instruments with low frequencies such as drums, bass, and rhythm guitar can create a cumulative "wall of mud" that can be extremely unmusical. Careful equalization can clean up a mix and give your music clarity and punch. Too much eq can lead to an unnatural sound, so a delicate and knowledgeable touch is essential.

Compression is used on individual instruments in order to keep their volume levels more consistent. Vocalists, for instance, often sing with a wide dynamic range, meaning they sing loud and soft in the same song. This makes it hard to determine the proper recording level. Although you could adjust the volume control on the recording console while watching the singer perform, anticipating these volume changes is difficult. A compressor automatically reduces the gain (amplification) when the input signal (singing volume) exceeds an adjustable preset level. Because of this electronic limit on the volume, the mike input can be turned up to allow quiet passages to be recorded at a high enough level to be heard clearly. The loud passages are quieter, the quiet passages are louder, so the dynamic range is "compressed." Acoustic guitar and bass sound particularly smooth and solid when run through a compressor.

Digital delay units are devices that hold a signal in electronic memory, then release it after a short time period, which can vary between one millisecond (1/1000 of a second) to 10 seconds or more. By combining this delayed signal with the original, many different effects are achieved. A delay of 50 milliseconds to one second combined with the original signal creates an echo effect, similar to shouting into a very large room with smooth walls. A delay of between 15 and 35 milliseconds creates a doubling effect, particularly noticeable if the original signal is in one stereo channel and the delayed signal is in the opposite. Setting the delay from 0 to 20 milliseconds can create a weird effect known as flanging, used extensively on Jimi Hendrix's amazing album *Electric Ladyland*. Be careful with delay; if overused it will only complicate the arrangement, sort of like adding extra players who constantly play after the beat.

Reverb is the natural sound of room acoustics. Singing in the bathroom is an example of how reverb can add depth and dimension to your voice—or any other instrument you care to bring in the shower stall. Sophisticated technology has created digital reverbs with multiple "programs" that simulate hundreds of imaginary rooms of different size and sound reflection characteristics. In the early days of recording, reverb chambers were exactly that: acoustically isolated rooms with hard, shiny walls; a loudspeaker at one end; and a microphone at the other. The original signal was fed to the speaker, picked up by the mike, and added to the original signal at the console. Again, be judicious with reverb. Nothing screams "DEMO" more than tons of reverb on everything. Currently reverb is not as popular as it was in the '70s.

TECHNIQUES AND TIPS

Here are some suggestions, common recording techniques, and miscellaneous ideas you may find helpful when in the studio:

1. Bass guitar usually sounds the best when plugged directly into the recording console via a "direct box," or DI. This is a small box that takes your high-impedance guitar signal and converts it to a low-impedance signal required by the mixing board. This will give you the pure sound of the bass guitar pickup. Compressing the signal while recording will give the bass even more presence. You'll need a strong bass level in the headphone mix or no one will know what you're playing. If you are achieving a particularly great sound from your amp, use it by miking the amp and record-ing it to a separate track. When it's time to mix, one or the other will sound better, or use a blend of amp and direct signal.

2. The easiest (well, not so easy) way to achieve a full sound on gui-tars and vocals is by doubling the part exactly. If done precisely, **107**

your parts sound absolutely huge. The Traveling Wilburys took this to an extreme, with all four of them playing the exact same part on acoustic guitar, then rewinding the tape and making four additional passes in the same way. That's 16 guitars playing the same part, and that's a big sound. Vocals sound great doubled, especially choruses. The trick when recording the "double" is to carefully balance the headphone mix so your old part is slightly louder than your live voice. The sooner you lay down the doubled part after you've recorded the original the easier the doubling is, because the memory of your first performance is fresh in your mind. Many vocals on hit records are doubled so carefully you never notice.

3. A popular rhythm (or lead) guitar sound is achieved by sending the guitar signal through a digital delay unit set to a very fast delay, like 5 to 10 milliseconds. When you mix, put the original sound on the right and the delayed signal on the left, or vice versa.

4. When you mix a song, each instrument is placed in a position either to the left, to the right, or any point in between. Clock settings are often used to describe these positions: the middle is "12 o'clock," hard right is "3 o'clock," left is "9 o'clock," and so on. The guitar panning trick mentioned above is equally effective at 10 o'clock and 2 o'clock.

5. Sometimes when recording a song, the performance doesn't really settle into a "groove" until after the first verse and chorus have already been played. This is "first chorus jitters," and can be avoided by rehearsing the chorus over and over and over again in the studio moments before you record the track. Play the choruses a few times in the proper tempo, then tell the engineer to roll tape. Count off the song and go—the chorus that made you nervous is now old news and no longer intimidating. As a recording engineer, I've seen this technique work many times.

6. When singers wear closed-design headphones (solid earpieces) during vocal recording sessions, they sometimes sing flat. Why? Because the closed design dampens the vibrations of the little speaker inside the headphones, so they vibrate slower, making the singer think the track is a slightly lower pitch than it really is, so the singer sings flat, which to them is actually on-key. Have the singer slide one earphone off an ear, or switch to open-design

headphones that don't seal off your ears. Singing in the studio is tricky stuff, so the singer should try every style and pair of headphones in the room until he or she feels comfortable with one.

7. Try different lighting setups in the studio. Super dark is atmospheric but useless for any visual communication between players. Interrogation-level lighting kills any groove-vibe you may try to develop. Try colored lightbulbs, Christmas lights strung around the room, table lamps in strategic places—whatever helps you get the feeling. Avoid strobe candles or you could burn the place down.

PERSONAL REMINISCENCE: THE AGONY AND THE ECSTASY

I've recorded in plenty of studios over the last 23 years in all kinds of musical situations. I learned something new about recording at every studio. At Doppler Recording in Atlanta, my first-ever recording experience, I learned that you could get a great bass guitar sound by plugging directly into the recording console. My bass rig at the time was a huge homemade cabinet with an 18" speaker driven by a 300-watt amp, and the engineer discreetly suggested I go direct. I complied, and my bass never sounded better.

We recorded the first two Motels albums mostly at Sunset Sound, an L.A. studio used by many top artists. I learned that the sound of the band and the skill of the engineer have everything to do with how the record will sound, and the actual studio facility has very little sonic influence on the final result. How did I figure this out? Well, Van Halen's first album *Van Halen*, the Doobie Brothers' *Minute by Minute*, and our first album were all cut at Sunset Sound. These records don't sound remotely the same. A studio is just a building with people and equipment inside, and how they interact determines the end result.

> A studio is just a building with people and equipment inside, and how they interact determines the end result.

It was also there that I learned the power of not trying so hard, of just playing your instrument and relying on "feel." Our producer, Carter, gave me a 9:30 a.m. session call to do a piano overdub on

"Porn Reggae," a reggae-tinged track that needed some good, loose piano playing to add texture. Half asleep, I stumbled into the studio, slumped at the piano and played what I thought was a practice run-through. At the end of the song, Carter hit the intercom button: "Thanks! See ya tomorrow." From this experience I learned how easy it is to get totally caught up in one's head when recording and how sometimes a loose, casual attitude can be the best approach. Mental flexibility is a great quality to develop.

At Record One, a flossy L.A. studio, The Motels cut two albums that went gold and earned us two Top Ten singles: 1982's *All Four One*, containing "Only the Lonely," and 1983's *Little Robbers* with "Suddenly Last Summer." Here I learned two things: The first was how to really approach recording as an art. Along with producer/engineer Val Garay, we worked on song arrangements literally from the bottom up, starting with the bass drum pattern and adding a drum at a time, then the bass guitar, then the other instruments. We determined the best key and tempo for each tune. Only when key, tempo, and arrangement were solidified did we begin recording.

The second thing I learned was the meaning of "playing in time." Since most of the tracks were cut "live," I found out how hard it was to play along precisely with the bass and drums. Val would play back the tape and "solo" the keyboard part against the bass drum and snare, and yes, I found that rhythmically I was all over the map. It takes tremendous concentration to play precisely in tempo. When you do, the track has a wonderful, unified feel. And what made it easier to play on time? I had to train myself to not look at the keyboard at all. I kept eye contact with the band, especially the drummer, and I concentrated on listening to the drums in the headphone mix, not my keyboard part. Learning this took time, and I was aided, to put it politely, by the producer attaching a piece of cardboard to the top of the keyboard so I couldn't see my hands. Oh, the brutality! Punching in the few missed notes was easy because my mistakes were *on time*.

The most fun I had was probably a session I did for Tom Petty in 1989. He was working on an R&B-style track and he wanted a sort of '60s Stax/Volt horn section. I showed up at Heartbreaker guitarist Mike Campbell's home studio armed with all four of my saxes. Producer Jeff Lynne was there, noodling on Campbell's guitar synth ("Listen—I'm writing the new Pink Floyd album") and he, Petty, and Campbell told me what they wanted: 22 sax tracks! I walked to the tracking room, which was the garage. For visual contact Campbell had a video camcorder in the garage connected to a TV monitor in the control room. So, surrounded by kids' bicycles, a lawnmower, basketballs, and all the usual junk people store in their garage, I proceeded to play one sax riff, triple track the same part to fatten it up, play a harmony part, triple track it, and so on. The end result was a studio-created horn section of baritone, tenor, and alto saxes, 22 tracks in all. We had worked efficiently and quickly, yet not as if we were in a hurry. I loved the feeling of working with three such talented artists, and the sheer feeling of alertness gave me a calm, steady thrill I recall to this day. The track, "Down the Line," was the "B" side of the single "Free Fallin'" and is included in the Tom Petty boxed set *Fast Forward*.

There is plenty of frustration involved in learning how to play music in a studio environment, but the good moments feel so good they far outweigh the bad. Work toward those magic moments—they are waiting for you.

MAKE YOUR OWN RECORD

Dear Mr. Edison,
I can only say that I am astonished and
somewhat terrified at the result of this
evening's experiment. Astonished at the
wonderful form you have developed, and
terrified at the thought that so much hideous
music will be put on records forever.
—Sir Arthur Sullivan (musical half of Gilbert
and Sullivan), referring to Thomas Edison's
demonstration of the phonograph in 1888

t used to be simple. If you didn't have a record deal, you didn't put out a record. If you did have a record deal, the record company did all the work of designing, manufacturing, and promoting your product.

Then things changed. The do-it-yourself ethic born of the '70s punk movement helped put an end to this dichotomy and created the first wave of non-record-label releases. One of the basic philosophies of D.I.Y. seemed to be that anyone could form a band, record the band's music, and issue it on the band's own label. This attitude lives on in the '90s in a world populated by fewer major labels, an abundance of small independent labels, and a glorious assortment of affordable home recording equipment. New audio technology has put digital recording gear in the hands of anyone with a few thousand dollars. At the same time, the cost of putting out a CD project has never been lower. Increased competition and better technology has improved the quality of tape duplication. Who the heck needs those big, stupid, multibillion-dollar music conglomerates anyway?!

Before we continue, understand one thing: Recording and creating a CD is time-consuming and expensive. You can easily spend $3,000 to $5,000 and more (much more) on recording and production costs. Without an audience base and/or a careful marketing and promotion plan, you may end up with nothing more than a reduced bank account, a garage full of product nobody wants, and a bruised ego. Without stomping on your dreams too hard, let's try to put the situation in perspective.

Bands often have a highly unrealistic view of what happens when they release their own record, feeling that the world and the media will beat a path to their door *just because they put out a CD*. Here is the all-too-common scenario:

1. The band spends time and money on recording and mixing a bunch of songs; then they decide to "put out our own CD" and they order 1,000 from a CD manufacturer. Everyone else is doing it, so why not?

2. They find a friend who's good at drawing Metallica logos on his school notebook to design the graphics, almost guaranteeing that special "local product" look.

3. After many complications and delays involving the CD mastering, graphic design, and production, the CD finally arrives. General celebration and partying ensues. Fame is around the corner! The world is definitely waiting for this one!

4. After giving away plenty of copies to friends, they mail some CDs to record companies ("Attention: A&R"), bring a few to the local radio stations, and put a whole bunch on consignment in various record stores.

5. Now it's time for the CD Release Party. They even play some other gigs and mention that the CD is for sale at the table in back of the club. "You guys are great, but I just spent my last dollar on beer. Do you take Visa?"

6. Time passes, the CDs sit on consignment in record stores like lonely orphans, the radio stations probably play it on the "local music" segment a few times, and any record reviews in the local press fail to mention where you can buy the record. More time passes. And more.

7. Months later the band is depressed because they put out a record and it wasn't a hit. Premature cynicism toward the music business sets in. A demoralized band member quits and now the group photo on the CD is outdated. Fade to black....

My intention is not to make light of these efforts but to strip away any fantasies about what happens after you make your own record. In a word: nothing, unless you create a demand for your music, your promotional resources, you must create this demand yourself. How is this done?

You create a demand for your record—and *you*—by playing lots of gigs and developing a following. When you do finally put out a record you have already created your own market for it and therefore it will sell to your fans. Not only does it feel good to have a following for your music, but you can actually make money! A CD that may have cost you $5 to create can be sold for $15, creating a 200% profit. Sell a thousand CDs and you've made $10,000. Wow! The key is to have a thousand people that want to buy it. Obvious, no? But many bands think the record is going to do all the work for them. Developing a following takes talent and hard work. This leads

> ...If you have a devout following of 1,000 fans, you should definitely make your own record, and quick!

me to state Jourard's Rule: If you have a devout following of 1,000 fans, you should definitely make your own record, and quick! If you have a somewhat smaller or more sedate following, you might want to think about it for a while.

OK, you've thought about it and you still want to put out your own record. Now ask yourself this question: *Do you need to do it immediately?* Would it be better to wait until you have a larger following, more and better songs, and a few more gigs under your belt? Tough questions, but this book is here to make you tough. Stand up straight while you're reading this!

Many bands go about the situation backwards; they put out a recording first and then try to build a market for it (their audience) without honing the necessary songwriting and performance skills. Of course, you may simply want to create your own record for far less logical reasons: personal satisfaction, for the thrill of being able to give records away to family and friends, to get better gigs, or to feed your insatiable ego.

CDS, CASSETTES, AND VINYL

When it comes to recording, there are three formats you can choose from: CD, cassette, and vinyl. Let's discuss the pros and cons of each. Vinyl, unfortunately, died a cruel and premature death at the hands **115** of the major record labels who, always thinking of the consumer's best interests, figured they could make a higher profit margin by killing vinyl and switching to CDs. Despite certain sonic problems (scratches, warping, skipping, and surface noise), albums were pretty darn great, if for no other reason than the large packaging size (288 square inches) that served as the canvas for some classic artwork. In the case of graphic design, bigger really is better.

The main problem with vinyl is that, aside from a few collectors and college radio stations, hardly anyone in the commercial marketplace listens to records or even owns a turntable any more. The majority of vinyl today is used in dance clubs and for live rap performances that involve "scratch." Unless you're making music to be played in dance clubs this format should not be your first choice. Yes, there is a growing renaissance of small labels releasing 7" 45 rpm singles, but this is more of a collector's market than a format geared toward mass marketing and sales, such as our new friend the CD.

Cassettes are still the easiest and most economical method of reproducing your music. Tape duplication is relatively cheap and the quality of tape has improved greatly. More importantly, everyone in the world has a cassette player. Your first recorded release should probably be on cassette. Why? Not only are cassettes less expensive and quicker to manufacture than CD or vinyl, but you can make as few as 25 to 50 copies at a time, which may, no offense intended, be your current market share. However, the graphic inserts (called "J cards" or "O cards" according to their shape) are usually printed in minimum lots of 500 or 1,000.

Still, the flexibility of the cassette format is unrivaled. For example, you could start by ordering 100 tapes and assembling them with 100 of your graphic inserts. The money you receive from tape sales of the first 100 finances your next order, and the process is repeated until you've used up all 500 to 1,000 of your inserts. This approach may be low-tech but it works wonders for your cash flow. For this reason alone the cassette format may be your only option.

Cassettes are duplicated from a master tape in one of two ways: real time and high speed. Real-time duplicating requires many individual cassette decks hooked up to a master sound source, usually a DAT player. The tapes are recorded at normal "real-time" playback speed of 1 7/8 ips. This creates first generation copies of the highest possible quality, but it's also expensive because of the time and equipment involved. For instance, a tape duplicator I know has 125 decks used for "real-time" duplication!

The more economical high-speed method, used by record companies and manufacturers making a thousand tapes or more, is called a *bin loop*—a special "endless loop" tape copy of your master, that consists of Side One recorded forward and Side Two recorded backwards. This tape loop master is loaded into a "bin-loop master reproducer," a playback machine that stores the master tape in a special freestanding bin. The audio output of this machine is hooked up to a whole bunch of "slave" tape decks that record both sides of the program simultaneously on a length of bulk blank tape at a high speed, often 64 to 80 times normal. Then, in a separate manufacturing step, the tape is wound onto an empty cassette shell, assembled, and labeled. This high-speed manufacturing process costs less per unit but the sound quality is not as good as "real-time" duplication, although the use of digitally recorded bin loops has improved the sound quality immensely.

Though not as glamorous a format as the CD, cassettes are definitely the way to go when you want your music reproduced with a minimum of expense and delay. Most college radio stations will play cassettes as well as vinyl and CDs for their "local music" segments.

Unfortunately, most bands feel that making a cassette somehow doesn't mean as much as putting out a CD. Poppycock! Let's say you write great material, spend money at a good studio getting a good sound and performance, and then only have enough left in your budget to put out a cassette. Another band with a similar budget decides to scrimp by recording at the cheapest, worst-sounding studio in town, choosing to spend the vast majority of the money on CD manufacturing costs.

Which recording would you rather hear?

In spite of the flawless logic I've just presented, the CD is undoubtedly the current standard, and for some artists is the only format worth considering. Let's talk about how to connect with the manufacturer.

CHOOSE YOUR BROKER WELL

Whether you decide to turn your mixed master tape into a CD or any other format, you'll be working through a *broker*, a salesperson (or organization) acting as a liaison between the manufacturer and your band. In addition to local or regional brokers who have relationships with manufacturing plants and printers, there are large national CD makers with in-house graphics and printing departments. You've probably seen their ads in national music-oriented magazines. If you choose the CD format, any broker you choose will "outsource" the pressing of the discs, because there are only between six and eight CD manufacturing plants in the U.S. that accept shorter runs of 1,000 to 5,000. However, many brokers both local and national have cassette duplication equipment.

> Should you use a big national broker or a local source for your manufacturing needs? That all depends.

Should you use a big national broker or a local source for your manufacturing needs? That all depends. If there is a problem with your project (in either the audio end or the graphics), dealing with a large national broker can sometimes be frustrating and time-consuming. Although these larger firms do offer tempting, easy-to-understand volume-priced "package deals" that include graphic design and printing, you may get more personalized service and "hand-holding" from a local broker. Ask around and find out who has a good local reputation, check out the ads for the big national brokers, determine your particular needs, and make an informed decision.

ASSEMBLY

Assembling a CD project is a bit like assembling a car; there are many parts that have to meet at a particular time and place. First, your master tape has to be converted into a CD glass master, including the necessary PQ codes, the nonaudio digital information encoded on the disc that tells the CD player how to access each track, the play times, time remaining, etc. This encoding usually takes place at the CD manufacturing facility, and can cost from $100 to $300 and up. However, many local mastering services can now create a master CD that includes these codes, saving you the additional expense at the broker. In addition, the artwork (CD label, inlay, and booklet) must be designed, converted into color separations of a very precise size and format, and sent to the printer. Color proofs must be sent to you, the client, for review and possible revision. Finally, after approval of the graphics and a test copy of the disc, the artwork, CD, and "jewel box" (or newer alternate packaging) must be assembled, shrink-wrapped, packed, and shipped.

Knowing how complicated this can be and how many aspects of the project can be neglected or screwed up, do you really want to go with the lowest price? It's best to choose a broker who has a good, long-term relationship with each source (graphic designer, printer, manufacturing plant). This may not be the broker or production company offering the lowest price! The CD manufacturing industry is so profit-margin-oriented that brokers offering the lowest price may constantly be changing manufacturing plants and printers every few months in order to chase the best deal. If a glitch or problem occurs, they won't have much "clout" with the particular vendors.

So do some research. If you know other bands who have put out a CD, listen to and look at the result; find out who they chose to manufacture it. Stay away from the "too-good-to-be-true" offers, or you may end up with a garage full of CDs replete with cheap-looking printing, slipshod mastering, and low-quality discs. The profit margin is high enough on retail CD sales so that you can easily spend a little more for a quality product and still make money when you sell them.

TYPICAL COST BREAKDOWN

Many brokers, both national and regional, offer package deal prices that include graphic design, reference CD, discs, printing, assembly, and shrink wrap. If this one-stop shopping approach is appropriate for your project, great! However, you may need a more customized package, and it helps to know the price range of each component. Although these costs may be outdated by the time this book is published, their proportions should be about the same.

By the way, the most problematic and time-consuming aspect of any recording project is the artwork. As one broker told me, the graphic packaging is two-thirds of the work and all of the headache. You really should start working on the artwork while you are still recording so that everything except song titles and sequencing can be in production as soon as possible.

You can expect to spend between $500 and $2,000—and up—on good graphic design and film (the color separations used to print the artwork), including design costs, color proofs, corrections, and revisions. Remember, I said good graphic design. If you intend to provide the graphic inserts yourself, be sure to choose a printer that supplies graphics to the music industry on a regular basis, or the inserts may not properly fit the cassette or CD box. The desktop publishing revolution has certainly put graphic design capability in the hands of the masses, but this doesn't mean that everyone with a computer, a scanner, and a copy of Adobe Photoshop is a good graphic designer.

Most musicians don't think of package design as an important sales tool; they're wrong. Remember, people look at a CD before they choose to buy it, and a good cover can enhance your record sales. A talented freelance artist specializing in CD/cassette artwork might charge $900 for a complete graphic package, including design and film (color separations) and require one to two months to complete the work. Graphic design is one area you won't want to scrimp on; nothing screams out "Local Product!" more than budget graphics. Good graphic design is not cheap.

The compact disc, including jewel box, shrink wrap, and assembly will run about $1,400 for a thousand. A four-panel insert and inlay (the "back cover" of the clear case) costs about $395, and other designs (a six-, eight-, or ten-page CD booklet, mini poster, etc.) will cost appreciably more, partially because of higher design fees. Freight costs on a thousand CDs can run from $50 to $150. So, including graphic design, manufacture, assembly, and shipping, a thousand CDs may cost between $2,500 and $3,000, not including the recording costs. And, while we're on the subject, let's talk about two neglected or misunderstood aspects of the record preproduction: sequencing and mastering.

SEQUENCING

Sequencing determines the order of the songs on your recording and is very important! I have recorded CD projects for several talented artists who decided to put the strongest, most commercial material near the end of the album instead of the beginning. Don't save the best for last—your listener may never make it that far. Generally speaking, put your strongest material near the front. Established artists have already earned the trust of the listener and can take more chances with sequencing; you won't have that luxury. The first 20 seconds of a record are the crucial moments when the listener makes a decision about the music and the production value. If the song grabs the listener's attention, he or she will more likely reserve judgment until further into the album.

There are countless sequencing theories, and record producers have their own philosophies involving song keys, tempos, where to place the "single," etc. Up-tempo tunes work well as starters; one producer I worked with always put the "obvious single" as track three, figuring that the first song should be uptempo, the second track should continue the energy level, and after the catchy third "hit single" track the listener was committed to the rest of the record. If you think of the song sequence as a sort of

> *If you think of the song sequence as a sort of sonic seduction, you are on the right track, pun intended.*

sonic seduction, you are on the right track, pun intended. In the days of the two-sided album, sequencing took on a different aspect because you tried to end Side One with an "album turner," a song that made the listener want to flip the LP. CDs, of course, have only one side, so you must sequence knowing there is no "pause" in the program. Refer to Chapter 7 for further tips on sequencing; the same theories we used to determine the order for live performance are appropriate for your album. Try to make listening to your record an audio journey.

MASTERING

There is much confusion regarding the word "mastering." The final mix of your recording project is called the "master tape," and pressing plants make a "master" from which the copies are made. You may have taken your tape to a studio with a hard-disk editing system in order to change the sequencing of the tunes and adjust the length of time between songs. This too can be considered a type of "mastering." True mastering, however, is a final "audio massage" of the music before production and duplication takes place.

All major label releases are mastered at places cleverly known as "mastering studios," and these facilities exist (with a few notable exceptions) in music biz cities like New York, Los Angeles, and Nashville. But why do you have to continue to adjust the sound of your music? Weren't you finished when you made the final mixes?

Not quite, unless every aspect of your recording and mixing sessions was absolutely flawless.

You may have recorded songs at several different studios, and as a result, the output levels may vary. The monitors (loudspeakers) used at a particular studio may have emphasized a particular frequency range, misleading the engineer into thinking there is more of a certain frequency on the master tape than is actually there. For instance, some recording studios, due to a combination of room acoustics and bottom-heavy speakers, create mixes with a "false bass." Tracks recorded in a studio with this problem sound full and fat when heard on the studio monitors, but thin and wimpy in the real world. Sloppy mixing or a poorly balanced monitor amplifier may lead to a noticeable discrepancy between the volume of the left and right channel. Furthermore, the entire finished mix may sound, well, just sort of weak. Getting sounds on tape is a true art.

A mastering session can raise the overall level of each track and then match these levels for a consistent sound, balance the two channels of the stereo mix, add compression that will "pump up" each song, and perform precise tonal equalization for each track. How is this done? Let's drop in on an imaginary session in a studio, the kind used by major labels (and maybe you). These mastering suites consist of an acoustically balanced room, high-quality audio monitors with an extremely flat (not favoring any one frequency over another) acoustic response, plenty of electronic sound-processing gear, and an engineer with very good ears.

Despite the necessity of great equipment, the key component is always the ears and musical good taste of the mastering engineer. Some engineers listen to the music very loud, others will listen at low volumes, some are ex-musicians who bring a musical sensibility to the session, others are strictly technical specialists who concentrate only on the scientific aspects of sound. Good mastering engineers can listen to a song and tell you exactly what frequencies are needed to bring out the vocal performance, or add more presence to the bass guitar. They also have the ability to perceive small differences in overall volume from song to song as well as in left side/right side balance. Each song may need a specific combination of compression, equalization, and leveling. For example, a particular song may have a drum track with transient peaks—brief loud passages that cause the overall mix to be generally lower in order to avoid audio distortion.

Running the mix through a stereo limiter will compress the dynamic range (reduce the difference between loud and soft passages), allowing the engineer to raise the overall level. This gives the track a punchy sound it may have lacked. In another case, a track may have a "muddy" sound from a combination of bass guitar, bass drum, and rhythm guitar contributing shared low frequencies. The engineer may choose to electronically remove all frequencies below 30 cps, thus cleaning up the track. This type of audio cleanup work is what good mastering can offer.

After discussing with the producer (or interested band member) the sonic manipulation needed to improve each song, the mastering engineer notes these changes and makes a new, sonically improved master based on your master, running each song through the appropriate gear. The resulting mix is sent through a Sony 1630 PCM (Pulse Code Modulation) device and is recorded on a broadcast-quality Sony U-Matic 3/4" format videocassette recorder, a format vastly more stable than tiny DAT tapes. Another storage form gaining popularity is the CD-R, or *recordable compact disc*.

These so-called state-of-the-art mastering facilities have rates upwards of $300 an hour. Local mastering facilities often offer similar type services for around $40 an hour. Sophisticated software programs such as ProTools allow the engineer to load your original studio mixes into a computer hard disk. Once inside the computer, your music has entered the wondrous digital domain of millions of digital ones and zeros. The engineer can now change not only the order of the tracks but also the sonic content of each song (as mentioned above) to improve the overall sound.

The quality of the equipment your music is being sent through is as important as the skill with which this equipment is set and adjusted. Here's an example of the equipment chain in one local mastering studio. The DAT master is played on a Sony 7010 DAT recorder ($2,000), and the analog outputs of the deck are run into a Focusrite eq ($3,500), then into a Summit compressor ($2,500 to $3,500), then finally to an Apogee AD500 analog-to-digital converter ($2,000). The final master may be stored either on a DAT tape or a CD-R. Good equipment plus a good mastering engineer equals a better sounding final product. Choose your mastering studio as carefully as you would a recording studio.

As mentioned before, the introduction of affordable electronic gear has been a mixed blessing. While it allows almost everyone to have fun with music, it also allows people who have no real skill at running a recording studio or mastering facility the ability to declare themselves in business as audio engineers. Translation: A technoweenie without any musical sensibility can screw up your project bad! Listen to the before and after versions of your songs and make sure you like what is happening to them when using one of these smaller-scale mastering studios. Remember, someone who charges $40 an hour for mastering and who still needs to read the manuals is no bargain at all. Trust your ears.

Out of the frustration caused by the sometimes shaky quality of submitted master tapes, mastering is now being offered by CD brokers at extra cost. Ask questions when shopping around. Unless you have a professional performing these mastering services, you are better off leaving your tape alone!

PROMOTE YOUR PRODUCT

OK, now you have a garage full of CDs or cassettes. How do you get them to the rest of the world? Will your product help get you a record deal? Is the world desperately in need of one more independent release?

Let's put your new record in the context of what else is out there.

Stated simply, there is a glut of musical product in the marketplace: 250 and 500 records are released on major and indie labels *every month* in the U.S. This doesn't include the thousands of artists (such as yourself) who choose to release their own recordings. You are competing with all of them.

> Stated simply, there is a glut of musical product in the marketplace...

There are two main differences between self-released records and a label-released product. First, the perceived credibility issue: At a record label, at least someone else besides you is convinced of your music's commercial possibilities. Obviously, the mere existence of a recording means nothing in itself. Anyone with a master tape and a checking account can put out his or her own record.

The second key difference is promotion and distribution. Record labels spend a vast portion of their budget on magazine advertisements, special promo items (posters, T-shirts), independent radio promotion, tour support, record store displays, promotional videos, etc. Record labels have access to a large distribution network involving sales reps, product warehouses, and a staff whose job is to ensure that the record is in as many stores as possible. Without distribution, the hottest record in the world isn't gonna sell. You can hear a band live and hear their song on the radio, but if the record isn't in the stores you can't buy it. Distribution is beyond important; it's vital.

When a major label releases a record, the record itself is only one part of a huge coordinated push to promote the act in the media marketplace. Radio airplay, touring, video, contests ("Have dinner with *Bulimia!*"), and coverage on TV, radio, and in the press—all of these promote the recording and work together to increase sales. Take away any one component and the system doesn't work. Once you see this you will understand how difficult it is to promote your recording the same way the Big Record Labels do it. However, bands like Fugazi and artists like Ani DiFranco have created their own labels and have toured without record company support but with great success—and on their own terms.

The standard approach is to put your record on consignment in as many stores as will take it. The drag is having to check with stores periodically to collect the money from sales.

You may want to try a more aggressive approach. Shop your finished mixes to an indie label and try to get a pressing and distribution deal (P&D) wherein they agree to release your record for a percentage of the sales receipts. You get the prestige of being on a label and they get a share of the sales. However, approach this kind of deal with caution; sometimes the label has questionable distribution and even more questionable sales tracking methods. A label may want the option but not the obligation to release future records, and this may not be to your advantage. Investigate thoroughly before committing yourself.

Another approach to setting record sales is to cut a deal with an independent distributor. There are hundreds of indie distributors throughout the U.S., and they make their money by selling records to stores at a profit. But distributors need a reason to stock your record. The fact that your record exists is not reason enough. If your band has a large following and a regional tour planned, the distributor may see dollar signs in the near future and accept your record. You play the gigs; the audience buys your record at record stores the next day; and you, the store, and the distributor all make money. However, distributors often hold back payment as long as possible and—depending on your clout (or lack of it)—sometimes forever. Check out the reputation of any distributor you do business with, and talk to other bands that have done business with them. Sources of indie distributor listings are in the Information Sources section at the end of this book.

This brings us back to the Real World: The best and simplest promotion is still playing live and selling your cassette or CD at gigs or through your mailing list. It may help to think of your record as one component in your career plan, rather than the focus of your efforts. Playing in a band really comes down to this: You want as many people as possible to be attracted to your music. If you gain a loyal following of supporters who are genuinely moved by your songs and performances, selling records won't be a problem.

HOW TO GET SIGNED

Over the years there have been different approaches to attracting record company interest. In the '70s you would cut some demo tapes, make an appointment with an A&R rep at a label, and squirm in your seat as they listened to the first five seconds of each song and then returned the tape with the vague comment of "not bad—needs a little work—let me know where and when you're playing."

The '80s approach centered around finding a good entertainment lawyer who "shopped your tape" to various high-powered record execs with whom the attorney "had a relationship."

Current trends consist of a search for the "almost-sure thing"— signing a band that already has a regional buzz, a rabidly enthusiastic fan base, plus their own self-released record that has sold plenty of units. Hootie and the Blowfish come to mind. A&R people at record labels, notoriously hesitant about signing unproven talent, are only too happy to nab a band that's already sold 50,000 units on their own label or through an independent.

Putting your product on consignment at local music stores is a productive marketing move only if you play a lot of gigs and people are aware of your existence before they walk into the store. Bring your record to local radio stations and ask them to listen for tracks that would be appropriate for their format. A good station will take a chance on a song that works for their "sound," and this type of break has often been the start of a successful career. The Cars had a song on the radio in Boston well before they signed a record deal. Many stations (especially college radio stations) have a "Local Music" program, and nothing beats the thrill of hearing your music over the public airwaves. You can send out notices via your mailing list asking that people call the station and request your songs.

PERSONAL REMINISCENCE: I DID IT MY WAY

I too have put out my own record. When The Motels disbanded in 1986 I needed some serious music therapy, so I formed an R&B band called Locomotive and decided to learn and play every sax song I ever loved. We learned 55 songs, many of which were sax instrumentals. I wrote six originals in a decidedly R&B vein. After gigging for six months we figured it was (of course!) time to make a record. However, back then CD manufacturing was not yet afford-able, so we decided to make a thousand LPs and a thousand cassettes. The initial tracks were cut at what was once Glen Campbell's studio, a small room in Burbank where he had recorded "Wichita Lineman." It was now a $150-a-day studio that catered primarily to heavy metal bands and featured an Akai 12-track recorder, a strange digital format that used special VHS-style cassettes. After we finished recording, we transferred the masters to a 24-track tape and mixed at a different studio.

> Bring your record to local radio stations and ask them to listen for tracks that would be appropriate for their format.

We had the music, what about the artwork? At this point I was working as a computer salesman, and this 17-year-old whiz kid working next to me pushing chips into motherboards had a textbook on probabil-ity that caught my eye. On the cover was a well-known photo of a train wreck at a Paris train station from the 1890s, the locomotive dangling from the second story of the building toward the street below. I wrote to the French company who owned the photo, ask-ing if I could use it. They wrote back in French. I couldn't read French. In despair I looked in the Yellow Pages and located the Franco-American Chamber of Commerce. Yes, the receptionist said,

I speak fluent French. OK, she told me, I'll translate this letter you have if you buy me lunch. Within the hour I showed up with a Big Mac, fries, and a Coke, so she read it. It said I needed to send 140 Francs via International money order for the nonexclusive right to use the photo. I located a bank that wrote international money orders and sent it off. Two weeks later I received the photo. Tommy Steele, the art director at Capitol, did me a huge favor and designed the album layout. The graphic was so striking I ordered a thousand posters duplicating the album cover and mailed out albums and posters to 130 college radio stations and various indie record labels. I got the list from the broker who handled the logistics of the album manufacturing, a fellow with the unlikely and very L.A. name of Tabb Rexx.

What happened from all this? Through follow-up calls to radio stations I learned that the record was receiving "light" airplay, mostly during a station's R&B/blues segments. One L.A. station, KLOS, played the record on the weekly "Local Licks" program frequently, and that felt good. But what did people like most about the project? The poster! I got more calls from people all over the U.S. who had seen it at the college radio station or in someone's office or home. People loved that poster and wrote asking for extra copies. Ahh, the power of promotional goods. Never underestimate them! So I now have an attic full of cassettes, albums, and a few posters. Did I get a record deal through recording my own album? No. Did I make money selling it at gigs? I sold 15, I think. So why did I do it? Because I got a big dose of artistic gratification I sorely needed, and the world got a cool poster of a train wreck. Sometimes that is enough.

CHAPTER TEN
MANAGEMENT, BOOKING AGENTS, AND LAWYERS

The way you pick your professional team will either set your career and finances up for life, or assure you a place on the Electric Prunes tour.
—Donald Passman, from All You Need to Know About the Music Business

his is the chapter you may have dreaded. Who are these people anyway? Why can't we just play music for the people, man? Because it is, after all, called the music *business.*

The music business is a world filled with percentages. Album royalties are calculated as a percentage of the list price. Song performance royalties are a 50/50 split (50% each) between the writer and the publisher of a song. Yet only a small percentage of CDs earn back their recording and production costs.

This concept affects other areas of the music biz as well. Managers, booking agents (also called talent agencies), and, increasingly, lawyers all operate on a percentage basis. For example, an attorney who has been instrumental in arranging a record deal may receive 5% of the advance as his fee. A manager who contributes time and effort toward building a band's career is entitled to her percentage of the income, usually 15% to 20%. Booking agents routinely earn 15% of the artist's negotiated performance fee. Business managers, the people that handle and keep track of the money you finally do receive, often charge 5%. And the remainder is taxable by your friend the United States Government! Ouch!

If this scenario makes you want to switch to something less financially complex, like mowing lawns, cheer up: Virtually every big-time recording artist employs a manager, a booking agent, and a lawyer, and everyone involved makes money. The success of the situation is due to teamwork. Bands are teams of players, and in the same way that a baseball team has trainers, coaches, and assistants, your team needs a support system too. And, not surprisingly, these support players need to get paid.

When starting out, many bands do fine without any support personnel. You certainly don't need the services of a lawyer if your immediate goal is to learn some songs and get a gig. In terms of management, you may have a band member with organizational skills and a head for figures (the mathematical kind) who acts as a combination manager/booking agent. That's great! However, if your ambition includes playing gigs out of town, out of state and beyond, having a well-planned career, and signing a publishing or record deal, it will help to know where these other players—managers, booking agents, and lawyers—fit into your long-range plans.

MANAGERS

Since the name of this book is *Start Your Own Band*, I'll say something that isn't technically correct: There are at least two kinds of managers. We all know about the superstar managers who handle the big-time bands like The Rolling Stones, R.E.M., and so on. Well, those major-league managers are busy and probably won't want to return your calls just yet. But there is another direction you should consider: Hiring someone you can trust to do most of the non-music-related work that every band faces.

After a group has been together for a while they realize that it takes a lot of time and energy to get gigs, record demos, assemble promo kits, organize mailing lists and mailers—all the non-music stuff. However, to succeed as a musical entity, most of a band's time and energy should go toward working on the songs and their performance—i.e., the music. Any time spent working on band business is time taken away from the core of the enterprise: learning, writing, and performing songs. Practically speaking, a band seeking gigs is a business enterprise, and every successful business puts one basic concept into practice: the division of labor. By hiring someone you trust to take care of these tasks, you and your bandmates can concentrate on the music.

This type of manager is really a combination manager, booking agent (often with a short list of clients—you), and public relations person. I know of several bands who have hired managers with no "clout" in the "big-time" sense of the word, but who instead are enthusiastic supporters who spend their spare time working for the band and getting compensated accordingly. One obvious way a manager gets paid is by taking a percentage of gig money, maybe 15%.

However, if you are only pulling in $100 a gig, $15 may not attract anyone as a manager. It helps to be a little further along with your career so that a percentage of your earnings is somewhat attractive to the person. Depending on how many band members you have, giving the manager an equal share may make more sense. Each member in a five-piece band makes 20%. Adding a manager/member whose contribution brings in extra income gives everyone 16.67%. If the manager brings in one extra gig per month, and sells band T-shirts, tapes, and CDs at each gig, this could easily pay each member back more than the 3.33% they contribute to management costs. Of course, every member of the band must have faith in the manager. Many bands have a member who somehow ends up doing a lot of this kind of booking and hustling up gigs, and they are usually the person most willing to find a manager—because they're sick of doing all of the extra work! It is really worth considering this kind of management arrangement, as informal as it sounds. There is plenty of business to be taken care of when your band is building a following on a local and regional level, and an extra person doing this work can really help your career evolve much more quickly. Think about it. A close friend or loyal fan with spare time are two good possibilities.

> There is plenty of business to be taken care of when your band is building a following on a local and regional level.

What about the major-league managers? What do they accomplish for their percentage? If they are honest and talented, they can build your career to its maximum potential and be well worth every dollar they earn from your income.

A manager needs to have an understanding of how your music fits into the marketplace, an ability to look into the future and see how your band can be presented in the most attractive way, a flair for organization, and a network of industry connections that enable them to put their plan into action. The job of a manager includes: helping you get a record deal and a publishing deal; determining how much you can or should receive as an advance; helping you with the choice of a record producer (when the time comes); controlling your image through merchandising; choosing how to present

your act in the media; finding other team players like lawyers, business managers, and booking agents; working to get you a good opening slot on a national tour (or designing your own headlining tour); and generally acting as a buffer between you and the rest of the world. This is perhaps the most important job. Artists are by definition creators; managers should do all they can to keep them away from direct contact with the business side of life, while at the same time keeping them well informed.

The basis of every good band/manager relationship is complete trust in one another. Without trust there is no sense of teamwork. Not only does the band need to believe in the manager, but the manager needs to know that the band is equally committed to doing whatever it takes to build their career.

However, unlike lawyers, airline pilots, or electricians, a manager doesn't need any credentials to start doing business. There are unscrupulous management-types (as opposed to competent managers) who are simply hustlers and scam artists. These people talk a good game, and are expert at determining what a band wants to hear and feeding it to them nonstop. They have no love for or interest in music—it's the money they want. Giant clues that you are being conned include constant name dropping ("So David Geffen says to me…") and the insistence that by simply signing a management contract with this person your troubles are over. These types often have great personal charm, persuasiveness, and a serious motor-mouth, leading you to conclude that yes, they probably could talk anyone into doing anything, so why not have them on your side? Despite your reservations, this relentless in-your-face onslaught often succeeds in planting a nagging doubt in the back of your mind: If we tell the guy to get lost, we might be kissing our ticket to fame, fortune, and stardom goodbye. Well, relax. Being good at figuring out what someone wants to hear and then saying it over and over again is certainly a talent. But tackling the difficult, time-consuming, and hard work of developing a band is a separate talent, and hustlers have neither the interest nor the ability to commit to such a task. Furthermore, management-types like this usually begin pressuring you to sign an exclusive management contract early in the relationship. **This is a giant warning sign!** Once you have entered into a legally binding agreement with someone who is incompetent and at cross-purposes with your goals, your troubles are compounded. If you can't break the contract and you eventually obtain new management, you will be paying two commissions, one to each manager. You want to avoid paying out 30%, so be very careful with fast- and smooth-talking manager-types. Trust your instincts and always consult a lawyer before signing any agreement regarding exclusive personal services. Charm is not the same as vision and commitment.

How do you attract a respected, powerful, and competent personal manager? This is difficult, since they are busy working with their superstar clients, something not only just as time-consuming as building a new artist's career but also much more lucrative. A more likely situation is that of attracting the attention of a major manager's assistant—someone genuinely interested in your band, who is eager to make an impression with the boss and also to establish themselves as talents in their own right. The assistant can handle the day-to-day affairs of the new artist, and when clout is needed, their boss can step in and wield that hard-earned clout.

A third alternative is the most realistic: middle-level management, often a small, young management firm representing developing "alternative" bands. These bands are beyond the start-up phase but not in the large-time yet; they may have a self-released single or CD, or maybe a deal on an indie label. What these managers lack in large-scale clout they more than make up for in dedication, enthusiasm, hard-core energy, and street smarts. These managers often act as booking agents as well, giving them further control over how they build a band's career.

Although every band wants to connect with someone who is higher up and further along in their careers than the band is, the real world tells us that you will probably attract people roughly on par with your current level of success. Play gigs, make tapes, grow an audience. Just work. Eventually you will confidently seek and attract the attention of a manager who will see a professional, dedicated act worth representing. If you want to attract professional management, be a professional band.

Hey! Enough of my yakkin'! Let's get inside the head of a couple of actual managers, and see what makes them tick.

BARBARA DOLLARHIDE: YOU GOTTA LOVE THEM

What does a manager do? What leads a manager into his or her chosen career? When does a band need management? These questions and more are answered by Barbara Dollarhide, the sunny, energetic, and experienced manager of Goodness, Mike Johnson (bassist for Dinosaur, Jr.), Stuntman, and Anodyne, all up-and-coming acts based in the Pacific Northwest. Read and see things from a manager's viewpoint. Trace the path of Carrie Akre, a singer/songwriter whose band Hammerbox is signed to a major label, then dropped, then they break up, she forms another band, is signed to an indie, then picked up by another major label. Don't look for career patterns here, folks. No two stories alike!

MJ: When do you think a band needs management?

BD: It depends on the band. Bands, first of all, have to understand that managers can only handle four to five acts on the roster, because it's incredibly time-consuming to work with bands, and that also there is a limited number of managers because it's a risky field to be in. Most established, credible managers are going to look for talent that have proven themselves on their own, built up a following, a fan base, have at least recorded some kind of demo, who have put together their own press kit, and have been getting a decent local draw. There are even some L.A.- and New York-based managers that won't even pick up a band until they know they have a [record company] offer, or genuine label interest already there. Because without the record there's no income at all, besides a few local shows, which doesn't pay the bills.

> Normally it's going to take a band a year to figure out who they are musically, personality-wise, and to build up any kind of fan base.

Normally it's going to take a band a year to figure out who they are musically, personality-wise, and to build up any kind of fan base. That's the norm; there are always flukes, bands that take off really quickly, and there're bands that take two to three years. A lot of bands think that because they've written a couple songs and they're playing together now, they need someone to work with them. That's not the case. They need to have at least a full record's worth of songs written, and have really figured where they're going, musically, and how they work together. Very seldom does the original lineup from day one end up being the final lineup of the band, there's usually going to be transition.

MJ: What does a manager bring to the table that a band member can't?

BD: The general goal when you're managing a band is get them to the point where all they're concerned about is writing, recording, and performing. Where they don't have to worry about anything like, everything from major issues like recording and publishing contracts, and trying to find those deals, to making sure they're at sound check on time, making sure they have enough guitar picks when they get to the show. Basically, just getting them to focus on their part, because that's their job: to write those great songs, to perform those great songs, and to record those great songs. They shouldn't have to worry about all the petty bullshit that gets wrapped up into the music business. That's the ultimate goal.

MJ: Do you find there's a lot of babysitting and hand-holding required of some bands?

BD: Some bands, yes. A band is a family, and with any family there's problems. So there's always going to be conflicts and fights and sibling rivalry. That's usually where some of the biggest problems come in. And that's always going to happen during touring and during recording, because there will always be different opinions on how things should be done, and different personalities that all of a sudden have to be together all the time. So part of my job is trying to help them survive that.

What I do is advise and counsel; I don't make any decisions for the band. I can't do that because it's their career. All I can do is say, "These are things I think are going to help your career, and this is why." Or vice versa.

MJ: How does a manager develop clout?

BD: Time. Having developed contacts during the time you've been in the business. Anybody can say, "I manage bands," but unless they've developed the contacts, through time and perseverance, and also developed a level of respect in the business, then the people they call on the phone aren't going to pay attention to them. But once you reach a certain point, the people will take your calls, and they'll open the packages you send them.

A lot of A&R people look at managers as a resource to find out about new talent, because they're in L.A. or New York and I'm managing bands up here in Seattle—so I can tell them, "This is one I picked out to work with because I think they've got the potential to **135** make it, so you should check it out." So you've got a better chance of them paying attention to the band. But it doesn't guarantee. Many bands have this idea that if they sign with a manager it means they're going to get a record deal. It doesn't mean that at all. If nobody else besides the manager sees the talent or potential, it's just not going to happen. All the manager can do is help get people to go out and find out about them. Whereas they may not have bothered to find out about them otherwise.

MJ: Give me an example of how you've worked with an artist or band to guide their career.

BD: I was an avid fan of Hammerbox before they were signed to A&M Records. I went to C/Z because of Hammerbox, and I worked the record there to radio and video and retail and press and every other way I could. When Hammerbox signed to A&M, I was still with C/Z at the time, and Carrie [Akre, the vocalist] said to me, "Someday you and me are going to work together, somehow, some way." They were being managed by their legal representation at the time. So the record came out on A&M, and then Hammerbox broke up, and Carrie started working on songs with different people around town.

A&M had an option called the "Leaving Member Provision," that says when the band breaks up A&M would have the first option on anything that any member chose to do after that, and A&M were considering exercising that option. So Carrie called me and said, "A&M want me to demo some songs, and I'm not sure how to deal with this, and I want to drop my current management, and I want you to manage me." So I did a little dance of joy because I knew that anything Carrie touched would be beautiful, and started working with that. She got the band together, after a few changes.

The Leaving Member Provision in any contract is not the most appealing thing to be involved with. And A&M was very busy; they had 60 releases scheduled for the upcoming year, and they said if Goodness were to put a record out, it wouldn't be until a couple years after the fact. So they recorded a demo, and it came down to the fact that the vice president of A&R knew that Carrie wasn't too enthusiastic about being there, he knew A&M were too busy, so we were able to get out of the deal. And it was a very friendly thing. Goodness's first show sold out. We did a great blitz on Seattle saying this is her new band, so we got a nice good start.

MJ: How did you do that?

BD: I got every newspaper to write about it—and I was the only one, there was no label, no one helping. I got KNDD to mention it because their program director was a fan of Carrie's as well. And the college stations announced it, and she had name recognition—it hadn't been that long since Hammerbox had broken up so the name was still in people's minds. So we got a good start here, and then the band decided they wanted to put out their own CD. But that meant that I'd be putting out a CD, but I wasn't a record label, and I didn't know if I wanted to be a management/record label. And then the guys from "Y" [Records] approached us. So we hooked up with them.

Goodness has been organic the whole way. They started off with a lot of people wanting to find out about them and it's just grown since then. And the record I used to shop to other labels, because the band was interested in going to a larger company. Interest generated rapidly, and they had four labels in the running, and in the end there were two that the band had an interest in, and the one they finally chose was Lava/Atlantic. Both Atlantic and Lava wanted the band, and Lava was distributed through Atlantic, but Lava has fewer releases, so there's more of a focus, and that was part of the appeal

> *Many bands think they need a manager so bad that they jump at anyone who's willing to do it...*

with Lava. "Y" Records' distribution was extremely limited, so we made a deal with Lava/Atlantic to rerelease and slightly repackage the CD, and it was rereleased nationwide February [1996].

That's the other thing bands often don't understand. They think the hardest part is getting signed to the record label, but once you get signed that's when the hard work really begins. That's when you're expected to tour nonstop, and be writing when you're not touring, and recording when you're not writing or touring, and doing promotional radio visits or special press days.

MJ: What about the trust level between you and the band?

BD: It's got to be 100%. If it's not there, the relationship's not going to work. Many bands think they need a manager so bad that they jump at anyone who's willing to do it, but theoretically it's a lifetime relationship: It's a marriage, a commitment. It's different from other **137** relationships; the agent, the lawyer, the label. You talk to the manager every day. You've got to be open, you've got to be able to have fights if you have to and yell at each other.

MJ: Is it a handshake deal or a contract relationship?

BD: Most of the biggest managers have been known to not have a contract. The highest risk you run is you get a band signed and then somebody or someone at the label says, "You need higher-powered management than what you've got." And they fire you, and you don't get your money. And that's a genuine risk. But I make abundantly clear at the beginning of the relationship that this is what I charge, and this is what I'll do for you. I don't require paperwork in a contract. Industry standard is 15% of gross. There're times when I've had bands on tours where they're making $50, $100 a night, and I'm not going to take my money from that, although legally I have every right to.

MJ: How does a band hook up with good management?

BD: A lot of managers find out from word of mouth or other bands, because they'll have them play shows with each other. Doing your research by calling anybody and everybody you know and asking about who's out there, getting phone numbers if you can, trying to network. Talk to bands they manage first, find out what they have to say first. There are books that list management, like the *Pollstar Management Directory, The Yellow Pages of Rock, Recording Industry Sourcebook*. They're not cheap but they're out there. Pollstar I like because they list the management roster. References are the best.

MJ: Do all successful managers have to love the music of the bands they represent?

BD: In my opinion, yes. Because management is hard, and it's draining. And unless you're proud of what you're working with it's not going to be worth it.

MJ: What advice would you give to a young band to help them build their careers?

BD: The first thing they need to do before they think of anything else is write some good songs. Nothing's gonna happen otherwise. Then they need to learn to play those songs well, and sing those songs well. Vocals are very important, especially for a rock band. Anyone who forgets about that initially is going to be hurt. You need patience, because it will take time. Try to build a local fan base however you can. Don't get concerned about the business side until you've got songs and performance.

DENNIS TURNER: STRATEGY + TALENT = SUCCESS

Dennis Turner has managed saxophonist Kenny G since 1984. Despite what certain jazz and pop critics have offered regarding his music, Kenny's career rather eloquently speaks for itself. He has sold 30 million albums. Most musicians I know would be "glad" to sell this particular number of records. Many critics feel that you can't be this successful and have a really quality product. Hootie and the Blowfish has suffered a similar analysis from the experts. I suppose this kind of philosophical rambling has a place in the world but so does selling 30 million albums. Yet all the talent in the world isn't enough. You need management. In this interview, Dennis reveals his early music roots, how he met Kenny, and how they worked together to take both of their careers into overdrive.

Dennis started his career at the University of Nevada Las Vegas as the concert chairman in charge of bringing musical acts to the campus. In 1972 he moved to L.A. and began working as a booking agent for club and concert venues. The agency he worked for handled Neil Diamond, and through this connection Dennis met Diamond's manager, Ken Fritz. Dennis began working for Fritz Management in December 1975. He worked with Ken for 13 years, signing such artists as George Benson, John Hiatt, and The Motels, and eventually became a partner in Fritz–Turner Management.

Kenny G heard about Dennis through his work with George Benson, a jazz artist who had broken into mainstream pop with his big hits "Masquerade" and "On Broadway."

When Kenny met with Dennis in 1984 to discuss a possible management relationship, Kenny's reputation and record sales within the current R&B music scene were slowly developing, but Kenny, like Dennis, wanted more…

DT: We sat down and had lunch, and I was so impressed with his intelligence, his sincerity, and his general vibe that I signed before ever studying his music. I heard his album one time I think.

MJ: Did he strike you as someone who was very ambitious?

DT: Yes. I felt that he had researched it well, he knew what he was doing, he knew who he wanted, and he wanted me, and that's how it worked out. He was added to the Fritz–Turner roster. So I started working Arista and putting him out on tour as much as I possibly could.

MJ: Tell me what you did to build momentum.

DT: Well, I focused 100% of my energies on his project and I came up with an idea. I went to Claude Nobs of the Montreux Jazz Festival and I hooked up with an airline, and somehow was able to get 16 round-trip tickets from various places in the United States to Switzerland. Basically it was a contest we threw that would be "Win a chance to see Kenny G perform live at the Montreux Jazz Festival." And we ran that in about 15 cities, and we gave away a pair of tickets on VH1 in each city plus one national pair, when VH1 was in its infancy. Basically it was just radio driven; people had to go into a record store to sign up for this thing and we had tens of thousands of applications. That was one aspect, and that got him a lot of press.

We basically broke through touring. I was an ex-agent and consequently I put him on the road as much as I possibly could; he was out working continuously in clubs and in concerts. We weren't using tour support, he was actually making enough money because of this hip R&B following that allowed him to do that. He was selling out 400 and 500 seat clubs and we were able to cut the deals tightly enough that he would make enough money to survive. [Kenny was booked through Peter Shiels at the William Morris Agency.]

> *Basically it was just radio driven; people had to go into a record store to sign up for this thing and we had tens of thousands of applications.*

MJ: Who had a higher level of success in their respective fields, you or Kenny?

DT: I had a higher level, primarily through my success with George Benson.

MJ: What makes a manager see the potential in a developing artist?

DT: Hopefully if their music is unique to the manager's ear it's gonna be a labor of love anyway. That's what Kenny was for me for many years, before we made a dollar, it was a labor of love. It was something that I passionately believed in, and I felt that I could break him.

MJ: Was your plan just tons of exposure, figuring that his talent, if displayed to enough people, would create the success?

DT: That's basically it. Of course, tons of exposure is very hard to come by. We generated the foundation by touring. I was able to put him on some George Benson dates, he did a George Benson tour where the audience just flipped out for him, the audience would just go wild for him, so that was a start. Then we got him on the *Tonight Show*.

MJ: How?

DT: Just tenacity. The record company and myself. I knew the TV show producer and he had taken a special interest in Kenny because he'd heard his music, so between the agency (William Morris Agency), the record company, and myself we were able to put that together.

MJ: With "Songbird," what part did you have in that?

DT: We convinced a guy named Don Ienner, who's now president of Columbia Records, to try and take a shot with a single on Top 40 radio. Donnie was head of promotion at Arista at the time. Myself and a lot of other people convinced him that this was worth a shot. And then Clive (Davis, president of Arista) wrote personal letters to everybody in radio saying, "You gotta take a listen to this, this kid is very special and you gotta take a listen to this"

MJ: I remember being amazed at the time, hearing a saxophone instrumental on Top 40 stations.

DT: Yes. And "Songbird" started to take off…but mind you, that particular album, *Duotones*, had already sold 400,000 units before we tried to get Top 40 ads.

So the substance was already there, it was just a matter of working on it. The foundation we built through concert touring. The exposure we had through VH1 and various other media outlets coupled with a great album, so the timing was right. Then we were able to capitalize on it through the Top 40 single, the CHR (contemporary hit radio) single, which was "Songbird."

MJ: How do you attract other artists? How do other artists get to you, how do you choose them, and what is that process?

DT: Basically it's relationships you build with record companies, agencies, lawyers, business managers, and they're the ones that are gonna feed you, especially lawyers and business managers and agencies are going to refer you. You simply determine, number one, is this the kind of music I like, and number two, is this someone I think I can get along with, because that's important in my relationship, the person themselves. I'm not interested in managing assholes.

MJ: You gotta like the music, you gotta get along with them. But there's gotta be more than that.

DT: There has to be a potential for them to be successful. You've got to see it in them. They've got to want it.

MJ: You gotta see the hunger.

DT: Yeah, but you know what? I don't like to see rabid people either. You know what I'm saying? The look of that rabid dog.

MJ: What advice do you have to artists that are trying to get good management?

DT: That's the age-old question and it's a very tough one. The initial step of course is to try and get on showcases where you can get exposed in front of anybody, be it a publisher, somebody from BMI or ASCAP, somebody from the National Association of Songwriters (NAS), all these organizations do showcases. Get on the showcase circuit and try to get your name around town, get a buzz going, just a low-level buzz so you can get some kind of interest.

Then, you would hopefully attract a lawyer, because lawyers get paid whether the artist is successful or not, theoretically. A lot of them do defer—I say defer, not waive—their attorney's fees. At that point it's easier to get a lawyer than it is to get a manager because a manager doesn't earn anything. Develop as many friends as you can within the publishing community that spawns talent, which is the BMI/ASCAP/NAS kind of vibe, and then try and get into the club circuit—I would think you'd have to do it primarily in L.A. or New York.

MJ: To what do you account your success, which is evident?

DT: Limiting my roster to artists that I feel have a tremendous potential and are also basically good human beings. Also, tenacity and good sense.

BOOKING AGENTS

When you first start out playing live performances, most likely you will be your own booking agent. In Chapter 7 we discussed techniques of getting club gigs. You can also book your own club tour, either regional or even national if you have the time, patience, and organizational skills. Several books mentioned in the Information Sources section at the back of this book are useful references when planning a tour. Eventually, if you're ambitious, you'll need a booking agent. A good booking agent will simplify the business side of your band and get you better gigs, taking a percentage of the performance fee, varying from 10% to 15%. Top agencies such as the

William Morris Agency, ICM (International Creative Management)

and CAA (Creative Artists Agency) do not as a rule book developing bands. There are, however, a large number of booking agencies that deal exclusively with bands who are working their way up through the club circuit. This is where you should start your plan for world domination. How can we find out more about these agencies?

Hey! I know. Let's call up Liz Garo, head of A&R and publicity at Restless Records in Los Angeles. Liz will share some of her thoughts on agencies, based on her 15 years of involvement in the music biz as a booking agent, tour manager, promoter, and co-owner of an underground club.

LIZ GARO: LET'S WORK TOGETHER

MJ: How can a band hook up with a booking agency?

LG: There are independent booking agents who are very qualified—sometimes even more so than the bigger agencies—to book tours for developing or new bands. Some of the best and most respected agents are Go Ahead Booking (Stereolab, Spinanes), Lovely Booking (Silkworm, Babe The Blue Ox), Van Go (Spain, Capsize 7, Possum Dixon), Rave (16 Deluxe, Doo Rag), and Red Ryder (Squirrel Nut Zippers, Kill Creek).

MJ: What makes a booking agent good?

LG: Someone who returns your phone calls! A desirable booking agent is someone who is capable of getting a band from here to there in the most effective and manageable way. A booking agent should work closely with band and label, if there is one, in terms of where the band wants to go, where the key markets are in which the music is getting a response. The agent in a sense can

> The agent in a sense can function as an important element in helping to market and develop the band...

function as an important element in helping to market and develop the band by getting them into the right clubs in front of the right audience. A good booking agent is someone who is aware of the band's needs as a traveling group, and won't have them drive 16 hours to get to just one show that won't be well attended, or to have the band play in the wrong kind of venues.

Because a lot of independent booking agencies are small operations, usually one or two people, they can't take on a lot of bands to represent. The up side to this is that these agencies are able to provide a lot of special care and attention to the act. The downside is that these agencies can't afford—financially or time-wise—to have a growing roster of talent.

If a new band is booking their own tour they can send a tape to one of the smaller agents to see if there is a band touring in a similar time frame and market that they can go out with. A band can try to hook up with an established band that is already making the rounds—the best way to do that is meet other bands and form a kind of friendly alliance where you can help each other out.

Indie agents are usually very passionate about music and truly care about the bands. They are familiar with and sensitive to the less-than-glamorous side of touring—long drives in a van, crappy sound systems, playing to an empty room. The indie agents have for the most part either played in bands, gone on the road as a tour manager, or been a promoter themselves, so there is a level of understanding of what needs to be done.

When any agent is looking at a band to book they are going to want to know what kind of live show a band puts on, when the band will have a record released, and if the band has played out before. It is very important to an agent—especially the small ones who don't have the time to make babysitting a full-time job—that a band is capable of being responsible, able to get to sound check on time, and know how to deal with people once they are there. An agent wants to pick up a band that will help out with promotion and will take care of their own merchandising and participate in general, as opposed to a band just thinking now that they have an agent everything will be taken care of. On an independent level that is just not the case.

MJ: What makes a bad agent?
LG: Someone who doesn't prepare enough in advance and someone who doesn't follow through. It's really crucial to plan ahead when booking—about two to three months in advance—and also to follow up with every venue that you send a package to or pitch a show to. Ideally, too, you want to get an agent who is connected to a lot of other bands and agencies and to someone who is just connected to the whole music network. It's important for an agent to be aware

of new clubs and promoters and of who's going out on the road looking for a support band.

MJ: What kind of signing do agencies require, and what percentage do they take?

LG: It varies, the bigger agencies sign contracts, the smaller agencies usually don't, but some agents do. Sometimes it's for two years, sometimes it's for a specific number of tours. It's not very common on the developing artist level. Agencies usually collect 10% or 15% plus expenses—phone calls, postage.

MJ: How do bands get paid?

LG: Usually the bands will collect the money at the end of the show and at the end of the tour they give the agent 15% of their lump sum. On certain high-paying shows ($500 for a show), agents will ask for a deposit or a percentage of the guarantee.

MJ: How much do bands get paid on this level of touring?

LG: A relatively unknown band will usually only get a door percentage (a percentage of paid admissions), which can average out to maybe a little more than 30, 40 bucks—depending on venue attendance. A band that has a small growing buzz can maybe get a guarantee of about $100 or more. If you do have a strong, respected agent working for you, they can often get better money because of their relationship and history with the club. If a club knows that an agent represents some bigger names and the agent is trying to get a show for one of their baby bands, the club may try and give the booking agent a good spot for the developing band in hopes of getting the bigger name act down the line. The majority of music industry work is about relationships and it is truly defined by the inner workings between agents and clubs.

MJ: What's some good basic advice for a band that wants to tour?

LG: Be sure to prepare far enough in advance—don't decide in late September that you want to tour in October. Also, instead of tackling the entire country, try to go out just regionally at first—it's sometimes easier to conquer a smaller territory rather than doing something nationally. Just use common sense and be cool to people, be courteous to everyone you meet, because impressions really do matter. Touring can really be a great way to see the country and it is an invaluable learning experience for a band in how they function as a unit and how they play. How a band survives a bad tour can say a lot about their commitment to playing and being together. For touring **145** to make sense for a band, a band needs to repeat the process—go back to the markets you've played in and build from there.

In terms of hooking up with an agency, a lot of agencies pick up bands through referrals and recommendations from other bands. And if an agent sees a band is working and doing it themselves, that's going to make a band that much more appealing to an agent. They already have a growing fan base and there's a sense that the band knows how to tour.

LAWYERS

OK, no lawyer jokes. Yes, it would be sweet if people could just reach agreements, hug each other, and go home happy. Sorry, wrong planet! When it comes time to negotiate a record contract, you'll want the best lawyer you can afford, mainly to do combat with the lawyer on the other side. What a system!

Often, a band will have their initial contact with an attorney soon after being asked to sign a contract by a record label, production company, or personal manager. If so, you'll need an attorney special-izing in music law, someone who has extensive knowledge of the current standards of record royalties, service fee percentages, length of contracts, and all that fascinating legal stuff.

> *Often, a band will have their initial contact with an attorney soon after being asked to sign a contract by a record label...*

In addition to offering legal expertise, a good attorney often serves as the calm voice of logic and reason in an environment where the very thought of any record deal often causes band members to salivate while visualizing Ferraris and yachts. There is nothing glamorous about signing a bad deal! A good lawyer can serve as a sounding board for a band with troubling questions. Here are some examples: A friend of the band wants to be our manager, what should we do? A producer wants us to sign a development deal that will give him 50% of our advance if he gets us a deal—is that fair? (No.) My partner and I started this band and we want to set up a corporation that hires the other band members, how do we make this work? How do we register and protect our band name?

This type of question needs the help of a good attorney to be answered fully. It is helpful to start a relationship with an attorney early in a band's career, perhaps one recommended by another band, a manager, or other trusted music biz friend. This can save you a lot of heartache down the road as you begin receiving different offers from people in varied areas of the music biz.

Enough theory. Let's check in with Peter Laird, an L.A.-based attorney who represents musicians (Bon Jovi; Peter, Paul and Mary), entertainers (Dolly Parton, Bette Midler), and many other show biz figures.

PETER LAIRD: ENJOY THE PROCESS

MJ: What is the role of major record labels in terms of band development?

PL: My perception is that bands primarily come up through small labels, not only in Seattle—I see it all over. And it's a healthy trend. It's difficult in any field of entertainment but perhaps more so in music for any huge company like MCA or Sony to have its ear to the ground and its feet on the street and all that. They try, but it more genuinely comes from smaller independent people who really put in the time and effort with new talent to develop them.

MJ: When the buzz phrase was "My lawyer is shopping my tape," when was that a typical way of getting a record deal?

PL: Certainly the '70s and part of the '80s, but I think it tailed out at the end of the '80s.

MJ: What do entertainment lawyers need to know as specialists?

PL: Two things: One is basic contract law. The other is now known as intellectual property, meaning not only copyright but the whole area of intangible property rights that artists get paid for one way or another. You've got your copyrights on your music, you've also got the right to your likeness on the T-shirt that they sell at the concert, and all of those things you have to know. Trademarks, band logos—they are also intellectual property, meaning the property rights that go along with a creative endeavor.

MJ: At what point in a band's career does it become necessary to work with an entertainment lawyer?

PL: When somebody puts a deal on the table for you. Most importantly, when an offer is made to you in writing, whether it's for a record deal, a publishing deal…that's when you need a lawyer. Maybe you need someone in advance of that point, because when something's put on the table that means usually there's some gener- **147** al understanding of what the general terms of the deal are going to be, so maybe you need a lawyer if you don't have anyone else speaking for you, like a manager. So it's either at the point when an offer is on the table or when there's serious interest.

MJ: What are some typical "beware" situations a young band should look out for?

PL: What typically happens is someone will come to you with what is known as a production deal, meaning you will sign to them—for all intents and purposes what amounts to a record deal. They get the exclusive rights to your recording services for some period of time. They also may get publishing rights and merchandising rights. Now, if they go beyond that and also try to get management, that's a huge warning signal, if they're going for everything under the sun! But it's not uncommon for a legitimate production deal to include recording services and some interest in your publishing, not all, maybe 50%.

The problem is, if you're in what the industry calls—and it's not a derogatory term—one of the "baby bands," is to set it up so that if whatever the situation is doesn't work out, that you're not tied up unnecessarily for a long period of time. Make sure of two things in this sort of deal: One is you can see if it's not successful it's going to end, and two is that it's a fair deal. What's a fair deal? It depends on what the production company is bringing to the table. Are they bringing a producer, are they just bringing money, do they have some way to advance the project beyond just sending it to the record companies trying to get interest?

Another red flag is if it's all going to cost the band money. Anybody could figure that out, if you're going to a production company and somehow it's going to cost you out-of-pocket. That's way out of line. Typically it's the production company doing the investing, so that keeps them in line to some extent. Obviously a production company isn't going to be spending tons and tons of money on a project that they see going nowhere, but they may have tied you up contractually.

MJ: Are all the good entertainment lawyers in either L.A. or New York?

PL: There are handfuls of other places, some good ones in Atlanta, Miami, Chicago, San Francisco, and there may be some in Seattle now. It's not absolutely critical you get someone in Los Angeles or

New York; it's more important to get someone who's obviously

bright and is going to put in the time and effort to protect your interests. It's not rocket science, you know. It was more important when the primary function of a lawyer was to get the deal in the first place. And that's really not the case these days.

MJ: How do entertainment lawyers get paid these days?

PL: Entertainment lawyers in general have over the last 20 years evolved into percentage-based compensation. The traditional lawyer compensation is on an hourly rate. Lawyers in the entertainment business started going into a percentage business, typically 5%, quite a while ago. This made sense in a lot of ways, because a lot of bands basically couldn't afford the hourly rates of lawyers to do deals. If you were a band that got discovered and had a record deal offered to you it's unlikely you would have the, let's say,

> ...You would pay for your lawyer out of the initial revenues that came to you from the record deal.

$5,000 to $10,000 to have a lawyer negotiate the deal for you. So you would make an agreement with the lawyer that if the record deal went through, the lawyer would get a percentage of the advance you were paid by the record company, the "up-front" money. So you would pay for your lawyer out of the initial revenues that came to you from the record deal.

MJ: So it's really a "spec" [speculative] deal for the lawyers, right?

PL: It was truly a spec deal for the lawyers because they would take on representation of many bands on that basis and not all of them would get signed, so the lawyer would be putting in a lot of work and in some cases the deal falls apart for whatever reason. This 5% trend started by the early '80s. A few people started and it just grew and grew.

Two things have happened over the years. One, it's become the standard and not the exception. Two, the percentage has gone from encompassing a way to pay your lawyer for negotiating your first deal to being an overall business relationship just like you have with your manager or your agent, where the lawyer is going to represent you in everything you do and for that is going to take 5% of all your gross revenues.

MJ: Let's say your booking agent takes 10%, your business manager (e.g., **149**

*your accountant) takes 5%, your personal manager takes 20%, and your
lawyer takes 5%. Now you've got 60% of your gross revenue left, and then
you're taxed at, let's say the top end, 40%. You're left with 20% of where
you started. Any comments?*

PL: [laughs] Well, the only comment is, there's two sides to that issue.
One is, it's incredibly important for any artist to be surrounded by
good business people, because if they're not, there's going to be trouble. That's the lawyers, accountants, managers—you name it. And all
of them play a different role. If the price of that is all those percentages, perhaps it's better than not having good people around you.

The downside to all of this is the artist is now supporting a huge
family and many artists wake up five or ten years down the road,
look behind them, and see this trail of people that they're supporting in quite handsome style and begin to resent it because they see
it as being all their creative efforts contributing to the success of their
career. It's not all their efforts; it's also the skills and the business ability of those people. Where's the balance between those two points of
view? It just depends, and it's case-by-case. Putting aside that general overview of how much talent has to pay for their business people:
I have some concern about lawyers about being partners with
clients. In some cases it makes sense, in other cases maybe our focus
starts to shift and the lawyer becomes more interested in making a
deal than protecting them in the long run. A large part of what
lawyers do is protect you, and to let you know not just what the
good points of a deal are but what the pitfalls are. If my compensation only comes from the deal happening, I may be less inclined to
point out the pitfalls.

*MJ: Any comments on management? What about a band hiring someone, at
a percentage, to help with business that even a starting band needs to cover?
Is it easier to get a lawyer or a manager interested when you're starting out?*

PL: It depends. It's probably easier to get a manager, because a manager can be anyone from a high-powered Hollywood-type guy who
knows everyone there is to know and represents a lot of big talent,
to the guy who's gonna carry your amps and get you from bar to bar
and go up and get the $125 you're going to make when you're play-
ing that bar. Most managers start at that lower level in some fashion.

It is an important thing, because in general, artists should not represent themselves, even on a low level, even to the local clubs. It's a
creative thing, and your ego is tied up in it, you can't be objective

about it, and if there's someone who is honest and has your best interests at heart available to you it's a good thing to have. Obviously, the potential problems come for one of those one in a thousand or one in a hundred thousand bands that become a big success—can this person grow with you and adapt to your needs as you grow? Or are you going to have to move on to someone who is more adept at whatever those needs are as you grow? And it becomes a very painful thing for young bands who have someone who's been loyal to them for five years and seen them through every lousy bar in an area, then they have a record deal and a national tour and this guy doesn't know how to function.

With any luck there's a way to bring those people along with you. I wouldn't avoid having those people. I think those people are important, almost from the get-go.

MJ: Any final thoughts on what bands should do?

PL: I'll say this not as a lawyer but as someone who has been around a lot, seen a lot, talked to a lot of people, and heard a lot of stories from people who have been at every level of the ladder, the top, the bottom, and everywhere in between.

I think the most important thing is to enjoy the process, because almost without exception, I believe the best time for an artist is before they are successful, the happiest time, the most rewarding time (and I'm not talking about financial rewards), the most creative time. It becomes much more like a job when you hit, and it's a very difficult job. So everyone's eye is always on the prize—"Gee, if we could only become the next whatever-it-is." And that's a good goal, and you need that goal to make it a business and a career. But don't forget to have fun along the way because the best times are going to be those times.

THE RECORD DEAL

I had signed a very bad deal with Specialty.
If you wanted to record you signed on their terms
or you didn't record. I got a half cent
for every record sold. Whoever heard of
cutting a penny in half!
—Little Richard (1932–)

art and commerce are shaky friends at best. This chapter's goal is to expose you to the main areas of the music business addressed in a typical recording agreement. Dwelling on all this number-crunching stuff is not the point; you're much better off concentrating on your job: writing, playing, and performing music. Leave the specific details of this business stuff to lawyers and managers.

For many musicians, nothing is more sought-after then the legendary, proverbial "record deal," and this concept is often viewed in rosy terms as a sort of blissful state of grace that will only lead to guaranteed success.

Nothing could be further from the truth.

To illustrate my point, here's a hypothetical situation. Your band, *Five O'Clock Shadow*, is playing at your cassette release party to a packed audience at a local club, when a man shows up wearing gold chains, dark sunglasses, and an oily smile. He introduces himself as Bobby Fabulous, and his rap goes something like this:

"I love you guys! I'll sign you right now! I've heard your tape and you show promise. Here's the (record) deal: I will pay you $100 as an advance against your album sales, which my company, Trust Me Records, will keep close track of. You in turn now owe me six albums. I own your publishing, and you can't record for anyone else. I also retain all merchandising rights. I'll charge half of the video budget and all of the tour expenses against future royalties, and everything is cross-collateralized. If you don't know what that means, great! You'll find out soon enough when (and if) your second album sells 500,000 copies and you still don't make any record royalties because proceeds from the second album are paying off the debt you incurred from your (non-selling) first album. Whaddaya say?"

I suggest a polite "No thank you, I just ate."

A record deal is all in the details. Let's drop the fantasy-laden aspects of stardom for a moment in order to take a close look at what a legally binding agreement between an artist (you) and a corporate entity (the record label) actually is. First we'll examine several common types of artist/label relationships, and then turn our attention to "deals" in general—from both the view of the artist and the record company. But before we start, let's broaden the definition of a record deal. Nowadays there's no such thing as a standard deal. Recording contracts vary widely, from Janet Jackson's $80 million deal all the way down to a verbal agreement (over pizza and a six-pack) between a band and a small, independent label.

VARIETIES OF RECORD DEALS

The music business has developed into a multibillion-dollar media machine, encompassing major record companies, independent labels of varying size, huge retail stores, interactive CD-ROMS, MTV, and video/record producers who have become, in many ways, artists in their own right. All these factors have helped expand the variety of legally binding agreements that most people think of as a record deal. Let's look at a few.

The Classic: Your band signs directly with a record label to make a certain number of records within a specific period of time. The label gives you an *advance* (more accurately: loans you money) when you sign, and you deliver the end product of your recording sessions (mixed, equalized, and sequenced recordings known as "masters") to the label, who press, distribute, market, and promote the CD or cassette. As you would suspect, the amount of this *advance* is negotiated prior to signing, and so is another key factor in any record deal: the *royalty rate.* This is the amount of money the artist receives for each recording sold, and is expressed as a *percentage* of the suggested retail list price (or SRLP) of the CD or cassette. The SRLP is currently around $15.98 for CDs and $10.98 for cassettes. The royalty rate varies according to your so-called clout at the time of signing, rang-

to 13% for a new artist signing to a major label, 14% to 16% for an established artist, all the way up to 16% to 20% for superstar artists.

On a CD that lists for $16, a band would earn, in theory (at 9% royalty), .09 x $16.00 = $1.44 per CD. Why theoretically? Because the above-mentioned advance is *recoupable,* which means the record company keeps the artist's royalties until it gets its money back. If you were advanced $20,000, the record company would keep the first $20,000 in royalties and pay you whatever royalties you make from subsequent sales. We'll discuss this in more detail near the end of the chapter.

Here's a more down-to-earth example: You and your band make your own recording and deliver it to an indie label along with your camera-ready artwork (cheap and easy with today's scanner/desk-top publishing hardware). The label pays for the manufacturing and distribution of the CD, giving you a (negotiated) percentage of the receipts. This is a version of what is known as a *P&D deal,* where the financial contribution

> Without promotion, the records will sit in the record stores like neglected orphans wondering why they aren't being noticed, or in our case, bought.

of the label is simply pressing and distributing the record. Although this sounds like a good way to avoid owing the record company money, there's one thing often missing in a P&D deal: promotion. Without promotion, the records will sit in the record stores like neglected orphans wondering why they aren't being noticed, or in our case, bought. As we discussed in Chapter 9, promotion is a vital component in generating sales.

Another option is an artist/band signing a deal with a *production* company, who in turn reaches an agreement with a record label to deliver records from either a specific artist (you) or a number of artists per year. In deals like this you usually have to give up some of your song publishing or a portion of your royalty income. So why sign with a production company? Because the good ones are often owned or run by major producers, managers, promotion people, or some other music biz type with a good track record and therefore "industry clout." The right artist/producer combination often creates a kind of synergistic magic, like the Beatles with producer George Martin, or Quincy Jones producing Michael Jackson.

How about this one? A *corporation* is formed (with the help of an attorney) which creates an employment agreement with…your band. The corporation (we'll call it Your Band, Inc.) loans out your "artistic services" to a record label. The record label pays advances and album royalties not to you but to the corporation, which in turn pays your salary. This arm's-length approach to dealing with a record company can help create a tax break for the artist(s), who receive no money directly—and the corporation can form a benefit package like health insurance. The big success story of 1995, Hootie and the Blowfish, have done this. When you sell 13 million records, forming a corporation as a tax shelter is a hell of a good idea. Why? Top personal income tax: 39.6%. Top corporate income tax: 34%.

DIFFERENT STROKES FOR DIFFERENT FOLKS

As you can see, there are many ways of "getting signed," just as there may be several reasons why you want a deal: a desire to see yourself on MTV, a passionate love for writing and playing music, or maybe to fulfill your lifelong dream of owning a car that actually runs most of the time. These are all valid reasons and can be included under the heading "Artist's Perspective."

Try this exercise, if you can stand it. Briefly change viewpoints and look at things from the record company's perspective. They want only one thing: to make money. Ouch! And although your band might be taking the *artistic* risks with your controversial, 23-minute tribute to Ozzy, the label is taking all of the *financial* risk, because as a new artist you have little or no track record, i.e., sales history. Major labels with highly successful acts such as Gloria Estefan, Janet Jackson, and Van Halen often try to balance their financial risks by signing new, unproved artists. These acts are offered "new kid" contracts lopsided in the company's favor. How lopsided? Well, what could be more lopsided than a contract that says the label can drop the artist at any time, yet the artist has no freedom to walk away from the contract? This is often the case in a typical contract designed for a new band. The "pay or play" provision inserted into many contracts states that if the label decides not to retain an artist *for any reason at all*, they can decide against recording, and choose instead to pay each member union scale (currently $271.73 per musician, per tune) for their (nonexistent) performance. If a clause in your contract states that the minimum number of tracks per album is ten, and the label dropped you, total career earnings from your contract could be a whopping $2,717.30. Not exactly fantasy stuff.

Therefore, it may be helpful to view a record label simply as a bank that loans you money to make a record. Since the only collateral you have for the loan is future earnings, the label writes up a tight little contract defining their share of the profits as much in their favor as legally possible.

Many musicians placed in the highly touted position of signing with a major label are often young and unsophisticated, neither interested in or willing to look closely at the details of a contract. Don't be one of these people! To further complicate things, an unethical lawyer who has signed an agreement with a band to "get them a record deal" by a certain date may fail to negotiate in the artist's best interest in order to clinch a deal, any deal, before the deadline. In contrast to this tragic affair, I know of one lawyer who, failing to get a fair deal for his client from a major label, broke off negotiations and withdrew from representing the artist, who was eager to sign. The artist may have retained another attorney, but the lawyer who dropped out has a clean conscience—knowing he didn't help sign someone to a terrible deal.

Wait a minute! Maybe you don't want to know much about legal stuff, right? You're too busy being an artist, a creator of sound and vision, unfamiliar with (and uninterested in) the business world. OK, and although I agree that you don't need to master entertainment law, you will eventually—while you stick to making great music— need to hook up with someone trustworthy and knowledgeable regarding music biz deals. As many starving musicians will attest, musical creativity doesn't automatically translate into business expertise. Record companies retain staff lawyers that do everything necessary to protect them, so when signing time comes, you will need representation too.

BLOW BY BLOW

Let's say your band, Blob, has been signed by Hey Now Records. What does this mean? Essentially, and in the charming legalese that lawyers thrive on, Hey Now Records is "hiring your personal services as vocalist and/or instrumental musician in connection with the production of records." Here are three major areas of a recording agreement, reduced to their simplest terms. As a member of the musical group Blob, you will:

1. Record exclusively for the record company for the "term" (length) of the contract;
2. Receive a cash loan ("advance") against future record royalties;
3. Repay this advance ("recoup") through earning a royalty on each record sold.

The specific numbers regarding these subjects (*length* of term, *amount* of advance, *percentage* of royalty) are usually the main focus of negotiations between you and the record label, or more specifically, your lawyer and theirs. Let's explore each of these critical bargaining points in order.

TERMS OF CONTRACT

Agreeing to "record exclusively" for a label is self-explanatory. Without this agreement you could theoretically have three records out on three labels, and be competing with yourself on the charts. You might like this but record labels don't. You can, however, be a sideperson on someone else's record as long as you aren't the featured performer on the selection.

> *Each of the aptly named option periods lasts until eight months after the release of the record specified for the period.*

The "term" of a typical contract is usually expressed not as a specific period of time (for instance, three years from the date of signing) but as a combination of how many records you owe the record company, and how much time must pass between each record's release date. This term is usually set up as an initial period and a sequence of option periods. The *initial period* lasts from the date you sign the recording agreement to eight months after the release of your first record. Each of the aptly named *option periods* lasts until eight months after the release of the record specified for the period. Record companies do this so you can't squirm out of your deal by stalling until your contract runs out. So a "five-album deal" might be in the form of an initial period (your first record) followed by four option periods of one album each. Option means just that: They have the right *but not the obligation* to record and release additional albums, *if they so choose*. If your first record is a flop, it might be your last one with that particular record label.

Options are always more favorable to the label than the artist. Why? Two reasons: You don't have a similar option to leave the label if you choose, and the record company just might get a bargain. If you signed a typical "entry-level" deal with a low-royalty rate and then had a huge-selling first album, the label would happily renew your option: They have a platinum artist signed at an entry-level royalty rate. Record labels' contracts usually include a long string of these options periods to hedge their bet.

MONEY, MONEY, MONEY

Let's talk about the "advance" you receive from the label when you sign. The record label spends money *on your behalf* to create and promote your recording. All of this money must be paid back through the royalty earned by your band, Blob, from each record sold by Hey Now Records. So how is this "advance" written into a contract?

Nowadays this money is actually named the "recording fund," and is designed to cover all the combined recording costs as well as any amounts payable to your band as a personal advance. Recording costs can include a lot more than you may realize—studio rental, tape and related supplies, musician's union scale, in many cases the producer's fee and advances, equipment rental and cartage, accommodations if needed, CD mastering, and all the sushi and beer you scarf while making the record. Although overly simplified, here's a good rule of thumb: If it goes on the record label tab, it will be taken out of your album sales royalties.

Record labels insist on calling this recording budget/artist advance a "recording fund" so that if the recording budget is exceeded for any reason, the artist's advance is automatically reduced.

One nice thing about all of these loans is that if the record flops, you don't have to pay the label back. If you're dropped, they simply write off the money as a business loss. However, if your record sells millions, your record royalties will be used for paying off all the recording and related costs.

WHAT ELSE DO I PAY BACK AND HOW?

What other expenses do record companies pass on to the artist? These can include *independent promotion*, the services of freelance people who have methods of getting records played on key radio stations. Depending on your clout, from half to all of these costs are charged against your royalties.

Tour support is essential for a new band trying to build a following and promote their record. These costs are completely recoupable (you gotta pay it back), and if you use some of the money to buy equipment, the record company will want to own the gear.

This is a good time to explain the miracle of *cross-collateralization*, a concept used by record labels to link the sales performance of one record with the other. According to this method, an album's expenses are not separate financial entities; they are part of your overall debt to the record company. Here's an example. Let's say your first record was a distinct flop: It cost $100,000 to make and only earned $30,000 in royalty income, leaving you in debt to the record company for $70,000. Your second release, which also cost $100,000 to make, is quite successful, generating $120,000 in song royalties. Does this mean you now get $20,000, the profit your second album earned? No. The $70,000 loss incurred by your first record is applied to your overall financial situation, which, according to the label, is simple: $150,000 in, $200,000 out, leaving you $50,000 in debt even though you have a big hit record. Record labels consider this accounting procedure common sense because it is all "money out versus money in" to them. However, this concept also explains how, after two flop albums in a row, a band can finally have a hit record and still be broke. That is why I feel obligated to repeat once again: *Every penny the label gives you is a loan against future record royalties.*

ROYALTIES AND MORE

Labels do all they can to minimize both the number of records they must pay royalties on and the amount of this royalty, which is usually expressed as a percentage of suggested retail list price. For your review, here are some current industry norms for record royalties: new artist signing to an indie label, 9% to 13%; new artist to a major label, 11% to 13%; established artist, 14% to 16%; ultra-mega-bigtime artist, 16% to 20%.

These royalty percentage rates are called "all-in" rates because they include the producer's cut of the royalty, which is usually 3% to 4%. If your "all-in" royalty rate is 10% and the producer gets a 3% royalty on each record sold, your royalty rate is actually 7%.

One of the ironies of today's music scene is that a producer is often a much bigger star than the act he or she is producing. Superstar producers like Mitchell Froom (Los Lobos, Elvis Costello) and Don Was (Bonnie Raitt) often command a 5% to 6% royalty. The record label is willing to pay (that is, loan you) top dollar for a producer with a track record; someone who is recognized in the industry as a known quantity who can guide a young, unproven band (translation: haven't earned $ yet) in a direction already proven to be a commercial success. This, of course, raises all kinds of thorny artistic issues we will purposely ignore for now.

> One of the ironies of today's music scene is that a producer is often a much bigger star than the act he or she is producing.

Suppose, after a highly successful debut album of high-energy rock, your band decides to record an album of traditional Norwegian drinking songs with cello and trombone accompaniment. Will the label have to accept it? No dice. Most recording contracts have a clause stating that in order to be accepted the album must be not only "technically satisfactory" (professionally recorded) but "commercially satisfactory" as well, meaning the label thinks it will sell to your audience. This too is a touchy subject between label and artist, with labels being notoriously narrow-minded in this regard. Ray Charles, known for his definitive R&B style, released an album of country music classics in 1962 called *Modern Sounds in Country and Western Music.* The record company blanched, the marketing people panicked, and the album came out and spent 14 weeks at Number One.

If all of the above seems confusing and complicated, that's because it is. These concepts are part of the everyday machinations of the music business and knowing they exist is part of your growing education. When and if you need to address these specific issues, a good lawyer is a must.

CHAPTER ELEVEN

PERSONAL REMINISCENCE: OUR LAWYER, OUR FAN

The Motels got signed from playing one club. As outrageous as that sounds, it's essentially true. To understand why, you need to know a bit about the music scene in L.A. in 1978. Bands and clubs were springing up in rapid succession. New Wave music was in the air. The Knack had already created a huge buzz in Los Angeles as a live act with their skinny ties, vests, and megapop material, including the unforgettable "My Sharona." I first saw these guys in '78 at a club called Madame Wong's. Essentially a Chinese restaurant on the edge of L.A.'s Chinatown, Madame Wong's had a small stage that was originally designed for a Polynesian song-and-dance revue. By night, Wong's became a rock club, and many bands got their start playing on that tiny stage. The Police played a surprise gig there one night. Bonnie Raitt would drop by and catch our show. Esther Wong, the original 90-pound Dragon Lady, took a genuine liking to The Motels, so we played there constantly, 38 times in all—seven times in one month. We would load up Martha's Checker station wagon with our equipment, drop it off at the foot of Wong's steep staircase, and schlep the equipment up a stair at a time. I remember every step of that staircase. E-v-e-r-y S-t-e-p.

A band called the Kats would often split the bill with us. They featured the Moore brothers: sax player Bobbyzio and singer Freddie, who was often accompanied by his sultry, husky-voiced young wife, Demi. No one knew back then!

One fan we developed was an attorney, Milt Olin, who attended many shows and helped us sort out the growing record label interest. He took a personal liking to the band and offered to help us get a record deal on a deferred-payment basis, which was good, since we were all broke.

L.A. was cooking in 1978-79. After The Knack had sold 5 million copies of *Get the Knack*, an album that cost $6,000 to record, record labels were going nuts, signing almost any L.A. band with their name on a bass drumhead. Label interest could be described as a shark feeding-frenzy. First one label would demonstrate interest in a band, then another. A third label would then court the band, figuring the act must offer something of value if two labels were already interested. Then, as the media reported the "heavy label interest," most of the other majors would become involved, possibly out of pride and competitive spirit more than a genuine interest in the act.

After we'd played about 30 gigs at Wong's, Milt became our legal representation. Capitol Records was the first to show interest, and although we had received many more offers from competing labels in subsequent months, Milt felt that Capitol was the place for us. We began tentative negotiations with them. Meanwhile, we would take various meetings with label reps at a Hollywood Mexican restaurant called Villa Taxco. Many a burrito we ate, as each interested label would play "meet the band" and pick up the tab.

One of the most amusing moments for us was a meeting we took with Joe Smith, at that time head of Elektra Records. He had become interested in the band very late in the game (and it seemed like a game at this stage), so we met at his offices at his request. He was in a time squeeze—he had to leave to catch a plane in about 15 minutes. He gave a very abbreviated and succinct pitch for his label while he repeatedly glanced at his watch, in the end suggesting we get together "in a few weeks and talk about cutting some demos." Ha! A few days later we signed to Capitol Records. Milt's initial instinct—to sign with a label that wasn't playing "follow the leader"—proved correct. Many of the bands signed in the Great L.A. Signing Frenzy of 1979 released one album and were promptly dropped when record sales proved less than fabulous. Capitol stuck with The Motels through two albums that sold only moderately well, and that loyalty paid off on our third and fourth albums, each of which sold over 500,000 copies. We also earned gold album awards from Canada, Australia, and New Zealand. It helped that Capitol was part of EMI, which had a major presence in music markets all over the world.

As our attorney, Milt also arranged for each of us to form our own publishing company, and we retained all the publishing rights to the songs on our albums. A good attorney, especially one who has an emotional investment in your band, can be a tremendous asset when you begin attracting record label interest.

CHAPTER TWELVE
MENTAL TRAPS TO AVOID

He that is without sin among you,
let him first cast a stone.
—Jesus, John 8:7

Working with people is difficult,
but not impossible.
—Peter Drucker

band is many things—a creative endeavor, an exclusive club, a musical outlet, and often a collective shot at the Big Time. No matter how you view it, a band is a specific group of people with personalities. And, dear reader, these personalities have been known to clash. For a band to succeed, each member must be able to appreciate, or at least tolerate, the other members.

This is easier said than done. As a veteran of countless bands (eight), I have noted certain behavior patterns that surface, regardless of musical style, particular lineup, or decade. Recognizing these traits is the first step toward conflict resolution. Every one of the situations and roles listed below is a kind of trap, a counterproductive stance that can be examined and, with any luck, discarded. Recognize anyone? Maybe…you?

THE I'M-IN-FOUR-BANDS MEMBER

This increasingly popular approach was originated and perfected in Los Angeles (Opportunity City) and exported everywhere. Afraid of any commitment to one musical situation, these musicians try to be everywhere at once under the guise of "covering their ass." After all, they figure, one of these bands will succeed, so they're playing it smart. Problem: Each band is only receiving a 25% commitment from this wise one. Scheduling rehearsals and gigs approaches mathematical impossibility. Two or more of these scaredy cats in a particular group are the kiss of death. Possible cure: being fired from all four bands in one week.

THE REVOLVING-BAND-SLOT PROBLEM

For some reason, many bands have one instrumental position—drums, guitar, keyboard, or whatever—that is always being vacated, and then filled by a new musician. Is it bad luck, fate, or some form of karma? Who knows? This problem tends to self-perpetuate for two reasons. First, whoever fills the slot is always the newcomer and rarely feels like a true member of the band. The new member also knows that the band existed before he or she joined and most likely will carry on when he or she leaves. Second, a band often grows used to whatever stylistic quirks the previous member had, making the new member even more of an outsider.

So how does this problem start? Often the band leader has some mythical ideal in mind for the instrumental position that no living, breathing person could ever fulfill. You know: "We're looking for a drummer who plays like John Bonham, and you're just not that guy." Of course, neither is anyone else in the world. Possible solution: Adapt to the new player's strengths and weaknesses and don't compare them stylistically to previous members or pie-in-the-sky ideals. Would you want to be judged by those standards? Try to break the chain of events that leads to the new member feeling alienated and never "good enough." Forget about past players and keep an open mind toward fresh musical input. In fact, the new player may take the band in an unanticipated and highly original musical direction, but only if the rest of the band is willing to stretch and take artistic chances. By the same token, if the new player's personality is compatible with the others, and he or she is open-minded, you may have found your final group member.

THE I-AM-THE-REAL-GENIUS-IN-THE-GROUP SYNDROME

A.k.a. The Tragic Burden of Greatness. This sweetheart is often the chief songwriter, but in many cases the best musician (drums, guitar, lead singer) ascends to this self-appointed throne. Behavior traits include chronic lateness, intolerance for any practical or creative input whatsoever, a deep feeling that the other members are lucky to be working with The Gifted One, and…well, you get it. If these people truly have talent, they hold it for ransom with their personality. Working with one of these tormented souls requires judgment;

maybe they *will* get a record deal. Do you think this will mellow them out? Coping techniques: quitting, buying and using boxing gloves and a heavy punching bag, transcendental meditation. Good luck.

THE I'M-A-GREAT-BIG-BABY PLOY

This person is often the youngest member and may in fact be a gifted musician, making this role a close relative of the Genius Syndrome listed above. Not uncommonly, their degree of talent is usually accompanied by a perfectly matched level of irresponsibility, making it tempting to simply fire the little giggle. Usually late to rehearsals and always late to soundchecks and gigs, unable to perform simple memory tasks such as remembering picks, strings, or spare drumsticks, the "baby" in the band heavily relies on support from other players. After all, the baby will claim, "I'm trying as hard as I can." Babies rarely own a car and often don't or won't drive. What do the other band members get from this situation? A reassuring sense of superiority, since every one of them is more responsible than the G.B.B., plus a strange sense of camaraderie based on mutual tolerance of the G.B.B.'s "I don't wanna grow up" behavior.

> Not uncommonly, their degree of talent is usually accompanied by a perfectly matched level of irresponsibility...

These types often drift from band to band, thanks to their obvious musical talent, only to wear out their welcome as soon as their true personality begins to surface. Possible solutions: a long talk, buying them a wristwatch and alarm clock, chipping in for counseling sessions, bemused tolerance. This is a tough one, because the G.B.B.'s massive insecurity makes confrontation almost impossible.

THE MY-SONGS-AREN'T-TAKEN-SERIOUSLY COMPLAINT

A popular whine. A band has been blessed with a songwriter who has spent years honing his or her craft, working constantly and obsessively. A body of work emerges, creating a musical identity for the band. The group attracts a following based on this serious commitment to writing songs. One night at rehearsal the bass player, who has decided that songwriting is a piece of cake, offers his first composition: "I wrote it in ten minutes!" Popular consensus: yechh! The singer hates the words, the guitarist refuses to learn the chords. Ego crushed, the bassist broods and develops a chip-on-the-shoulder approach to learning new songs. Solution: If you want to be taken seriously as a writer, put in the time. Dabbling in songwriting is a dangerous hobby. Remember, the singer is the one who has to stand up there and do something with those lyrics you're so proud of.

THE ISN'T-THIS-BAND-A-DEMOCRACY? CHALLENGE

Directly related to the previous paragraph. No band is made up of all leaders, yet a band with no leader, either musically or otherwise, is a band with no identity. One person, often in partnership with another, is usually the core around which a band is formed. This core could be anything—songwriting talent, stage charisma, organizational skill, or the "vision thing." Successful bands are not, as a rule, democracies. At best, band members respect and support the leader(s), musically and emotionally, intensifying the artistic thrust of the band. This helps create the "winning team" approach that every successful band embodies. Seriously. If you have a problem with one member having more power in the decision-making process, there is a simple option that's always available: quit. The key member in a band makes the band; if he or she didn't show up for the gig, there would be no gig. In The Police, this was Sting. In The Pretenders, Chrissie Hynde. Apply this simple test to bands you love.

So how do band members work together to make playing in a band a tolerable, even joyous relationship? With humor, or not at all. Try to develop "in-jokes" that make no sense to outsiders. Take turns listening to each other when conflicts arise; sometimes just being heard is remarkably therapeutic. Throw a band party every now and then. Learn to share the joys of working and playing, and more importantly, to share the horrors of that out-of-state gig that paid $27.50, the flat tires in the rain, the where's-the-audience gigs. Ultimately, the aptly named Golden Rule is hard to beat. Loosely paraphrased: Try treating others as you want to be treated. You may find yourself in (Praise God!) a Completely Jerkless Band.

PERSONAL REMINISCENCE: THE VOICE OF EXPERIENCE

I've been in bands with members who exemplified each of the above roles, and I've been a textbook example of a few of those roles myself. My post-Motels R&B band Locomotive had the great revolving-door keyboard slot filled by several players who were in many bands at once, thus combining two roles in one! In fact, I'm getting mad just thinking of how Locomotive's last gig never happened because of that. Grrrr! Here's what went down: I had decided that Locomotive had served its purpose and arranged our farewell gig at a favorite Pasadena venue called Toe's Tavern. I never actually met Toe but I loved his club. In a bittersweet, sentimental mood, I booked the date and began calling my friends, inviting them to the big final blowout. Alas, our keyboard-player-of-the-month couldn't work on that particular night—he had a gig with one of his two other bands. Silently cursing his name, I phoned the club and cancelled, rang all my friends with the sad news, then called on the Lord to give me understanding.

A week later, on the day of the now-cancelled gig, guess who called me? The keyboard player. You know the rest: "Hey Marty, the gig I was going to play with the other band was cancelled, so now I can play your farewell gig. Marty? Marty? Are you still there? Who let out that blood-curdling scream? Hello? Hello?"

FIVE STORIES

If at first you don't succeed,
you're running about average.
—M.H. Alderson

TRUE ADVENTURES IN MUSIC

here are countless ways to be a musician in the music business. However, most of us are only aware of one aspect of an artist's career—the high-profile moments, the so-called "Big Time." What hasn't been revealed as fully is the period before and after the Big Time. This chapter explores not only the Big Time, but a generous share of the time spent on either side.

There is plenty of middle ground between having no employment or artistic success in the music business and experiencing massive fame. For most musicians, life is not an MTV weekend fantasy; it consists of hard work, missed and found opportunities, and the ups and downs of life itself. The stories in this chapter illustrate the myriad ways in which intelligent people have been lured into music's web of delight and disappointment; how they have survived career lows *and* highs, and how early musical experiences left a lasting impression.

If you're at a stage in your musical journey that feels like a dead end or if you think everyone else breezed directly from their first gig to MTV *Unplugged* status, think again. Read the following true adventures in music. Almost without exception every one of these musicians struggled, groped, came close to giving up more than once, yet continued working until—eventually—opportunity did knock. One artist found out his band's audience wasn't in the U.S. at all, but overseas. Another artist switched his career focus to songwriting after a long period as drummer for a very successful band. Yet another tale explores events leading up to the formation of an all-instrumental band with a great gimmick. Our final story traces the lengthy path of a devoted musician whose chance meeting with **171** a talented young singer led to big, big success for both parties. Every one of these stories contains nuggets of wisdom embedded in the narrative. Try to find them.

Los Straitjackets: Playing Music Is Fun

If you ever walk into a club and see four guys onstage playing brilliant surf-music-inspired instrumentals while wearing gold medallions, burgundy turtlenecks, and multicolored Mexican wrestling masks, then you've just encountered Nashville's Los Straitjackets. They drive crowds into a frenzy with their flawless musicianship and antic stage presence. Equally as important, they make a living touring and playing the music they love. The birth and growth of Los Straitjackets only makes sense in looking back; otherwise, it seems to be an utterly random series of events that led to the creation of a highly original and successful band. They did it their way, and it is paying off.

I spoke with Danny Amis, one half of Los Straitjackets' guitar arsenal. A lifelong music fanatic, he grew up in Minneapolis listening to his older brother's record collection, which included instrumental albums by The Ventures, The Shadows, and Link Wray.

MJ: What was your first experience playing in a band?
DA: We were called The Overtones, and we did punky instrumentals. This was back in 1979. The punk ethic was to be unconventional, and I figured playing instrumentals was loyal to that sentiment. We broke up in 1980, and I moved to New York, where I was invited to play bass with my buddies, The Raybeats. They had a big following in Europe. I was the youngest member of the group and I enjoyed the touring and the lifestyle. But all the talk of big dollars and all that stuff went to my head, and I became obnoxious—no one wanted to be around me and I got fired. I learned a lesson, though: You've got to keep everything in perspective, and for someone in their early twenties that can be hard.

After that I got a gig as the sound engineer for [Minneapolis's] Beat Rodeo for a couple years, 1983 to 1984. I didn't know anything about equipment but I knew what sounded good. I still loved playing guitar though, and during the '80s it seems that pop music shifted away from guitars and toward synthesizers and sequencers, which I hated. I figured that Nashville was a place where guitar was still the featured instrument on the music scene, so I went to check it out. I took a guided tour of The Nashville Network and I overheard two stagehands mention that they needed an audio engineer that night. Through sheer luck, I got the gig.

I learned a lot working at TNN for ten years. I met many of the top singers and players in country music. I did a show once with Duane Eddy, Chet Atkins, and Les Paul playing guitar together. I was doing monitors and it was kind of intimidating. Les Paul was plugged straight into the board and he told me to put some delay on it for him, and I'm thinking, "Oh my God, this is the guy who invented it!"

Through working with such a wide variety of artists, I learned that a professional attitude and a real love for music were two keys to success in the music field. Some artists had a good attitude, and some didn't. You could tell by an artist's vibe if they were going to be successful or not. It was a great learning experience.

MJ: Tell me how Los Straitjackets got together.

DA: I was in a club in Nashville one night in 1992 and I heard a band called Lynxtail, who played all these great instrumentals by Link Wray and the Ventures. I was amazed and pleased to find someone playing my favorite style of music in a successful band. I introduced myself to the guitarist, Eddie Angel, who came from upstate New York. During this same period of time I also met a great drummer, Jimmy Lester, who worked in various bands.

> Through working with such a wide variety of artists, I learned that a professional attitude and a real love for music were two keys to success in the music field.

It was a fun project at first. Jimmy and Eddie called me up. Jimmy was playing with Webb Wilder at the time and Eddie was in between groups. We did some instrumentals; we were called The Straightjackets then. We did two or three dates here in Nashville and that was it. It was a short-lived thing because then Jimmy had to go back out on the road and Eddie started another band [Planet Rockers]. Eddie left town for a while, then moved back to Nashville in 1994. I think it was Jimmy who said, "Let's get the Straightjackets back together." It was just a three-piece the first time around, I was playing bass back then, with Eddie on guitar and Jimmy on drums. For the second version we decided to make a few changes. I switched over to guitar since I had a lot of instrumentals I'd written, and we added Scott Esbeck on bass. When the four of us got together and played with Scott on bass it really sounded great, we were kind of amazed at how good we all sounded together, and I said, "Man, we gotta get this on tape, let's go into the studio and record." And about two months later, after we'd rehearsed about four times, we went into the studio and cut the album in a day and a half.

MJ: The record sounds great. Tell me about the recording process.

DA: It was a studio with two Alesis ADATs, synched up to make 16 tracks. Our engineer, Brad Jones, is very good with mike placement and he's got a great sounding room over there. Nothing fancy, we just set up and did it, and my friend Ben Vaughn happened to be in town. He's an old friend of mine, he's put out quite a few records of his own as an artist. Ben has also produced albums by Ween, Charlie Feathers, and Arthur Alexander, and he offered to produce the sessions.

We just went in to cut a demo tape and we laid down 14 songs in a day and a half. We sat back and listened to it and said, "Man, this is good enough to release." Because we cut everything live. So much time is wasted in studios. You can really keep your costs down if you just rehearse the songs, know them, then go in and cut them live. We overdubbed a couple of things, fixed a couple of guitar parts, but that was it.

The rough mixes sounded so good that we hired a professional mixer to finish the project, Roger Moutenot. We decided to shop the songs to labels as a complete album. I started making lots of tape copies, and with Ben's help we targeted indie labels we thought might be interested. Rykodisc and Eastside Digital passed, Hightone and Watermelon wouldn't take my call, and Rhino liked it but were only putting out reissues at the time.

MJ: Did you have a promo kit at the time?

DA: When we mailed the tapes we didn't have the photos ready yet so we sent them out two weeks later, along with refrigerator magnets.

MJ: Refrigerator magnets?

DA: I went into an office supply store and saw these thin rectangu-

lar magnets designed for business cards and thought how perfectly ridiculous it would be to create fridge magnets with our picture on them. I just glued them on.

MJ: I have to ask how you decided on the wrestling masks and matching outfits you wear when you perform.

DA: Eddie and I were trying to figure out a unique way to present the band on stage. So many bands at the time had either the standard "grunge" look or the standard "metal" look, and it all seemed so conformist. We didn't want to look like just any rock 'n' roll band, we wanted to really stand out. I happened to have these wrestling masks. I don't know why I bought them. I got them from a street vendor outside a wrestling arena in Mexico City. Wrestling is a very big deal down there. The wrestlers in Mexico are like superheroes, kids are really into them. I said, "Well, what if we wore these?" It seemed like a good idea, so I went back down and bought a whole bunch more, brought them back, and we found four that fit. And those are the ones we wear.

MJ: So two weeks after the record companies got your tape, they got the fridge magnets and a photo of four guys wearing wrestling masks?

DA: Right. And a label out of Boston called Upstart, affiliated with Rounder Records, went for it. I really liked Upstart's attitude, and they were immediately enthusiastic about our music and our style. Our lawyer said the royalty deal was fair so we signed. They offered us a contract and an advance that more than covered our recording expenses. We called the record *The Utterly Fantastic and Totally Unbelievable Sound of Los Straitjackets.*

MJ: What were your recording expenses?

DA: Twelve hundred dollars.

MJ: How do you tour?

DA: We just pile in the van with our stuff. We don't have a lot of equipment. We don't need a lot of equipment. Nobody needs a lot of equipment. We don't need a P.A. It's really just three amps and a drum set. We just throw that in the back, and we've got enough room in the front. I bought a used 1992 Ford Club Wagon for $10,000, which is the van to tour in, I think. It's the extended one. We've got enough room to stretch out and have all of our equipment. We just rent two rooms at hotels for the four of us. It works.

MJ: Tell me about the unique merchandise you sell at gigs.

DA: After we play and change out of our outfits, we bring out a **175** roadcase with our promo stuff. I figured this stuff added to our image with the masks, so we offer the fridge magnets, buttons, rulers ["Los Straitjackets Rule!"], trading cards ["Collect All Four!"], and coffee mugs. We don't sell our CDs at gigs because we want people to buy them through record stores.

MJ: Is Los Straitjackets what you do for a living?

DA: Yes. We've only been doing this a short time. We're keeping our expenses down, we don't have any road crew with us, we can pile all our equipment and us into one van. I also take care of the business and that makes me the spokesperson since I know what's going on and what's coming up. I use a laptop computer to store itineraries, band income and expenses, and create mailers. I call the booking agent regularly.

MJ: How did you get a booking agent?

DA: I just asked all my club owner friends, "Who's a good booker?" and the Mongrel name kept coming up. We sent Mongrel a CD and told them we were ready to tour. The agency said to look them up when in town, so when our tour brought us to San Francisco, we visited the booking agent's offices, had a beer with them, and let them know we weren't a bunch of 20-year-olds, that we were professionals. They then felt obligated to see us play, and that night we put on a real good show. They signed us up immediately.

> So many bands' songs and attitude seem to be saying, 'Everything sucks.'

MJ: I saw you on the Conan O'Brian show. How did you get on without a manager hustling for you?

DA: Conan's sidekick, Andy Richter, had heard of us through Upstart, and had already used our music as background for some of his comedy routines, so he called our label and we got on the show. We've been on several times since.

MJ: You guys combine excellent music with a hilarious visual act. It's really show biz.

DA: We're there to entertain people. You have to have a positive, professional attitude. So many bands' songs and attitude seem to be saying, "Everything sucks." Well, everything doesn't suck. Playing music is fun.

STAN LYNCH: MANY IRONS IN THE FIRE

By any measure, Stan Lynch has enjoyed enormous success in the music business, if only for the fact that he played drums for 19 years as a member of Tom Petty and the Heartbreakers. For ten albums, Lynch laid down the beat on rock classics such as "Breakdown," "American Girl," "Refugee," "The Waiting," "Stop Draggin' My Heart Around," and more. Armed with plenty of drive, humor, musical talent, and a serious work ethic, Lynch seems to be making the transition from drummer to songwriter/producer with relative ease. His "story" of how he drove from his hometown of Gainesville, Florida, to L.A. in 1975 and gradually built an enviable career in music is a classic example of perseverance meeting opportunity. Now residing in Florida, he travels frequently to L.A. and Nashville, producing records and writing songs.

MJ: What were some of your early childhood music memories?
SL: I remember my father liked Ferrante & Teicher records [two pianos], which I really liked too, and I also remember soundtracks: *The Threepenny Opera*, *The King & I*, and *The Sound of Music*. I especially remember hearing, on my father's Fisher stereo, Ferrante & Teicher playing *Exodus*—the sound of that moved me, it conjured images to me, before I even knew what the word meant, it seemed profound and big.

MJ: What about your first record purchase?
SL: That would be "Whatever Shape (Your Stomach's In)" by the T-Bones [a 1965 instrumental that became an Alka-Seltzer jingle]...I bought it because it had a drum break in it that went "boom bapbap duntduntbap, boom bapbap didididiboomboom..." It turned out to be [studio drummer] Hal Blaine. I bought it and just practiced that stupid fill on my practice pad. It was my first rock record. I was only ten, it was like 1965. I wasn't aware of The Beatles....The first album I bought was Eric Burdon and The Animals. I dug The Rolling Stones' album *12x5*... I didn't like pop music, I liked weirder stuff; I bought [Jefferson Airplane's] *Crown of Creation*. I had a big green mono radio and I would listen to this one station in Miami. I remember at one point thinking, "Wow, there's like seven rock bands! How am I gonna keep track of all of this? There can't possibly be any more. The market is flooded!" I listened to The Lovin' Spoonful, Paul Revere and The Raiders. I remember thinking back then, "These drum parts are as hip as the guitar parts."

MJ: How old were you when you got a kit, and started gigging?

SL: Around 14 or 15. The first gig I had was with Flash and The Cosmic Blades at the Newberry American Legion Hall, the Watermelon Festival. I'd played at several parties, but that was the first real gig. I'd been in knucklehead bands, jam bands, but that was the first gig. After that it was the Styrophoam Soule, an actual working band. We wore dickeys. They had a horn section, so we played Chicago, and Blood, Sweat & Tears, all that bad boogaloo faux black music.

And I was making tons of dough, probably $150 a week, living at home. I financed my first major drum kit, the band had a big-time show, with lights and a big P.A.

MJ: So this is the way that you learned how to play, how you got your chops?

SL: By playing in cover bands religiously, in the Styrophoam Soule, a year and a half, it was three gigs a week 30 weeks of the year, almost like touring—we played five sets a night. I was around 16 years old. I clocked a lot of performance time even before I was out of the eleventh grade.

[At this point, still in high school, Stan hooked up with yours truly on bass guitar and vocals, a certain Steve Soar on guitar, and Road Turkey was born, a three-piece band playing covers and originals. I eventually switched to keyboard, and a four-piece version of Road Turkey played clubs and bars extensively throughout the South from 1973 until December 1974. In February 1975, Stan moved to L.A.]

SL: I was going out there to "make it." I drove my Volkswagen van, with my drumset, my share of the P.A., and $100. A friend of mine in Laurel Canyon let me rent his basement. Back then you could live pretty comfortable in L.A. for $150 a month. And I slept in my van a lot.

MJ: How did you get in a band out there?

SL: Remember MCS [Musicians Contact Service]? I signed up with them as a "drummer that could sing." I got a call from these guys who had moved from Texas, Slip of the Wrist, who were managed by Bill Hamm, who was a big deal—he managed ZZ Top, Johnny Winter…that was their big ploy over the phone. So I drove out to Pasadena, and jammed with them, got the gig, we played bars. I played with them for a year, it was a good life. They were real rock 'n' rollers from Texas, and they really taught me stuff about playing down and dirty, simple, and in the pocket.

MJ: How did you hook up with Tom Petty?

SL: Benmont [Tench, Petty keyboardist] was making demos, and he called me to play drums, then said he needed a bass player, and Ron Blair [first Heartbreaker bassist] was living next door to me. Blair and I went to the session; Benmont had brought [Heartbreaker guitarist Mike] Campbell. We were there to play Benmont's material. I think Petty showed up to play harmonica.

About two weeks later I got a call from Tom, who said quite bluntly, "You want to start a band?" I was kind of interested, but I was torn, because I was in Slip of the Wrist; they were gonna go to Texas and tour. I talked to Slip of the Wrist about it, agonized over it, I told them all up front, "Look, I'm really torn, I wanna do this, these are all old buddies of mine." Mark [Stimpson, SOTR guitarist] was the one who told me to do it, just said, "Look man, if you guys are close to getting signed you oughta do it."

Petty said he had a record deal. Then Tom and I flew to Tulsa and we recorded "Luna" that night, just me and him in Leon Russell's old church recording studio. I played keyboards on it. It was so weird. It was one of the few times Tom and I had any real musical communication other than "Stan, play the drums."

MJ: So then we've got 17 years of you playing drums as a Heartbreaker.

SL: I think it's closer to 19 years.

MJ: At the moment that you left the Heartbreakers, what was going on in your mind, in terms of looking ahead?

SL: I was very scared, frightened. Frightened to death.

MJ: Were you frightened in a physical feeling, like pit in the stomach?

SL: Like curl up on the hardwood floor and cry.

MJ: How long were you totally floored by it?

> It was one of the few times Tom and I had any real musical communication other than "Stan, play the drums."

SL: I'd say a solid year. I just worked my way through it. The only thing I knew how to do was work. I did songwriting, I did that stuff with The Mavericks, with the Eagles, I did that album with Toto. [Stan wrote songs for these artists.]

I had always kept my publishing finger in it the whole time I was **179** with the Heartbreakers, as my side job, to try to get songs cut. In the '80s I did pretty good at it, I got songs cut here and there [by Don Henley, the Byrds, Ringo Starr]. In the '90s I was getting pretty serious about it. The band started doing very little. Tom was only making a record every two years and most of those were solo records. When my relationship with the band was over, it was just time for me to do the other thing more; I just went into it full throttle, my work with Don Henley.

MJ: How did you meet Henley?

SL: Through another musician, Danny [Kootch] Kortchmar. He liked the way I talked, he thought I was a funny, glib guy. He said, "Man, you're one funny motherfucker, man, you gotta start writing this shit down." He sent me to the other room and I started writing this shit down.

And I kind of played a little dumb, I kind of played like, "Oh, I really don't know how to write." Meanwhile, I'd been trying to write, I'd had a publishing deal for ten years. I was trying to keep it kind of fresh, and I kind of bluffed.

And the next thing I knew he said, "You know, Henley and I got this track, we ain't got the words down for it yet. Man, you ought to take a shot at it." I did. It was called "Drivin' With Your Eyes Closed" and it made it on that *Building the Perfect Beast* record [1984].

The next record they were working on, *The End of the Innocence*, I started doing more, and Don was actually asking, "You got any tracks for me?" He solicited my input more, and I came to the party a little more armed for the next record.

MJ: Did your relationship with Henley help you get other gigs in production and writing?

SL: I'm sure it has. It's caused people to acknowledge that I have a life beyond being a drummer.

Kootch said it real well to me: "I can name the drummers on one hand that crossed over from being drummers to other things. It's very rare; so don't get nervous if it's not working fast." He told me it was gonna be an uphill battle.

I remember calling Kootch and saying, "Look man, I'm no longer in the band."

Kootch, without missing a beat, says, "Sounds like you got a promotion to me."

The bottom line is, if you're not doing your own thing, you're doing someone else's thing. Which is cool, if you love it. But when you're bored with it, when you're no longer contributing to the greater good of the project, it's time to move on. Make your move.

MJ: How did record production come about?

SL: By doing demos that people liked the sound of. In the case of Henley, you'd send him a track that he'd write to, and he'd say, "I like that track, let's get in the studio and do it again. What guitars did you use? What kind of pedals did you use? What'd you do?" So you go in to re-create your demo, and by virtue of that, you're "producing." I'm just now starting to get trusted by young bands to produce.

When you cut to the chase, it comes down to this: If you take music as your life's work, you'll never be disappointed. But if you take music and you wonder why you haven't gotten the correct response from it daily, you'll only be disappointed.

You really just take music as a theme park; you don't really know what ride you're gonna get on, you just kind of go, "Fuck it, I'm going to Music Land, and I'm gonna get in there, I'm gonna pay my money," or in this case you just pay your dues, just put your time in, and you get into the park, and you don't know whether you're gonna ride on the Hit Parade roller coaster, or the production Tunnel of Fun, or the drummer Wheel of Fortune, you just get in there and rock out. It's just a big theme park, complete with every huckster and clown and yuckster.

MJ: Was there a particular moment, after the Heartbreakers, that you saw hope for your future in the music business? Name a moment.

SL: I felt really good when the Eagles album was at Number One, I felt good when the song I wrote and produced with them was on the radio ("Learn to Be Still"). At the same time that was on the radio, The Mavericks had a Top Ten [Country] album. I had [written] a Top Ten single ("I Should Have Been True") on a Top Ten Country album at the same time I had a song on a Number One pop album. It was an unbelievable week.

And while this was going on, the Petty greatest hits record was Top Ten too. It felt like I was in business for myself for the first time. It didn't matter if I toured (played drums) with any of them. None of these bands wanted me to tour!

MJ: Any advice to people starting in this business?

SL: If you're a kid and you want to be in the music business, learn as much music as your brain can retain, because you're gonna want it for later. Just when you think that you don't care about that kind of music, somebody's gonna ask you if you've heard it, and how do you help re-create it. So don't be a musical snob. Music is a language, and even words that you think you're not gonna want to know, learn it, there'll come a time when it's just the right word to use. You need to know that stuff, and if you're a snob, you're just going to end up saying, "Yo! Hey! Dig!" And that's what your music vocabulary's gonna sound like and you're gonna become very boring very quickly.

Keep a really open mind; keep a really open heart. It's more than technique. Technique's the part that almost anyone can do. They can put a monkey on the moon! That's easy. Now, how do we make the monkey interesting? That's the hard part. And that comes from the heart, and the way you communicate with people is a big deal in music.

As corny as it sounds, it's not about being just rich and famous. You will get to be "rich and famous" if you're good, but it's a byproduct, it's not the product. You've got to love music.

BOB WELCH: THE ENDLESS CAREER

Bob's tale is complex, unique, and rife with simple moral lessons. It's the story of a guy who grew up in Beverly Hills, whose first love was jazz records, who slowly got the hang of guitar and pop music, and through a remarkably random path found himself in Europe and out of work just in time to join Fleetwood Mac as a singer/songwriter/guitarist. Simple, huh? When opportunity knocked, Bob answered the door, invited it in, and made a big pot of tea.

> This is mostly the story of a talented musician who capitalized on his good fortune.

It's all in here: a genuine love of music, a bit of actual musical training, plenty of experience in playing and recording, shrinking soul bands, career-enhancing phone calls, shifting band personnel, fake bands and lawsuits, lengthy tours, serendipitous meetings, and yes, being in the right place at the right time. This is mostly the story of a talented musician who capitalized on his good fortune. Staying in the game was Bob's strategy. Can you imagine trying to plan in advance any of what you're about to read? Not me, by a long shot.

MJ: How did playing music enter your life?

BW: My dad got me a little three-quarters-size guitar when I was about six years old, and I took guitar lessons from a session guy. His name was Tiny Trimble, a big fat guy. He taught me elementary stuff, "Little Brown Jug," stuff I could play on one string. In elementary school I took clarinet lessons. Then puberty started kicking in. The early rock era was starting and the clarinet was not cool. It was totally a nerd instrument. I was kind of getting embarrassed, with girls and all that stuff, and I remember kind of accidentally on purpose dropping my clarinet case on the playground. I was running to catch a bus, and the case flew open and it broke into a million pieces.

From then on I got my guitar back out, which at that point only had four strings on it. Me and some of my friends and my sister's friends would walk around the beach on Balboa Island singing Ricky Nelson songs at the top of our lungs and stuff. I was 13 or 14.

MJ: What music did you listen to? What was the first record you bought?

BW: The first rock thing of course was Elvis, "Don't Be Cruel." I remember standing in front of the mirror and lip-synching to that. I got interested in Elvis when I was about 15, but nothing serious, just doing imitations. Then toward the end of high school, in L.A., it was all a surf band thing. We used to go down to the Rendezvous Ballroom in Newport Beach and watch Dick Dale and the Deltones when I was 15.

So I began trying to put bands together. I wasn't really thinking about music, but I liked the idea of playing in a band and it was beginning to be the hip thing, and let's be honest, *it seemed like a really good way to get girls* [italics mine] given that I wasn't an athlete or anything.

MJ: I'm hearing this from a lot of people.

BW: A lot of people kind of started that way.

MJ: So when did you finally put something together?

When I was going to UCLA and my friend Tony Lytle called. He had this band up in Portland, Oregon, called Ivory Hudson and the Harlequins, which was a ten-piece rhythm and blues show band. Tony asked if I could come up and try out as the guitar player and I jumped at the chance.

By the time I tried out I had really been practicing. I got the job. It was seven black guys and three white guys. We would do James Brown's whole set. We would do Martha and the Vandellas tunes, we would do an Ike and Tina Turner song, a B.B. King song, a Bobby "Blue" Bland song, real show-stopping stuff.

This was my first professional band. We were playing every night, we made it down to L.A., and we lived there for the next seven years. Ivory Hudson and the Harlequins pared down and changed their name to The Seven Souls, we got a manager in L.A., started playing a lot of the R&B clubs, opening up for Ike and Tina Turner, James Brown, and all the rhythm and blues acts at the time in L.A. We started to become a really big draw on our own in this club in the Crenshaw district of L.A. called Maverick's Flat. On any given weekend we'd have Steve McQueen and Muhammad Ali drop by, people like that. We were a big local draw. Eventually that band broke up, and three of the members formed a trio in 1969 and we all moved to Europe. The trio was called Head West, and we had a record deal in France. For one reason or another there was a lawsuit where our equipment was impounded. It became a big mess, very depressing. So after a couple of years of that, that takes us up to 1971. Head West had folded, they had all gone back to the States.

Fleetwood Mac

BW: I was basically sitting on my butt in Paris wondering what the hell I was gonna do when my old friend Judy Wong called me from London and told me that Jeremy Spencer had disappeared from Fleetwood Mac in L.A. and they needed a guitar player and what was I doing? Well, I was sitting on my butt in my underpants wondering what I was gonna do. I had no band, I was running out of money, I was 26 years old and I felt the walls closing in.

MJ: *Who was this mystery woman?*

BW: Judy Wong was an old girlfriend of mine I had met seven or eight years earlier. She had gone to London in '65 and had gotten to know a lot of people. The Beatles period was happening. She got to know George Harrison's wife at that time, Patti Boyd. Judy was also friends at that time with Patti Boyd's sister, Jenny Boyd, who was Mick Fleetwood's wife[!]. It was kind of an incestuous scene where everybody knew each other. Judy was really plugged into that whole thing over there, she knew everybody, and she said, "Why don't you come over? I can't guarantee anything but I'll introduce you to everybody and see what happens."

MJ: *Were you ever asked to formally join?*

BW: My memory is really hazy on that, not because it was 25 years ago but because of the English habit of understatement. Over a period of a few weeks it became apparent I was going to be in the band, but no one ever said, "Well congratulations, Bob." It was very low-key, very subtle.

MJ: At what point were you starting to write these atmospheric, hypnotic songs like "Future Games"? Where did that come from, how did you demo them and show them?

BW: "Future Games" I wrote in Paris. I had a little Sony sound-on-sound tape recorder which at the time was a real miraculous technical innovation, but a cheap piece of junk by today's standards! I had a bunch of stuff on tape. There were no machines out until about 1969–70 where you could do anything like overdubs or sound-on-sound. On my Sony I could put on a couple harmony parts. The quality was horrible, but I had a few tapes and I could play them in addition to sitting down on guitar and playing, so the way I demonstrated them was probably a combination of both.

I initially really didn't know what they wanted me to do. My first thought was, "Well, they've lost two guitar players in the past two years, so I guess they're looking for a guitar player."

Even more than looking for a guitar player, they were looking for a singer and somebody to contribute material, so they were really interested in hearing my material. And "Future Games" turned out to be the title track of the first album I did with them, which was great. But that was totally unanticipated by me at the time, I had no idea what to expect.

> *I had a little Sony sound-on-sound tape recorder which at the time was a real miraculous technical innovation...*

MJ: And then with Bare Trees *[1972] you had "Sentimental Lady."*

BW: That was a song I had written while on the road with Fleetwood Mac, in New York, one that at the time I thought was really good, and they seemed to really like it. It was not the kind of thing that Fleetwood Mac had been doing but it really fit in the context of what was going on in 1972.

One Step Beyond

[Bob made five albums as a member of Fleetwood Mac, including 1973's *Mystery To Me*, which included "Hypnotized," a Welch-penned tune that still receives considerable airplay 23 years later. By 1974, however, legal hassles and general burnout ensued. It was time to move on.]

BW: So I kind of made up my mind I was gonna quit. I felt if I ever wanted to take a shot on my own, now was the time. At the same time Mick had found Lindsey Buckingham and Stevie Nicks and Mick said, "Why don't you stay in the band and maybe we could add them to it." Everyone agreed Fleetwood Mac needed some fresh input, because everybody was exhausted from the lawsuit and five years of nonstop touring. I kind of went back and forth and then decided, no, I'd leave.

So I left and decided to do this three-piece band called Paris. It was a hard-rock thing. We wanted to be Led Zeppelin, which is another reason I left Fleetwood Mac. I wanted to do more energetic music at the time, I really liked what Led Zep was doing.

So Capitol signed Paris, and we made a couple of records. Then Hunt Sales, the drummer, got a bad case of something called Bell's Palsy, so he couldn't play for six months, and during that six months I was sitting out in my apartment in Malibu writing all the songs that turned out to be the songs on *French Kiss*. That album was initially the third album in the Paris record deal. The deal was rewritten because Paris was officially disbanded. Paris just kind of gradually faded away.

Fleetwood Mac's promotion man was also promoting a band that was becoming huge, called Boston. Boston had this sound, a real formula thing that Tom Scholz had thought up, and I said to myself, "This is what I wanna do. I'm not gonna mess around with any eclectic, jumping-all-over-the-place, sounds-of-my-soul, music-of-my-mind type of deal. I'm gonna do a bunch of songs that are all consistent from one to the other, where there's a continuous thread running through the whole album like the old Motown albums used to be, like the Boston album is."

So I wrote a whole bunch of these songs, including "Ebony Eyes," which was a cannibalization of a whole bunch of different tunes and so on, and went over to [record producer] Carter's house one day and played him a whole bunch of stuff, and he said, "God damn, every one's a hit—let's go in and cut some of these things."

So Carter introduced me to [session drummer] Alvin Taylor, and we went in the studio and cut a bunch of stuff. Me and Alvin cut the basics with me playing a scratch guitar track, and then I put the real guitars on and played the bass too because this is what I'd done at home.

Christine McVie came in and sang some vocal parts, Stevie Nicks sang on some things, and Lindsey Buckingham and Christine—or maybe it was Mick Fleetwood, who at that point was my manager—decided to do one of my old Fleetwood Mac songs.

So we did "Sentimental Lady." It was pretty much Fleetwood Mac playing but it was going to be a Bob Welch record. Mick played drums, John McVie played bass, and Lindsey produced all the guitar things. It was lot of fun, and that was the one track that kind of stood out from the other tracks on *French Kiss* but in a really good way.

The general consensus at Capitol was that this could really be something. Me and Michael Seibert [Capitol promo guy] played the tape in advance for a lot of program directors. We went out at Capitol's expense and hyped all these record guys on the fact that the record was coming out.

Of course it didn't hurt that Fleetwood Mac had a Number One record at that point and that Mick was my manager. It was just one of those magical times. Fleetwood Mac's success was working for my benefit, and I like to think that my later success with that album helped them, and everything was just a big, wide, wonderful world. It was a big carwash, everybody splashing in there together.

I made four more albums on Capitol and two more on RCA. Work work work work. I ran into my share of problems, I ran into the disco era, and the great record company recession, which was '79–'80. After the disco era and the recession you had simultaneously the great Punk Revolution and then Fleetwood Mac and people like me and Steve Miller and Peter Frampton, we were like ancient history. I had a problem in how to define what my image was going to be. I liked certain elements of the new stuff but I wanted to keep certain elements of the old stuff. That was a pretty confusing time.

MJ: *How have you remained interested in music this long?*
BW: Only by taking the injections that I get every week (laughs). To be honest, I've gone through periods where I really hate music, **187**

where I can't stand the scene, the business, it seems phony and ruthless and stupid, and why would anybody…I mean, we're not curing cancer, why would anybody really give a shit?

The pop music scene can be really limiting. If you did have to exist on a pure diet of who's got the latest record out, what sounds are they making, what's the latest pop thing—and I did that for years—you'd go crazy. Anybody would.

If you open yourself up to those other areas [of music] it really provides perspective, and creative fuel. I find it very inspiring. One day I decided to give myself a challenge, there was about five minutes of *Madame Butterfly* that I really liked, so I said I'm gonna transcribe it, that's what everybody's supposed to do in music school, and I missed out on that. So I sat down for five days and did that. And it really gives me satisfaction, it's just pure satisfaction, it's got nothing to do with money, or a hit record, it's just pure

> …I just wanted to play onstage every night because I loved doing it.

musical goodness. And that's refreshing, and then you can try to write a song after that and feel like your brain has been kind of washed clean.

MJ: What kind of encouragement or advice would you give a kid who wants to play in a successful band? What should be the approach?

BW: Well, the way I first got into music, I just stumbled into it and it was just something I loved. I never thought more than one day ahead. I didn't have a career plan, I didn't know about gold records, sellout crowds, and groupies—I just wanted to play onstage every night because I loved doing it. I just loved playing guitar and being onstage. I didn't even know why I loved it. Later on I figured out, well, maybe it's because there's cute girls in the audience, and later on in Fleetwood Mac because we're making money at it. That's just a secondary effect; it's got to come from the heart.

Now it must be very confusing for younger kids, because there's magazines and MTV and it's been picked apart, and it seems like you gotta have the attitude first before you even care about playing your instrument.

I don't think that's the right way to go about it. You've just gotta love singing or playing your instrument or writing songs. You have to not care about wanting to be famous, about wanting to be rich, about wanting all the adulation and groupies and all that junk.

You don't necessarily have to have the Number One record in the country and the Number One band in the country to have a life in the music business.

CHRIS ECKMAN: SEEK YOUR AUDIENCE

You've never heard of The Walkabouts? That's OK, neither has most of America. But in Europe, where they have sold over 240,000 records, this Seattle-based rock band is a big deal. Ironically they don't even have an American record deal. Sometimes in order to find your audience you not only have to leave your hometown or state, you even have to leave the *country*! Group leader and chief songwriter Chris Eckman's story is one of persistence, many record company entanglements and complications, chance encounters with young record company execs, and a love for music that rather quickly separated him from a promising academic career. Find out how a young man and his band, described by their label as "hippies with big amps," built a successful career in Europe. I spoke to Chris at a Seattle recording studio where he was producing a Norwegian rock group who had flown over to work with him. As you will see, there is no such thing as a typical story. Truth is always stranger than fiction.

MJ: How old were you when you first picked up an instrument?
CE: When I was about ten I got my first guitar—it was a cheap acoustic. I took lessons for about four months, but the lessons were on Monday nights, and I had to miss Monday night football, so I eventually quit!

I stopped playing guitar till I was 15. Then I knew I wanted an *electric* guitar. I was saving money from a summer job I had, because I knew my parents would never buy me an electric guitar and amp. Then somebody tipped me that if you bought something at a pawn-shop, there's no way you can take it back. So I went down to a pawnshop and bought an amplifier and a guitar. And of course I brought it home and the first thing my Dad said was, "We're going down there and get your money back," and I said, "I bought it in a pawnshop, you can't do anything about it!"

I went to college in eastern Washington, and my first band was this punk rock spoof band. We played originals but also did covers like "Sweet Jane" and "I'm So Bored with the U.S.A." by The Clash. This was around 1979.

That summer I went up to Alaska to work at a fish cannery and I met Carla [Torgeson, vocalist and guitarist for The Walkabouts]. This place was about 300 people stuck on the edge of a peninsula in the middle of southwest Alaska. We were the only two people who had guitars, and after a couple weeks of seeing each other walking around with our guitars we said, "Let's get together and play." So we did. She played all this folk music, most of which I had removed from my record collection, and I was playing these originals, and listening to punk rock. We'd sit at the table and kind of stare at each other trying to figure out how this was supposed to work. We were there for a couple months, and we fell in love, we had this relationship.

And all this while my two brothers were playing in punk rock bands as bass player and drummer, and in 1984 we all ended up in Seattle together, so we said, "Let's try being in a band."

At this point, I had graduated with a B.A. in philosophy, and I was offered a full scholarship to go on and get my Ph.D. So I was thinking, I've always wanted to do the band thing, I'll just play a couple of club shows, then I'll go back to school and do all that. Of course, that never happened, because I started doing the band, and…I just sort of fell in love with that.

Our first gig in The Walkabouts was a barbecue party. We recorded an EP in 1985, put it out ourselves, and sent it out to college radio stations. It was called 22 Disasters. The title provided us with the worst review we've ever had in the history of the band. It was a one-line review from I think *Rockpool* magazine out of New York—it was like, "26 disasters, if you count the members of the band."

First Album

At that point, it was crazy, but we took out a bank loan to finance recording an album. It was $5,000. We'd already lost $3,000 on the EP. It took us almost a year to finish the album. We'd do it after hours, and squeeze into different places to do it, and when it was done, I saw Jonathan Poneman [cofounder of Sub Pop record label] on the street, and I asked him, "What label should I send this to?" and he said, "There's a label in Los Angeles called Wrestler Records," so I sent off a tape and literally a week later the guy called up and said, "I want to do this album," and we were just ecstatic. He said, "I'm gonna give you $5,000 for it," and I thought that's exactly what we'd paid for it, amazing.

But it turned into an absolute disaster; a year later we ended up getting the master tapes back from him. He never did anything with them, we signed a contract and he just didn't act on it. He never gave us the money, nothing exchanged. In the end our bass player's mom, who was studying law, posed as an attorney, went into his offices, and basically seized the tapes.

By around 1985–86 we had started playing clubs in Seattle, and we'd get about 100 people out—it seemed like things were moving forward. Then we went through a period, after this album *hadn't* come out, when our enthusiasm for the whole project was running really thin. We had played a show at a club and there were like 40 people, and we used to get 100. So we had a band meeting and said, "This is it. This has been fun, but we're moving backwards now, there's no sense in doing this." We had about $500 saved up in a band account, so we said, "Let's go into an eight-track studio and let's record the set we have now, and at the end of this we'll hand everybody a tape and say OK, it's been fun."

> We had played a show at a club and there were like 40 people, and we used to get 100.

And we went into this studio and then we started getting into it, we spent $500 and then we borrowed another $500 and kept patching together this project. At the end of it we took it to a friend of ours, Conrad Uno [of Popllama Records], he heard it and said, "If you resequence this thing, this is actually an album—I'd be happy to put it out." So what became our final demo was really our first album, *See Beautiful Rattlesnake Gardens*.

We got a few good reviews, a year passed, this is around 1988 now, and we got $1,500 together to record our second album. And we just went ahead and recorded it. We brought it to Conrad, and he said, "I'm losing money on everything I've got right now, I can't do it."

Meanwhile, Sub Pop [indie label who signed Nirvana] had just started, and our drummer Grant was working at Muzak along with Bruce Pavitt [co-founder of Sub Pop]. Grant takes this tape of our second album, *Cataract*, to work one day, and Bruce Pavitt says, "I'm quitting work next week, we're moving into offices; this is really turning into a real record label." So Grant says, "Maybe you want to hear this." And Bruce comes to work next day and says, "OK, we'll put that out."

So now we're on Sub Pop and we do this van tour, playing for 20 people.

In 1989 we did a six-song EP called *Rag and Bone*, and finally this one was paid for by a record label [laughs]. And that came out on Sub Pop, and we got a small booking agency out of New York.

MJ: How did you get a booking agent?

CE: Because we'd gotten reviews, even *Cataract* got reviewed in *Rolling Stone*, and *Spin*, so at this point we're starting to get a little buzz. While this is happening, Sub Pop is branching out into Europe, and we kept walking into Sub Pop every week saying, "You should send us to Europe," and they're like, "Nothing's happening for you there, all in good time." But finally, in the spring of 1990, they say, "OK, you can go over there, but you're gonna have to spend nine weeks for it to even come close to breaking even." And we went to Germany for the first time, we played for maybe 40 people, but we thought it was great, "Hey, there's 40 people in Cologne who know who we are, this is great." And we played all over Europe really, and ended the tour opening up for Tad and Mudhoney in London, I think we had like 20 minutes onstage.

But it became very clear that there was something happening for us there. We were doing all kinds of interviews; people wanted to talk to us. We just had this suspicion that it could actually work for us in Europe.

Europe Calling

In 1990 we recorded an album called *Scavenger*. At this point Sub Pop were negotiating a deal with Columbia Records involving four bands—each band was gonna get $40,000 to record a "real" album. So we hired this producer Gary Smith who had worked with The Pixies, The Chills, Throwing Muses. But still no contract with Sub Pop, who were still negotiating with Columbia. But they come up with the money, and halfway through the recording of the album, I get a call from Jonathan Poneman saying, "The Columbia deal is dead; we're going to stay independent."

And my stomach just dropped. We had this $40,000 record coming out on Sub Pop, and we'd never sold more than six or seven thousand copies of any album we'd done for them, and we still have no contract with them. So we say, "For everyone's sake we should find another label, this is too expensive of a load for you guys to carry, no one's ever gonna make their money back on this one." They agreed, and we spent almost a year trying to get on another label, but it didn't work. So in the end it comes out on Sub Pop, we do a tour through America, and Sub Pop is at the point where they're virtually bankrupt. Our records are sitting on the loading dock, they're not in the stores, they haven't been serviced to the press, we're out on the road, I'm ready to quit. Then [drummer] Grant announces he's quitting the band. We go back to Europe in winter 1992 to promote *Scavenger*, and the first show we played sold out, 550 people, in Germany, and we're thinking, "They told us nothing was happening over here for us!" The guy from Sub Pop Europe walks in the door with this stack of press one meter high, and says, "This album, everybody loves it, we've sold 16,000 copies of it, it's doing fantastic." So we go to Denmark—sold-out shows—and now we're thinking like, "Pinch me, when is this gonna blow up?" But it was really happening.

So we signed with Sub Pop Europe and released *New West Motel* which came out in 1993. And we went back to tour that album with no American record deal, and the shows went really well. Now this album's selling 25,000 copies.

And that's really our story at this point. Between then and now we still haven't been able to get a U.S. deal but each album we release in Europe sells more than the last one. We did an album called *Satisfied Mind* in 1993 that sold about 25,000 copies, then did one in 1994 called *Setting the Woods on Fire* that did 34,000.

Beyond Indies

At this point it became very clear that we had maxed out the Sub Pop thing, so we spent most of '95 negotiating a deal with major labels and we signed to Virgin in 1995 for all of Europe, but still nothing in America.

MJ: How does it feel to be an American band, living in America, and your audience is in Europe?

CE: When you're there it doesn't seem that strange because you're just a band and you're written about in the press and you go into a town and open up a paper and there's a big spread on The Walkabouts, so it all seems to make sense. It's only strange when you're here. It's not as hard for me as some of the other people in the band because I spend a lot of time in Europe doing business and other things, so I'm always getting this…"stroke" in a way. Frankly, it's nice to come back here and not have to be in a band, I can just be the guy, just walk around.

But it's strange. As much as I'd never trade the modest success that we've had over there, it is frustrating at times to think that you can't play in your own country. Because I don't think what we do is that esoteric.

MJ: Why do you think it's not working here?

> We drive around in a big tour bus in Europe with a road crew, and obviously if we came to the States at this point we'd have to start over.

CE: Number one, I think labels have it pretty well figured out what our gig is. We drive around in a big tour bus in Europe with a road crew, and obviously if we came to the States at this point we'd have to start over. And the labels know in their hearts we wouldn't do that, and we probably wouldn't. It's pretty obvious that we're not going to rent a van and go around for nine weeks and play for 20 people. And also, in a way, in some circles we're considered old news over here, we kind of missed our chance. So we're looked at a bit, I think, as damaged goods.

MJ: When do you think that chance was?

CE: In 1991, if *Scavenger* had done well. That album had everything going for it: It had Natalie Merchant and Brian Eno on it, had the hot "alternative rock" producer, everything about it was set up to take us to another level, which it did—in Europe—but it didn't work here. So that was our chance, come and gone. Whereas in Europe we doubled our sales; our last album, *Devil's Road*, sold 70,000 albums.

 MJ: What advice do you have for bands who are starting out?

CE: Do your own thing, don't worry about conforming to the

industry, because things come and go. If you're gonna be in it for the long haul it's best to just go inside yourself and find that thing that you want to do.

I think the worst thing a lot of young bands get caught up in is this idea that if you're not signed, and you don't have management, and you don't have any of this in the first six months, your whole career is a failure. Don't think of it as a career; think of it as something you do for your own reasons first. Because if things move on, you'll have plenty of time to think about it as a career, because it just becomes insane, the whole business side of it will almost dominate what you do. Unless you're really in touch with what you do artistically, that can really drag you down. So be into it for your own reasons.

PETE ANDERSON: "ALL I CARED ABOUT WAS MUSIC"

Pete is the musical partner and producer of Dwight Yoakam, a gifted singer and songwriter who took the music world more or less by storm with his first release in 1986 and has built a solid, successful career on his own artistic terms.

Without Pete Anderson's arranging and producing skills, Dwight Yoakam wouldn't have sold over 12 million records worldwide. Without Dwight's singing and songwriting talents, Pete wouldn't have so quickly built his career as a top producer and widely recognized whiz guitar player. The mutual support they give each other is a classic (and classy) example of how two people's collective raw talent, determination, and "people skills" can help forge great careers in the music business.

Pete: The Early Years

MJ: What was your first memory of music that moved you?

PA: I think the biggest impact was the fervor that Presley made. I remember seeing him on *The Ed Sullivan Show* when I was eight and thinking, "This is cool." I remember listening to popular music back then and the first 45 I bought was "Peggy Sue" by Buddy Holly. The first album that I bought was probably *Loving You* by Elvis Presley.

MJ: When did music kick in for you profession-wise?

PA: When I was about 17. I started a jug band. I didn't have a good ear for music, it was always difficult for me, but I had a lot of desire. We played coffeehouses, parties, we were the Turnpike Travelers, then changed it to the B-52 Blues. [Laughs.] Yeah, they ripped me off! I started getting into Dave Van Ronk, Buffy Sainte-Marie, and Tom Rush. Joni Mitchell was a local musician you could see for free, at the time, there in Detroit, back in '65, '66. She had written "The Circle Game."

MJ: What happened for you musically in the ten years between then and when I met you in L.A. in 1976?

PA: I really loved the guitar and got into the blues, bought a Silvertone guitar at a pawnshop. I remember seeing the Paul Butterfield Blues Band at a club called the Chessmate. I was blown away. I immediately bought the album, called up my friends and made them sit in my room and listen to it. And that album was full of liner notes about Elmore James, B.B. King, Albert King, all these people, and I just went to the record store and started looking for these people's records.

In '68, I quit my job, packed everything I had in a Volkswagen convertible, and drove from Detroit to Phoenix. I started going to jam sessions at the Fireside Chalet. In the back window of the bar was a skating rink, so when you were sitting at the bar you looked out and could see people skating. There was a jam session every Sunday, so I went there like a dog, I was there from the minute it started to the minute it ended, around 1 a.m.

I stayed in Phoenix till '72, had a bunch of blues bands, ran my course there. In the spring of '72, I moved to L.A. I started going around to guitar stores, and got a job working at a music store, Betnun Music, back in 1975, where I met you.

Four and a Half Hours to Change the World

MJ: You were an OK guitarist when I knew you at Betnun's, but you got a lot better. How?

PA: I went to GIT [Hollywood's Guitar Institute of Technology] and was working country music gigs, so I could go directly at night and apply what I'd learned that day at the gig. I would say, "Well, 'Silver Wings'—let me play a major scale harmonized in thirds for my solo."

MJ: So that's how you learned how to play, by playing bars in the San Fernando Valley?

PA: Yup. There was a key gig in there. Late summer of 1979, a booking agent gave Rick Tucker, a bandleader, my number. His guitar player was leaving and he needed a replacement. He called me up, said come and play. The club was called Mike's Pizza in Simi Valley, a big pizza parlor with a huge dance floor like a honky tonk. Rick's band was a four-piece: drums, bass, acoustic guitar, and electric. This guy made a living playing music. He worked Wednesday through Saturday at Mike's Pizza. Every other Sunday, Monday, and Tuesday he worked at a place called O'Mahoney's in Santa Monica. So what would happen is you'd play four days in Simi Valley, three days in Santa Monica, your gig would start right up again at Simi, so you'd play 11 days in a row and you'd have three off. So it was 11 on, three off.

> *♪ don't listen to anyone else when ♪ play in a band, just the snare and the hi-hat.*

Rick Tucker was a plethora of music. And he never had a set list; someone would come up and say, "Hey Rick, do a Beatles song!" And he'd just do five in a row! "Do Conway!" We'd do six Conway Twitty songs. So I had to know everything.

The thing about this band was, first it taught me to listen to the drummer. I don't listen to anyone else when I play in a band, just the snare and the hi-hat. Second, it taught me to practice. Basically I was practicing four hours a night, 11 nights in a row, and I remember July of '78, we played one full month, we played every day and twice on the weekends, so we were playing nine gigs a week for a full month. And if that's not a chop-builder I don't know what is.

I'd wake up and start working on my guitar, polish it, change the strings, clean it. Make sure my clothes were pressed, that I looked sharp, my clothes were tailored, my gear was right, my strings were right, case was perfect, my cords were wrapped, everything's packed, get ready to go, clean up, go to the gig, and my whole thing was, I had four and a half hours to change the world with my guitar every night in this club, and that's how I looked at it. I wanted to have everybody's attention when I played, not by outrunning the band but by being creative in the band format.

Dwight and Pete Meet and Create Heat

MJ: How did you hook up with Dwight Yoakam?

PA: I eventually got fired from the Rick Tucker band; he felt uncomfortable with me in the band after a while. So I took a left turn. I thought, "This stuff sucks, it's not even real country music anymore, what should I play? R&B." I became a guitarist for hire, whoever picked up the phone and called me, I'd work for them.

I had a pickup gig in the San Fernando Valley at a place called Ryan's Roundup, where I was playing in a band with a steel player called Boo Bernstein, and he was a mutual friend of me and Dwight's, so Boo invited Dwight to come and sing at this bar one night. He came in and sang a couple of Merle Haggard songs, and I think he was impressed because I knew the real licks to "The Fugitive" or something. He needed a guitarist, so he called me up. I went over to his house, listened to some of his songs. The songs were good but the singing was too affected, yet the lyrics and the way they were put together was really exceptional. We'd talk about stuff, and he was real green about things, "What's publishing? What's producing? What's record deals? How does all this stuff work?" I was 34, I'd been around the block a few times, so I started filling him in on stuff I'd learned about the business. I also remember encouraging him with his songwriting, saying, "Look, you've written really great songs here. The lyrics are great, nobody writes like this anymore." He was writing bluegrass, really straight Merle Haggard, country kind of stuff.

Don't Back Down

PA: I think Dwight always had confidence in himself, but two people having confidence in what you're doing can be really strong. One person, you can do it, but people can beat on you. When there's two there's really strength in numbers, and just two makes a big difference.
MJ: So you supported him in a very basic way.
PA: Yeah. We played clubs, playing his material and other material. It was a pretty good band, we could play bluegrass and rockabilly and stuff. It was more aggressive than my other country gigs. Dwight was very aggressive on the guitar. He's a good bluegrass flatpicker, and he can play real straightforward.

We consciously decided to add a fifth piece—we got a fiddler, and we started playing clubs and getting fired from every club because we wouldn't play the popular tunes, and I remember sitting down with Dwight and saying, "Look, you've got a great voice. Learn five of the popular songs. We'll play them at the auditions, we'll get the gigs, we'll play them whenever people request them and then we'll do whatever we want."

And he was like, "No, I don't want to do that, I just want to play my songs." This is in 1983, there wasn't a showcase scene for what we do, so I said, "You're talking about basically playing these clubs for free to play one set of your own music." Dwight said, "Well, that's what I want to do." And I said we should make a record.

We got into a studio behind a sewing machine shop on Ventura Boulevard, and hired an engineer. We cut the EP that became *Guitars, Cadillacs, Etc. Etc.*

In the meantime we were playing more and more. It finally got to where we could headline the Palomino and draw some people and we were creating a buzz in L.A. Steve Berlin, who was playing with The Blasters, not Los Lobos back then, saw us and said "You guys should play some gigs with us." The Blasters and Los Lobos were kingpins of the roots-rock scene, but they were always wanting to help people out. We ended up going to New York and Houston and Austin and opening for The Blasters, and that was really what put us over the top.

By the time we got to Austin, Paige Levy had called up from Warner Brothers, and she was really serious; she'd gotten the record, read the press, and wanted to see us and was interested in signing us. She saw us play at the Austin Opry House, thought it was great, and basically went out of her way to force Warner Brothers to sign us, in 1985.

Make Them Records, Boys

PA: The way that Dwight and I make records now? He'll call me on the phone and start playing his acoustic guitar and say, "Here's a song." He'll say, "Check this out," and he'll have a verse and a chorus, and I'll say, "Wait a minute," and I'll grab my guitar and say, "What if you do this?" and so on.

MJ: So you do it over the phone, even though you both live in L.A.?

PA: Yeah. We'll do it on the phone until I get a long list of 10 or 12 songs, and then I'll come over to his house, bring the list. We'll go through them. I'll say, "Play this one, play that one," and we'll think of drum beats, and styles we're both familiar with, like "Buck Owens" or "Merle Haggard" or "Johnny Cash" or "Gerry and the Pacemakers," whatever. We'll think of things in common, or grooves we think would work. And we'll just brainstorm, and I'll just make lists, and I write my comments down by the song titles until we feel **199** we have a really strong list of 10 to 14 songs, maybe a cover or two. We'll call up the guys, we've been doing this with for ten years, go into a rehearsal room, and he'll start banging on them; either Dwight or I will talk about what we envision for the drum beat.

MJ: Describe the room you use.

PA: It's a rehearsal room in North Hollywood, with a small one-foot-high stage and good monitors, very woody and cabin-like, junky kitschy handmade looking place. The whole band is there; bass, drums, keyboard, myself, fiddle, and mandolin, and the keyboard player plays accordion, organ, piano, and samples for synth sounds. Dwight on acoustic. We set up somewhat like a live gig, only Dwight faces the drummer instead of the far wall, sort of in a circle. So we play the tunes, brainstorm ideas, and tape everything with a DAT. And we time things too, with a stopwatch. We use a click track, that only the drummer hears, so we can put in a number for tempo.

> We've had a great run. I've had worse jobs that have paid less.

MJ: How many records have you done this way?

PA: All six of 'em. We've done eight altogether, one's a greatest hits, one's a live album. *Guitars, Cadillacs, Etc. Etc.* is over double platinum, *Hillbilly Deluxe* is platinum, *Buenas Noches from a Lonely Room* is platinum. The greatest hits record, called *Just Lookin' for a Hit,* had two new songs on it, that's close to platinum. Then we did *If There Was A Way*, that's almost double platinum, then *This Time*, that's double platinum heading for triple. We did a live record called *Dwight Live* that went gold, and then we did the new record called *Gone*, which is at about 750,000.

We've had a great run. I've had worse jobs that have paid less.

Philosophically Speaking

MJ: What have you learned over the years regarding playing, recording, and producing music that you feel has contributed to your success?

PA: In general, a producer has to leave his ego at the door. And it's difficult for an artist, but an artist has to subjugate his ego in the studio. And if two people are willing to do that, you have a good chance of making a great record.

You cannot make decisions based on your ego, you have to make sound decisions on what's right or wrong musically. Once I learned to control my ego, my producing got a lot better. I didn't always have to have the right idea, the idea that worked; I didn't care where it came from. Once I learned to encourage people who had a lot of good ideas, and not feel threatened by that, everything got better for me.

MJ: What advice would you give to someone starting out in the music field who would like to do some of the things you've done?

PA: The hard brutal truth? Be as objective as you can about yourself. The most important thing you can do or be is find out who you are as soon as possible. The earlier an age you figure out what you should be doing and where you should be going, the faster you'll get there.

My story is, I originally thought I was going to be a recording artist. But that's not where my talents lie, and if I'd known somewhere along the line I was going to go in this direction I might have ended up here earlier. I think it's dangerous to follow a muse that you don't have the credentials for. You're gonna come to the point where you go, "You know, I just don't write songs as good as these other people, so maybe I'm not gonna be a songwriter; maybe I'll be a bass player, or a road manager, or a booking agent." It depends on how far away from the center you fall.

MJ: What were you true to that made your life in music work?

PA: I never gave up on my dream. The thing that drove me the most was some kind of self-determination to be in control of my own destiny, which is basically self-employment. I tried to follow my muse, and to shed off the parts of me that didn't work, and continued to be honest about myself as an artist, a singer, a songwriter, a producer, and arranger as I went along, in relevance to my peers and other people that are doing what I'm doing, and comparing myself in an honest fashion.

MJ: Any last thoughts?

PA: Don't try to be something you're not. You need to be honest with yourself, and that's very difficult. It's a brave stance. You've got to be brave. If you're five foot two, you're not gonna dunk a basketball, it's not gonna happen. To find your space takes a lot of thought, a lot of self-analysis. Try to control your ego, work on your people skills.

We don't live in this world alone, we all interconnect with other people. I don't know anybody that does it by themselves. There's people that want it to appear that they do, but if you were a fly on the wall, you'd see that nobody does it by themselves.

CONCLUSION

The thing is to be able to outlast the trends.
—Paul Anka

W hat can we conclude from this vast swimming pool of information you waded into at Chapter 1, only to emerge dripping and shivering here at the deep end? Here, towel off and relax while I ruminate.

As you now know, there is a vast body of practical knowledge that is helpful as you start a band and keep it going in the direction you choose. We have covered plenty of this nuts-and-bolts stuff—technical territory involving shopping for equipment, preparing to record and recording, an overview of music copyright and publishing, making your own record, and other mostly material concerns. Now it's time to get a little, well, philosophical.

PLAYING IN A BAND CAN BE A JOB

For most people, a band starts out simply as a way to have fun with music. But many bands begin to build on the surprising energy that can spring from this "just for fun" attitude, going on to a full-fledged career in the music business. Yes, playing in a band can actually become a job, just like being a car salesman or bank teller. This concept is sometimes hard to grasp when you look around the rehearsal room at your "coworkers." But think about it for a minute: You work together as a team, with each player performing a specific task (drums, bass, guitar), you create a product (music and entertainment), and you get paid for this artistic output (never enough). If you begin thinking of playing in a band as a job, in fact a job you would like to keep, a job you love, then you may change your attitude toward certain aspects of your involvement. You'll get serious about how you organize rehearsals, how you promote gigs, writing songs, showing up on time in general, how you handle band finances—in short, you treat it like a business. The lifestyle aspects of being in a band can overshadow this business approach, and this is normal. In fact, there are two personality types inherent in each band member to varying degrees. I call these extremes the Lifestyler and the Musician.

The Lifestylers want to play in a band mainly because it looks cool. Fair enough. They like the idea of guitars and keyboards and drums and hair and wild clothes and having a practice place and driving around in a van and feeling like a member of a private club, which is in fact what a band is. They might be merely passable as musicians, and that may not matter.

> It is the hard work that produces the great songs, albums, and live shows, not some sort of magic.

The Musicians love listening to, playing, and writing music. They want to be in a band because it provides a greater outlet for their musical expression, as a player, a writer, or both. For them, it's an indescribable thrill to write a song and hear it performed by their band, or anyone else for that matter.

Most band members share a blend of Lifestyler and Musician traits, and since a band is (literally) a group effort, not everyone needs to be as fixated on music as the pure Musician, nor as fixated on clothes and attitude as the Lifestyler. Both are OK as long as the sum total of all these traits within a single band adds up to something original and entertaining.

I've talked to many highly successful music artists during the course of writing this book. Without fail, each one of them understands that he or she has a job—a different kind of job than most people, but a job nonetheless, with all the accompanying responsibilities, time commitments, successes, and failures that go with it. And they work hard! Touring, writing, doing interviews (some of them for this book), recording, meeting with lawyers involving contracts (not as fun as it sounds), and so on. It is the hard work that produces the great songs, albums, and live shows, not some sort of magic. I'm fixating on this "job" concept to hopefully carry you through times in your band career when things aren't all sweetness and light—the bad gigs, the personality conflicts, the periods when nothing seems to be going right. These demoralizing moments happen every day at workplaces around the world, and bands are not separate from this world.

Playing in a band is a job. Sometimes a job isn't so fun. But when everything is going well in a band situation, you'll know you have the best job in the world.

SOCIAL SKILLS RULE, DUDE!

As you may have gathered by now, the ability to work closely with other creative people in the music business is, pardon my French, gosh-darn important! Being affable, flexible, reasonable, and other positive words that end in "ble" will often get you further in this biz than raw musical talent. Of course, the nicest player in the world isn't going to get a gig if he or she has no musical ability. The reverse of this is also true: The best musician in the world isn't going to get the gig if nobody wants to be around him or her. Every person interviewed in Chapter 13 knew something about working with other people, either consciously or unconsciously. Everything you bring to the table counts. If you spend time playing scales and working on music skills regularly, take some time to analyze how you deal with other people in general. Nobody makes it alone, so the more people you have on your side the better your chance of success. Hey, you're welcome. Drive safely. You look marvelous, you good-lookin', talented thing. Get outta here, I love you. Gotta run. Call me.

CAN YOU BE HAPPY WITHOUT A RECORD DEAL?

The answer to the above question better be "yes" or you're in for a lot of heartbreak. Only a tiny minority of bands get signed to a record deal of any sort, and (please remember this), *only a tiny minority of signed bands get treated well.* In many cases a band doing well on their own comes to a crashing halt soon after signing a deal. How can this be? A few reasons. Personality traits magnify to bigger-than-life size when each band member suddenly finds themselves on the other side of the Great Divide—the "we have a record deal" side. Believe me. As Cyndi Lauper once sang, "Money changes everything." Record company cash advances, often more money than any member has seen before, can bring out all kinds of crazy behavior lurking within each group member. Does the word "greed" ring a bell? Furthermore, the A&R person who signed the band may have quit or been fired, leaving you on a label where you don't have an inside player rooting for your band and pushing all the right promotion and publicity buttons necessary for success. Furthermore (I'm almost done, record deal worshipers), you may record an album for a label that is accepted at first, then shelved and the band dropped, leaving your album in record label limbo, neither returnable to you (they own it) nor releasable (they won't). Without a record deal you could have put out the same record yourself and sold it from the back of your van if you had to.

Does this mean you shouldn't pursue a record deal? Not at all. You just need to put the *idea* of a record deal in perspective. In several of the interviews in this book, those interviewed mention how important it is to really enjoy the process of playing and of learning how to be a professional band. Bands that fixate on getting a record deal at all costs are focusing on the wrong subject. The subject, as you may have figured out by now, is great songs and great performances. A record deal may or may not be the byproduct of this focus. In fact, some bands and artists blow off the whole record deal concept completely while enjoying highly successful, self-directed careers. Here are a few examples.

Fugazi are a hard-core band with an anticorporate stance who release records through their own label, Dischord. They never charge more than $5 for a concert. Since 1988 they have slowly developed a very loyal fan base without mainstream press or MTV airplay. By their fifth album release they charted on the Billboard Top 200 with no commercial push. They did it their way, completely separate from the corporate music biz world, and it worked.

Ani DiFranco releases records on her own label, Righteous Babe. Her nine albums in seven years have sold a total of 500,000 copies, and she is a huge draw on the festival and college circuit. She sells them directly to her fans, and guess what? She doesn't get a 12% or 14% royalty per record, she gets a 100% royalty! That's right, you can make *a lot of money* selling your own records to your own fans. Laura Love, a Seattle-based singer/songwriter, has put out three releases, selling a total of 40,000 copies on her own label, the wonderfully named Octoroon Biography. These numbers are more impressive than bigger sales figures on major labels because the artist keeps all the sales income, not a percentage. You can have a very successful career, financially and artistically, completely outside the corporate music business circle.

WHO ARE YOU?

Fewer things are more pitiful than a musician who has been fired or whose band has broken up. Be careful! Unless you are the leader of the band, do not allow yourself to become so absorbed in band life that you disappear as an individual walking this earth. Why? Because you can be fired by the leader and then poof! There goes who you are. This is not a good position to put yourself in, believe me. For almost nine years, from 1979 to 1986, I would wake up in the morning and more or less say to myself "I'm a Motel." No, I wasn't losing my mind; that was the name of my band and I was proud to be a member. But when the band broke up so the leader could pursue a solo career (it was actually on a Friday the 13th, I swear), I went into your basic existential meltdown. Who was I? Could I get in another band? Did I want to? Was I even capable of doing anything else? The answer, of course, was yes, and you're reading the result.

> People tend to identify with their jobs, and when they get fired or laid off, the psychological consequences can be devastating.

This "I am my job" attitude is very common in the workplaces of the world. People tend to identify with their jobs, and when they get fired or laid off, the psychological consequences can be devastating. Being fired from a band that plays locally and is in the developing stages can be rough, but getting canned from a major act with albums and national tours under their belt can be a real blow to the player. Life can seem drab after all the glamour and adoring crowds. But the real world is where we live, and after a hopefully brief "poor me" period, you need to get it together and find another band or another occupation.

The problem, as I see it, is mistaking your ego for your true identity. The ego is a wonderful, shiny, and productive thing, constantly goading you into realms of material achievement through an insatiable appetite for self-approval. You know, "Hey everybody—over *here!*" Without your ego, you would have no ambition. An ego isn't a bad thing, but it isn't really you. In my more cosmic moments I visualize the ego as a big, bright balloon attached to me by a string.

Every year it gets blown up a little more, making it bigger and more noticeable—and more likely to break. Being in touch with the real you can help keep your ego, and the whole band thing in perspective. Having a sense of humor is often a reflection of this perspective. I don't mean wearing a clown outfit on stage, but just realizing that there really is a world out there not completely wrapped up in MTV, musical equipment, record charts, and pursuit of the Record Deal.

THAT ALL-IMPORTANT PERSPECTIVE

What do you do to relax, to detach from all the trivia and detail of day-to-day life? Yes, drinking a six-pack and falling down is one way, but you may find other ways to get a new perspective on not only the band thing but everything else. Meditation, yoga, exercise, periodic detachment from "business as usual"—all these things can really help you become a better band member as well as a better human being. The world of music, bands, and pop culture is seductive. Find a way to balance this part of your life with an activity or belief system that helps you stay grounded. If you want a long and productive career as a musician or songwriter you'll need to spend some time pursuing these other areas of life, not as distractions but rather as a source of strength to help you pursue your musical passion.

Whew! Heavy going there for a minute. One final bit of advice: have fun playing music, and whatever aspect of the business you pursue, *work it*!

Information Sources

Knowledge is of two kinds. We know
a subject ourselves, or we know where
we can find information upon it.
—Samuel Johnson (1709–1784)

 his is by no means a complete listing of everything, but rather an eclectic grouping of info sources I found helpful in researching this book. May this list aid you in the endless search for truly useful knowledge.

BOOKS

Bartlett, Bruce, and Jenny Bruce. *Practical Recording Techniques*. Indianapolis: SAMS Publishing, 1992. This is a very good overview of recording techniques that gives you enough information to understand what goes on in a studio, without too much technical detail.

Baskerville, David. *Music Business Handbook & Career Guide*. Thousand Oaks: Sage Publications, 1995. Academic, textbook-style overview of the music business, covering more than popular music. Helps you understand just how big the music business has become. Encyclopedic in scope; usually available in public as well as music school libraries.

Bleeding Heart Collective & MaximumRocknroll Present. *Book Your Own Fuckin' Life: A Do It Yourself Resource Guide*. Listings of DIY bands, venues, 'zines, radio stations, indie labels, and record/book stores for all 50 states and 62 countries. Radical, activist, cutting edge, cool. Updated yearly. The Bleeding Heart Collective, 4728 Spruce Street, Box 354, Philadelphia, PA 19139. Call 215-569-2477, ext. 3.

Cardinal Business Media, Inc. *Recording Industry Sourcebook*. This glossy 424-page spiral-bound publication has, among the fancy ads for recording studios, listings (including addresses and phone numbers) for major and indie labels, distribution, management, booking agents, record manufacturers, recording studios, concert promoters, attorneys, graphic artists, public relations firms, etc. Shows you in four-color splendor how many businesses depend on someone, somewhere, sitting down and writing a song. Unfortunately it costs about $90. *Recording Industry Sourcebook*, 6400 Hollis Street, Suite 12, Emeryville, CA 94608. Call 1-800-233-9604.

Davies, Ray. *X-Ray*. Woodstock: The Overlook Press, 1995. The "Unauthorized Autobiography" of Ray Davies, the founder and driving force behind The Kinks, one of the most influential groups of the '60s British Invasion. This is an autobiography in the form of a biography. Brilliantly written, this gives you a feel for the swingin' '60s scene as well as Davies's imagination, self-deprecation, and wicked sense of humor.

Erlewine, Michael, Vladimir Bogdanov, and Chris Woodstra, eds. *All Music Guide to Rock: The Best CDs, Albums & Tapes*. San Francisco: Miller Freeman Books, 1995. Covers 2,500 artists and more than 15,000 albums, from Abba to ZZ Top. Includes many informative essays regarding rock styles (Soul, Surf Music, Punk, etc.) and lots of additional info resources. Well-written reviews.

Forest, F. Alton. *Acoustic Techniques for Home & Studio*. Blue Ridge Summit: Tab Books, 1984. Out-of-print. Look for this book in your library. Very practical look at sound-isolation techniques.

Garo, Liz. *Book Your Own Tour*. San Diego: Rockpress Publishing, 1995. Describes how to set up a "van" tour, lists venues, restaurants, music stores, press contacts, and record stores for over 100 U.S. cities. Practical advice on vans, including a very cool description of how to build a van loft for equipment storage and sleeping space.

Guralnick, Peter. *Last Train to Memphis: The Rise of Elvis Presley*. Boston: Little, Brown & Co., 1994. This is one of the best music biographies ever written, covering the first 24 years of Elvis's life, up to when he was drafted. Cool sections on El's wide musical influences, demonstrating how the music that goes in your head eventually reappears, but always in a slightly different form.

Halloran, Mark, ed. *The Musician's Business & Legal Guide.* Englewood Cliffs: Prentice Hall, 1991. If you feel a need to wade through the details of musician-related law, this is the book. Shows you why they call it the "music *business."* Very well written and easy to understand.

Josefs, Jai. *Writing Music for Hit Songs.* Cincinatti: Writer's Digest Books, 1989. Extremely practical guide to writing pop songs, including music theory, lyric crafting, and common chord progressions. Heavy on the craft, light on the philosophy. Recommended.

Lewisohn, Mark. *The Beatles' Recording Session: The Official Abbey Road Studio Session Notes 1962–1970.* New York: Harmony Books, 1988. If you like The Beatles and listen to their albums, this is the Bible. Read how they cut ten songs for their first album in 585 minutes. Detailed descriptions of every recording session; endlessly fascinating.

Musician Magazine. *The Musician's Guide to Touring and Promotion.* Extensive directories of major and indie label A&R, music conferences, showcases, music industry websites, tape/disc manufacturers, and more. Pretty darn useful stuff, updated yearly. $9.95 postpaid to Musician's Guide to Touring and Promotion, 1515 Broadway, 11th Floor, New York, NY 10036, but call 212-536-5208 for current price info.

Passman, Donald S. *All You Need to Know About the Music Business.* New York: Simon & Schuster, 1994. Written by a top music industry lawyer, Passman, who tells you all you need to know and more about deals, publishing, merchandising, tours, songwriting, etc. His practical knowledge is immense, his writing style can verge on the cute and precious. Super-informative.

Rollins, Henry. *Get in the Van: On the Road with Black Flag.* Los Angeles: 2.13.61 Publications, 1994. If you think touring the country as an indie-label punk band is glamorous, read this book. This is the real thing; Rollins documents his view of the early '80s punk scene with seriousness and deadpan humor. Great photos.

Shemel, Sidney and M. William Krasilovsky. *This Business of Music*. New York: Billboard Books, 1990. Dry as the desert but loaded with info.

Smith, Joe. *Off the Record: An Oral History of Popular Music*. New York: Warner Books, 1988. Cool, informative interviews with 221 pop music biggies.

Sokolow, Fred. *Fretboard Roadmaps: The Essential Guitar Patterns That All the Pros Know and Use*. Milwaukee: Hal Leonard Publishing Corporation, 1993. A "how-to" book teaching movable patterns on the guitar fretboard that enable you to play chords, licks, scales, and progressions in all keys. Learning these patterns will improve all aspects of your guitar playing. Super-useful stuff.

Solgins, Adam. *Rock Names: From Abba to ZZ Top*. New York: Citadel Press, 1995. Find out what Steely Dan was named after and many more. Very funny.

Williams, Chas. *The Nashville Number System*. Complete and thorough explanation of this groovy musical shorthand. Includes handwritten charts of seven songs by different top session players. Available as a video. Contact Nashville Songwriters Association International (NSAI), 15 Music Square W., Nashville, TN 37203; 615-256-3354, or *Mix Bookshelf* (see page 216).

Zollo, Paul. *Songwriters on Songwriting*. Cincinnati: Writer's Digest Books, 1991. Serious interviews with 31 songwriters (Paul Simon, Rickie Lee Jones, Randy Newman, Frank Zappa, Roger McGuinn, etc.) by the editor of *SongTalk* magazine. Very revealing, especially the interview with Paul Simon.

MAGAZINES

There is no need to describe such popular magazines as *Rolling Stone*, *Spin*, *Musician*, *Downbeat*, and other highly mainstream periodicals. But here's a few you may be unaware of.

Acoustic Guitar. This is just a great monthly magazine. Includes transcriptions, useful technical tips, and cool interviews. $29.95/year. P.O. Box 767, San Anselmo, CA 94979; 415-485-6946.

Alternative Press. Sort of a cross between *Spin* and *Flipside*, covers newer bands. Includes reviews, new release listings, feature interviews, and "Burn the Manual," a useful technical column for musicians. $19.95/year for 12 issues, to Alternative Press Subscriptions, P.O. Box 1936, Marion, OH 43306-2036. Call 1-800-596-2318.

CMJ New Music Monthly. This petite mag calls itself "The Guide To New Music," and that's accurate. As well as reviews and feature articles on today's "alternative" artists, books, videos, and other media, CMJ arrives every month with a CD containing tracks from 20 new releases. Sure, the record labels pay for song placement, but it's a great way to check out a lot of new music without buying all those CDs every month. Any CD you like can be ordered toll-free. One year subscription (12 issues) for $39.95. Call 1-800-414-4CMJ.

Flipside. Massive bimonthly punk fanzine covering vast quantities of extremely indie music. A veritable Subculture Bible, it includes publications lists, interviews, reviews, local scene columns, et al. This is the stuff that eventually becomes "alternative." A living history of the DIY movement. $12/year for six issues. *Flipside*, P.O. Box 60790, Pasadena, CA 91116. URL: http://www.forfood.com/~indieweb/flipside/flipside.html

MAXIMUMROCKNROLL. A big monthly review of the punk and indie scene. Plenty of everything: irreverent, rude, and energetic. A sample issue has five local scene reports, ten band interviews, six book reviews, 28 opinion columns, 110 fanzine reviews, and 285 record reviews. $18/six-issue subscription. *MAXIMUMROCKN-ROLL*, P.O. Box 460760, San Francisco, CA 94146-0760; 415-648-3561, fax 415-648-5816.

Pollstar. "The Concert Hotwire." This weekly concert industry mag lists top-grossing concerts of the week (Boxoffice Summary), current Top 20 radio charts, top album retail sales, and tour schedules for virtually every act playing the United States. Special issues list concert venues, college gigs, who manages who, and more. At $295/year (or $95/90-day trial subscription) you won't want to subscribe; borrow a copy or check your library. Pollstar, 4333 N.W. Avenue, Fresno, CA 93705; 1-800-344-7383; 209-224-2631.

Song Talk. A quarterly publication of the National Academy of Songwriters. Extremely informative mag on songwriting thanks to extensive in-depth interviews—often 12 in an issue—with writers and artists. Inspiring stuff. Write or call for membership info: NAS, 6255 Sunset Boulevard, Suite #1023, Hollywood, CA 90028, 1-800-826-7287.

Tape Op. A quarterly that covers "music recording in the real world," with home recording tips and interviews with bands that have successfully recorded their own albums. Practical, useful information presented in a charming format. A real tool, for young bands on the move. $2/issue postpaid, *Tape Op*, P.O. Box 15189, Portland, OR 97293; 503-230-1089; e-mail address: fboa@teleport.com.

CATALOGS

2.13.61. Henry Rollins of Black Flag founded this book publishing company, named after his birthday. In addition to his cool books (including the classic *Get In the Van*), other off-the-wall authors are represented, plus CDs from his record label 213CD. 2.13.61, P.O. Box 1910, Los Angeles, CA 90078; 213-969-8043.

Jamey Aebersold Jazz Aids. For learning how to play your instrument, this catalog offers many superb and useful tools. Features over 70 different book/recording sets (CD/cassette/LP) that provide you with a great rhythm section playing blues and jazz standards. You play along with the recording on bass, guitar, piano, wind instrument, or whatever you play. Sort of like having a band that will play whatever you want for as long as you want while you practice on your instrument. You don't have to be a "jazz" player to learn from these. The catalog includes a vast listing of books and videos on theory, scales, patterns, and technique for all instruments. Contains enough instructional media to keep you learning for a lifetime. Highly recommended. Jamie Aebersold Jazz, Inc., P.O. Box 1244, New Albany, IN 47151-1244; 1-800-456-1388.

Bradley Broadcast. Caters mostly to radio and TV stations, and has a great selection of mikes, recording devices, audio processors, and a lot of equipment not available in rock-oriented equipment catalogs. A different selection of gear worth checking out. Bradley Broadcast Sales, 12401 Twinbrook Parkway, Rockville, MD 20852; 1-800-732-7665.

Carvin. This San Diego-based equipment manufacturer offers guitars and basses, amps, sound reinforcement, and many accessories. They have three stores in California but work mostly through mail order. Carvin, 12340 World Trade Drive, San Diego, CA 92128; 1-800-854-2235.

Disc Makers. This company is a large (five locations) national disc and cassette manufacturer, maybe the largest. The catalog offers a huge and certainly convenient assortment of "package deals" involving different combinations of CDs and cassettes in various quantities. They offer graphic design and many price/quality levels of packaging. For one-stop shopping they are hard to beat; for more control over aspects of making your own record you may be better off using a local broker with a good reputation. Call 1-800-468-9353.

Disc Makers Guide to Independent Music Publicity. Free advice on how to promote your act through media, record release, mailing lists, etc. Carefully spaced plugs for Disc Makers—but what do you expect? Worth every penny. Disc Makers, 1-800-468-9353.

Disc Makers Guide to Master Tape Preparation. Same idea here. Disc Makers, a large, internationally promoted disc and cassette manufacturer, offer this free 53-page booklet full of useful info on preparing a trouble-free master tape. Despite the plugs for Disc Makers (but of course!) this is good stuff. Disc Makers, 1-800-468-9353.

Full Compass. Another great mail-order resource to help you find the best price on a wide array of mikes, headphones, mixers, recorders, speakers, outboard gear, lighting, and more. Call for free catalog. Full Compass, 8001 Terrace Avenue, Middleton, WI 53562; 1-800-356-5844, 608-831-7330.

Mackie Product Line Brochure. I don't know Greg Mackie and this is not a specific endorsement of Mackie products. However, part of their philosophy is to educate potential customers, so Mackie catalogs always contain plenty of free and useful information about mixing consoles and their design, explaining subjects such as routing, eq, preamps, and even how to assemble your own mixer cables. You can learn plenty about mixing boards without spending a dime by reading these brochures. They also offer a free video explaining mixing concepts. You can't beat the price! Mackie Designs Incorporated, 16220 Wood-Red Road N.E., Woodinville, WA 98072; 1-800-898-3211.

Mix Bookshelf. "Information resources for music professionals." Seems to list every book ever written pertaining to the music business, maybe even this one. Includes sound effect and audio samples on CD, CD-ROMs, etc. Mix Bookshelf, c/o Whitehurst & Clark Inc., 100 Newfield Avenue, Edison, NJ 08837-3817; 1-800-233-9604, fax 908-225-1562.

Rainbo Records. These guys have been manufacturing records since they were called 78s. Another service that does huge volume work, including vinyl. Very retro info brochure. 1738 Berkeley Street, Santa Monica, CA 90404; 310-829-3476, fax 310-828-8765.

INDEX

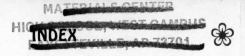